Secrets
of Superstar
Speakers

Secrets
of Superstar
Speakers

Wisdom from the Greatest Motivators
of Our Time and with Those
These Superstars Inspired
to Dramatic and Lasting Change

Lilly Walters

McGraw-Hill

New York   San Francisco   Washington, D.C.   Auckland   Bogotá
Caracas   Lisbon   London   Madrid   Mexico City
Milan   Montreal   New Delhi   San Juan
Singapore   Sydney   Tokyo   Toronto

McGraw-Hill

A Division of The **McGraw·Hill** Companies

1 2 3 4 5 6 7 8 9 0   AGM/AGM   9 0 9 8 7 6 5 4 3 2 1 0 9

ISBN 0-07-134707-0

The sponsoring editor for this book was Betsy Brown, the editing supervisor was John M. Morriss, and the production supervisor was Tina Cameron. It was set in Adobe Garamond by North Market Street Graphics.

Printed and bound by R. R. Donnelley & Sons Company.

McGraw-Hill books are available at special quantity discounts to use as premiums and sales promotions, or for use in corporate training programs. For more information, please write to the Director of Special Sales, McGraw-Hill, 11 West 19th Street, New York, NY 10011. Or contact your local bookstore.

This publication is designed to provide accurate and authoritative information in regard to the subject matter covered. It is sold with the understanding that neither the author nor the publisher is engaged in rendering legal, accounting, or other professional service. If legal advice or other expert assistance is required, the services of a competent professional person should be sought.
—From a Declaration of Principles jointly adopted by a Committee of the American Bar Association and a Committee of Publishers.

This book is printed on recycled, acid-free paper containing a minimum of 50% recycled, de-inked fiber.

*For my personal and wonderful superstar,
my husband, Marty Schermerhorn.*

Contents

Preface

Superstar speakers cannot be measured by how much they were enjoyed the day of the talk. A great movie entertains, and perhaps inspires. You laugh, maybe learn a few things. How much do you pay to rent a great movie or go the movies? With a great speaker you are also inspired, and laugh, but you will pay from $12,500 to $135,000 to bring one of these speakers to your company. Why the discrepancy in the worth?

Because great speakers create change. Their worth is measured, *years after the speech,* by the change their words create in the actions and attitudes of those whose lives they have touched.

Because of Those Words . . .

What has changed in the lives of the listener because of the words? What moments of truth and long-term applications happen in the hearts of those who encounter your words? What is really being remembered years after hearing a talk? If you knew that, you could create your speech around what is really being applied and remembered. Want memorable results? Study the qualities remembered!

This book will show you through survey research and analyzed results, flavored with interviews and anecdotes from Superstar speakers and from those whose lives they have touched.

I have orchestrated the reflections and wisdom of these two groups throughout this book. The first part of the book, "Who Are These Superstars?," will show you the person he or she is, or was, the person behind the persona, his or her wisdom and turning points, and how he or she overcame incredible adversity and failures to become a Superstar speaker.

In the second part of the book, "Creating a Superstar Speech," we show you the results of the words and *why, how,* and exactly *what* it is about these Superstar speeches that has created change in the lives of listeners.

Throughout the entire book you hear both from Superstars, in their own words, and from those whose lives they changed.

> *Great speakers affect their audiences in astounding ways. I believe this is because the great speaker flashes a light of recognition into our minds. We suddenly see a truth that was already there. Like a hunting dog who points his tail back, and his nose forward, when he first sees a bird. He recognizes it. The instinct awakens.*
>
> *The ideas great speakers present are like a mirror flashing a bright signal from a far-off power source. We are transfixed. We have been waiting for that very message. We already know it. We recognize it. We say to ourselves, "This is true. This is the confirmation I have been waiting for. I recognize it and welcome it like the electrifying sight of our nation's flag in a foreign land."*
> **—Dottie Walters**

Your talk must change actions and attitude. How better to decide on how you will create your talk than to study the results of those whose lives have been changed! Especially note vignettes of those who, because of the words of a Superstar, changed their journey:

> *As we were exiting a program by Mark Victor Hansen, my youngest boy, Devin, said, "Dad, does writing your goals really work?" I said, "Yes son, it does." But he wasn't interested in further discussion.*
>
> *A couple of weeks later, after an Ed Forman television program*

on goal setting, Devin said, "Dad, will you help me write my goals?" I thought to myself "yes!" But before I could answer, Brandon, our first-born son, said "Dad, will you help me write my goals, too?" And I realized though I had given up on Brandon, Brandon hadn't given up on Brandon . . . .

"Panic stricken" would describe my wife's and my reaction when Brandon was diagnosed with Down's syndrome, a birth defect in the cell chromosomes that for most results in mental retardation. That prognosis was not ok with us! So we looked around. We became aware of an eight-year-old Down's syndrome girl in Australia who could read, write, and speak three languages, was a whiz at math, and a virtuoso on the violin. We decided that if she could do it, Brandon could do it.

We began doing everything you can imagine: stimulation programs, vitamin therapy, a continuous stream of volunteers, a constant devotion of daily effort, everything. I became a Cub Scout leader so Brandon could be in Cub Scouts. I became a Boy Scout leader so Brandon could be in Boy Scouts. And more importantly, I occasionally took him and his brother to hear professional speakers. But in spite of much ongoing inspiration from speakers like the Rev. Robert Schuller, Dr. Wayne Dyer, Earl Nightingale, and Norman Vincent Peale, by the time Brandon was 10 years old, he still couldn't read, our momentum had slowed to a halt, and I had given up.

But when he said, "Dad, will you help me write my goals, too?" it sent a shudder through me. After working on his goals, every couple of days, Brandon came to me and asked "Dad, can we read my goals?" I began to think, "He really likes reading his goals, maybe it's time to try again to teach him to read." I'm proud to say that Brandon has completed reading his first I Can Read book!

And this outcome occurred because through thick and thin, we kept filling our minds and our hearts with stimulating ideas and information from some of the best professional speakers in the world today . . . .

—WILL SHERWOOD, SPEAKER, AUTHOR,
GRAPHIC DESIGNER

Quotes, like the one above, will be directly from those who heard the words of a Superstar that changed their life. As in Will's quote above, I will give a brief description of who they are. You will find that many times the Superstars I am profiling are talking about the experiences they have had in the audience of another great speaker.

Why Lilly Walters Wrote This Book

All my life I have been in the world of professional speakers. My mother was one of the premier women on the platform (see her profile). I sat and listened to her and other greats on the platform, the radio, and video. For 15 years I have, and still, run Walters International Speakers Bureau, where we track over 36,000 professional speaker. I have become a best-selling author on subjects about the world of professional speaking. I wrote the prequel to this book, the best-selling *Secrets of Successful Speakers: How You Can Motivate, Captivate, and Persuade,* and I co-authored *Speak and Grow Rich* and *What to Say When You're Dying on the Platform!* (For more information, go to http://www.walters-intl.com).

I love the beauty and power of the spoken and written word. This book will show you what I have known all my life: Your words can and do change lives. This book is the first I know of that attempts to find out what lasting effects those words had, all the hows and whys, years after the fact.

Who Are the Greatest Superstar Speakers of All Time?

By sending a survey to 4,000 people, I created a list of the top-70 Superstars speakers. I tracked those qualities most often repeated as the reasons for choosing these greatest Superstars. Throughout the book I have broken down these qualities in great detail. Whenever possible, the Superstars themselves, and the people whose lives have been impacted, explain why and how in their own words.

Reading this book will make you feel that you are at a great convention. Around you are master speakers: Lou Holtz, Winston Churchill,

Tony Robbins, Norman Vincent Peale, Zig Ziglar, Anita Roddick, Vince Lombardi, and many others, all talking about the art and craft of influence, inspiration, working with an audience. You will hear their personal stories, challenges, turning points, and strategies for handling their own growth.

I asked 4,000 speakers, meeting planners, and members of the press a question: "In your personal opinion, who is/are the *greatest* motivational speaker/s you have ever heard? And Why?"

The results showed:

Anthony "Tony" Robbins	Earl Nightingale	Maya Angelou
Al Walker	Ed Foreman	Naomi Rhode
Alan Keyes	Elizabeth Dole	Napoleon Hill
Anita Roddick	Florence Littauer	Nido Qubein
Barbara Jordan	Gen. Colin Powell	Norman Vincent Peale
Barry Spilchuck	Glenna Salsbury	Og Mandino
Bernie Siegel, M.D.	Ian Percy	Patricia Fripp
Bill Gove	Jack Canfield	Peter Daniels
Billy Graham	Jeanne Robertson	President John F.
Brian Tracy	Jesus Christ	Kennedy
Buckminster "Bucky"	Jim Rohn	President Ronald Reagan
Fuller	John Bradshaw	Rev. Bob Richards
Capt. Dave Carey	Keith Harrell	Rev. Robert Schuller
Capt. Jerry Coffee	Ken Blanchard	Rosita Perez
Cavett Roberts	Kenneth McFarland	Stephen R. Covey
Charmaine Pountney	Larry Wilson	Terry Cole-Whitaker
Christopher Reeve	Leo Buscaglia	Tom Hopkins
Deepak Chopra	Les Brown	Tom Peters
Denis Waitley	Lou Holtz	Vince Lombardi, Sr
Dewitt Jones	Margaret Thatcher	W. Mitchell
Dottie Walters	Marianne Williamson	Warren Greshes
Dr. Anthony "Tony"	Mario Cuomo	Werner Erhard
Campolo	Mark Victor Hansen	Willey Jolley
Dr. Sidney B. Simon	Martin Luther King	Winston Churchill
Dr. Wayne Dyer	Matt Weinstein	Zig Ziglar

This book would not be big enough to interview all of them, so I chose 19 to be the focus of this book. More will follow in Vol. II!

Where Are the Women?

In my survey results, you note a lack of women. In the top 25, there were only two: Dottie Walters and Maya Angelou. In the top 40, we add Elizabeth Dole, Marianne Williamson, Glenna Salsbury, and Patricia Fripp. Since I sent the survey to 4,000 of those I know, and who therefore know my mother (Dottie Walters), we can certainly argue the results would be biased in her favor. Since I think she is the greatest of all time, I think the results are right on target—and yes, my own bias is duly noted.

But where are the rest of the women with platform power? Why are they not being remembered? The results of this survey reflect what, from years past, is being remembered and used today. Well, in years past, men ruled the speaking platform. After World War II, Rosie the Riveter went quietly back into the home to mind the laundry and the children, and her voice was no longer as appreciated in the business world. When my mother took the platform in the 1950s, she was one of very few female voices.

We will certainly need an entire volume of just women Superstars soon.

Qualities of Greatness

What are the qualities and strategies of being and becoming a Superstar? The good news is there are thousands of qualities and strategies you can use. The, possibly, bad news is these often contradict each other. Why did one person "love" Tony Robbins' sincerity, while another would think he was "plastic"? Why does one person see Anita Roddick as the greatest life-changing speaker of all time and another can't imagine why she is even in this book?

There are many minds and hearts to motivate, with many paths that reach them. Some, like Zig Ziglar, Elizabeth Dole, and Norman Vincent Peale, give credit to their belief in their Christian beliefs. Others like Christopher Reeve tell of other sources of strength. This book will try to sort all of them out and help you see what made each speaker a "Superstar" in the hearts of those I surveyed. After studying these results, you can then create your talk, with the same Superstar impact, *by creating your own unique path to the heart of the listener,* based on your personal journey and experience.

So what *exactly* made those messages work?

I looked for common threads, then I compiled, tabulated, analyzed, and interpreted them. I broke these comments apart and attempted to track those qualities that were most often repeated as the reasons for choosing a specific speaker as a Superstar.

Figure 1 on the next page is an overview of the most monumental reasons why people were motivated by these specific speakers. Every reason on the list that follows is enormously significant and was mentioned over and over in my survey.

My thought before taking this survey was that when asked weeks or months later after a presentation, people would recall the stories more often than the message or content. They say things like, "I loved the way he told stories!" and "I loved her humor!" Yet note the huge disparity between the relatively low value/impact of stories versus the value/impact of a message.

Most speech courses and coaches focus on entertainment, story-telling, drama, and multichannel teaching techniques to deliver a "great" talk. They concentrate on avoiding the academic-world presentations, which are typically dry and heavily content-annotated to support their point or message. As this research shows, this focus is wrong.

So, why does everyone agree that those academic content-heavy talks are dull, but great speakers have great content? To find the answer this book helps you study what people are really retaining years later. What do respondents say about the meaning of "message"? The second part of this book, "Creating a Superstar Speech," breaks each of the qualities apart much farther and explores them in great detail.

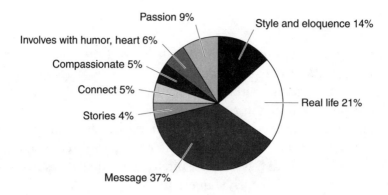

Passion 9% Style and eloquence 14%

Involves with humor, heart 6%

Compassionate 5%

Connect 5% Real life 21%

Stories 4%

Message 37%

Audience members recall and clarify . . .

Message

- *The content creates change!*
- *It was smart*
- *God was in the message*
- *Simple and easy to follow and understand*
- *Down to earth*

- *Focused*
- *Clear*
- *Practical*
- *Because his/her message and/or content was . . .*

- *Because of the ideas and wisdom that was . . .*
- *Because it motivated. inspired, me to . . .*
- *New*
- *Customized*

Real Life

- *Overcame adversity*
- *First to do it*
- *Character*
- *Integrity*
- *Who he is*
- *Life is an example*

- *Walk and talk*
- *True and personal stories*
- *Real life*
- *Humble*
- *Honest*

- *Believable*
- *Sincere*
- *Genuine*
- *Off platform issues*

Style and Eloquence

- *Uses words well*
- *Eloquence*
- *Voice*

- *Style*
- *Presence*
- *Appearance*

- *Charisma, personality*

Passion

- *Energy*
- *Enthusiasm*

- *Dedication*
- *Conviction*

- *Power*

Involves (by using humor and heart)

- *Tears and emotions*

- *Humor, wit, entertainment*

- *Audience participation*

Figure 1. Overview of the Qualities of Superstar Speakers and Speeches

Acknowledgments

To the Superstars who have contributed to this book! The celebrities who gave so freely of themselves, and the hundreds of professional speakers who shared their stories of how a great speaker changed their lives.

To the 24 people who took this book in its rough and hardly ready form, read it and ripped it and made suggestions to make it great: Leil Lowndes, Wayne E. Baughman, John E. Kinde, Scott Sindelar, Jason Wrench, Peter Francis, Hank Moore, Greg Sanders, John R. Haworth, Linda Henley-Smith, Michael Crow, Dennis Brown, Jim McJunkin, Kathy Yeram, Dottie Walters, Wally Bock, Anders Rasmussen, Nancy Gerber, Michael Bane, Edward Leigh, Donald W. Blohowiak, Lou Hampton, Dr. Deanna Berg, and Burt Siemens.

And to the many people who sent me history and research on the Superstars, such as Maggie Munoz, Vic Conant, and Nick Carter at Nightingale-Connat; Angie Ainsworth and Kevin Holtz in Lou Holtz's office; D. J. Harmeling at Robbins Research; Laurie Magers with Zig Ziglar; Jude Johnson and Renee Dunn with Deepak Chopra; Teresa Esparza with Jack Canfield; Boyd Criag with Stephen Covey; Lisa Williams with Mark Victor Hansen; Cindy Williams, Kerry Tymchuk, Carol Scott, and Kathryn Wilson with Elizabeth Dole; Sybil Light with Guideposts® and Ruth Peale; Karen Bishop and Tim Blanks for Anita Roddick; Bob Thomas at the Washington Speakers Bureau.

Secrets
of Superstar
Speakers

PART I

Who Are These Superstars?

There are hundreds of Superstars, past and present, that I will profile in future volumes. In this first volume I will tell you the story of 19.

In Chapter 1 I profile these 19 Superstars and tell you about the turning points in their lives and the special wisdom for which they are famous. In Chapter 2 I cluster their strategies for staying on top and solving problems to make comparisons easier.

You will see threads and basic truths that are common to Superstar Speakers.

Common Characteristics

- All have overcome amazing obstacles to reach their Superstar status.

- They're people who've successfully translated a life's work, study, accomplishment, and passion into the publicly spoken word. That's how they touch people profoundly—first a profound life, then a profound message.

- They persevered. If something didn't work, they tried something else, then something else, then something else.

- They are well paid for their skills and experience: per talk from $20,000 to $135,000.

1

Who Are They? How Did They Get There?

The person behind the persona is more motivating than the words the speaker uses. What are the setbacks, turning points, and philosophies that carried them through to their winning games? Their lives are peppered with failures and with *overcoming* those failures. Ah, sorry. Mom would quickly quote Bill Marriott at this point, "Failure? I never encountered it. All I met were temporary setbacks."

Maya Angelou

. . . Her rare style of song, poetry, personal stories, and inspirational messages made the connection each time I heard her.

The last time, after the speech, I was in the lounge of our hotel when I realized that Ms. Angelou was enjoying some much deserved relaxation time with some associates at a nearby table. I gathered my courage and went over to chat with her. After introducing myself, I told her that I'd heard her speak 10 years earlier and that she had literally changed my life. Because of her speech, I had made a decision to use my gifts to make a difference in people's lives.

Her reply?

"You just did."

— Gary Rifkin, speaker, trainer, energizer, Rifkin Training and Consulting

Maya Angelou, arguably the best-known poet in America. She is a remarkable renaissance woman: a speaker, a Tony-nominated, Emmy-nominated professor with over 50 honorary degrees, actor, teacher, playwright, producer, director, best-selling author, and social and civil rights activist. To top off a life filled with colors, she has worked as a prostitutes' madam, a nightclub singer, and has even appeared on *The Muppet Show!*

She gained worldwide recognition with the first of her series of remarkable autobiographies, the penetrating mega-best-seller *I Know Why the Caged Bird Sings,* which has sold more than 2 million copies since it first appeared in 1970. She is among the first African-American women to hit the best-seller's lists.

On April 4, 1928, she was born Marguerite Johnson in St. Louis, Missouri, and was raised in segregated rural Arkansas, Her adored brother Bailey, Jr., preferred "Maya" to "my sister," the nickname stuck.

Dr. Angelou, who speaks French, Spanish, Italian, and West African Fanti, began her career in drama and dance.

In the 1960s, at the request of Dr. Martin Luther King, Jr., Ms. Angelou became the northern coordinator for the Southern Christian Leadership Conference. In 1975, she received the *Ladies Home Journal* Woman of the Year Award in communications. She received numerous honorary degrees and was appointed by President Jimmy Carter to the National Commission on the Observance of International Woman's Year and by President Ford to the American Revolutionary Bicentennial Advisory Council.

In the early 1970s she became the first African-American woman to have an original motion picture screenplay produced, *Georgia, Georgia.* She was also nominated for an Emmy Award for her acting as Kunta Kinte's grandmother in the TV mini-series of Alex Haley's *Roots.* Her best-selling autobiography *I Know Why the Caged Bird Sings,* was also turned into a two-hour TV special on CBS.

She has also authored many celebrated books, almost all autobio-graphical, but written in such an encompassing manner that we all can see ourselves within her persona. Her works include: *All God's Children Need Traveling Shoes, And Still I Rise, Gather Together in My Name, The*

Heart of a Woman, I Know Why the Caged Bird Sings, I Shall Not Be Moved, Just Give Me a Cool Drink of Water 'fore I Die, The Poetry of Maya Angelou, Now Sheba Sings the Song, Oh Pray My Wings Are Gonna Fit Me Well, Shaker, Why Don't You Sing? Singin' and Swingin' and Gettin' Merry Like Christmas, Wouldn't Take Nothing for My Journey Now. Among her numerous impressive honors are a Pulitzer Prize nomination for her works of poetry, *Just Give Me a Cool Drink of Water 'fore I Die* (1971) and *And Still I Rise* (1976).

Today Maya lectures in the United States and abroad. She speaks with the lilting cadence of the dancer she was trained to be. Just the sound of her low resonant, expressive voice filling the room brings poetry to mind, language laced with hues and shades of stirring imagery.

> *When I attended my very first book conference, in 1978, I had the good fortune to hear Maya Angelou speak. She referred to her "sheroes," both in literature and in life. This was particularly meaningful to me, for I had just published my first book,* The Quotable Woman, *which is filled with hundreds and hundreds of "sheroes," but I'd never heard that word before: Angelou coined it. I never liked the word "heroine"—especially in our drug culture, it has so many negative associations. I've been using the word "sheroe" instead ever since, both in my writing and my public speaking. Everyone, without exception so far, loves that word—and I always tell them, thank Maya Angelou! I do.*
> —ELAINE PARTNOW, AUTHOR
> AND PERFORMANCE MANAGER

Turning Points for Maya Angelou

Much of the content in *I Know Why the Caged Bird Sings,* comes from the early period in her life. When she was three years old, her parents divorced. Maya and her brother Bailey were sent to their grandmother and disabled uncle, in Stamps, Arkansas. She grew up during the Depression and helped her grandparents by working in their general store.

When she was only seven years old, on one of her occasional visits to St. Louis to see her estranged mother, tragedy struck. She was raped by her mother's lover. When she came out of the hospital, she told her family who had attacked her. Soon afterwards, the person was found dead. She thought her voice had actually killed a man! So she stopped talking. She was afraid her voice was dangerous and that even those she loved might be killed by her voice.

For five years, the voice that today is magical in its ability to lift and inspire was struck dumb. But I have heard she loved the sound of voices and words. She would sit quietly in rooms, imagining she was a giant ear, absorbing conversations and reading.

Years later someone told her if she really loved poetry as much as she said she did, that she would speak it!

So many turning points for Maya Angelou, each layering the next. Not ALL made her "better," but all made her stronger. As a teenager, she fought and won the battle to become the first African-American, and the first woman, conductor on San Francisco's streetcars. She became a prostitute at 18 and at one time found herself madam of two lesbian hookers.

In 1970, after changing her name and becoming a writer, she made a permanent mark on the nation's cultural scene with the publication of *I Know Why the Caged Bird Sings*. Over the years her books became popular, even catching the attention of then Governor Bill Clinton.

On January 20, 1993, she read the work she created for Clinton's inauguration, "On the Pulse of Morning," a tribute to the ethnic diversity of America. This was the first Presidential invitation extended to a poet since 1961 when Robert Frost was invited.

Maya Angelou's poem, "On the Pulse of Morning," changed the way I looked at myself and the world in general. Through this one poem I began to recognize that all of us are connected. I am not only adjoined to other humans, but to everything! We are inextricably connected to all life, even the rock, the river, and the tree. Humans are connected to every infant born at this very moment, as well as the mastodon hatched millions of years ago. Mother Angelou elevated me to such a place that I will forever be spiritu-

ally and psychologically linked in a functional way to this orb that we know as earth.
　　　—ALMAS JAMIL SAMI', LECTURER, PUBLISHER,
　　　AND AUTHOR OF *The Unshackled Mind*

Although very successful by the time President Clinton asked her to perform, this event propelled her into media Superstardom. *I Know Why the Caged Bird Sings,* jumped onto the paperback best-seller lists, and sales of Angelou's six paperbacks increased as much as 600 percent. In 1994, she was honored with a Grammy for Best Spoken Word or Non-Musical Album for "On the Pulse of Morning."

A 16-year-old pregnant and unmarried Maya watched enviously as ambassadors and diplomats filed into a San Francisco hotel to sign the United Nations charter. But not long ago she was an invited guest for the anniversary celebration of the charter's signing. No longer the longing, downcast spectator, she read her poem, "A Brave and Startling Truth," on the same stage with U.N. Secretary-General Boutros Boutros-Ghali.

Years ago Maya Angelou (about whom I had barely heard at the time) was interviewed on National Public Radio. She described with feeling and without apology the many obstacles she had to overcome along her way—including limited expectations of her and many roadblocks.

Her words inspired me to hold to my dream of being anyone I wanted to be. Well, my timetable was a little off, but at age 48 I make my living writing. I have Maya Angelou to thank. She represented the possibility that I could become anyone I wanted to be.
　　　—SUSAN COLANTUONO, AUTHOR, CONSULTANT,
　　　INSPIRATIONAL EDUCATOR

Special Wisdom of Maya Angelou

Maya wisdoms seem to focus on laughter, courage and love, three of the key ingredients in composing your life. Her message is that everybody has a chance to shine, everybody has poetry inside. Here are some of the "Maya-isms" for which she is often quoted.

- Leave footprints on the sand and laugh as much as possible.
- You pick yourself up, dust yourself off, and prepare to love somebody.
- We all come from God, trailing wisps of glory!

Les Brown

Les has inspired me in every way. I heard him give a keynote at the National Speakers Association meeting, "I came here 5 years ago in a bus. I am leaving here today in a Lear jet."

He galvanizes and mesmerizes an audience, and makes us want to go beat on our chests and go out and do new wonderful stuff. He has the power to pick up everything that Martin Luther King ever did and really have a dream and take the world forward.
—MARK VICTOR HANSEN

Les Brown served three terms in the Ohio State Legislature and is a very popular professional speaker, voted by Toastmasters International as one of the world's five best speakers for 1992.

Les Brown is renowned. No, not as in "His Band of Renown," that's another guy. As in renowned professional speaker, author, and television and radio personality.

In 1986, Les entered the public speaking arena on a full-time basis and formed his own company, Les Brown Unlimited, Inc. The company provides motivational tapes and materials, workshops, and personal and professional development programs aimed at individuals, companies, and organizations.

Les has had no formal education past high school, but with persistence and determination he has initiated and continued a process of unending self-education which has distinguished him as an authority on human potential. Les Brown's passion to learn and his hunger to realize greatness in himself and others helped him to achieve greatness. He rose from a hip-talkin' morning DJ to broadcast manager; from community activist to community leader; from political commentator to three-term legislator; and from a banquet and nightclub emcee to premier keynote speaker.

In 1990, Les recorded his first in a series of speech presentations entitled "You Deserve with Les Brown." This was awarded a Chicago-area Emmy and became the leading fund-raising program of its kind for pledges to PBS stations nationwide.

He is the author of the highly acclaimed and successful books, *Live Your Dreams* and *It Ain't Over Until You Win.* He is the former host of *The Les Brown TV Show,* a nationally syndicated daily television talk show which focused on solutions rather than problems. Les is a speaker and author. He designs specialized coaching programs for corporate leaders, sports leaders, and entertainers that helps them attain high levels of effective communication.

As the publisher of SUCCESS *magazine, I was hosting a conference attended by more than a thousand highly successful entrepreneurs who had paid a substantial amount in fees and travel expenses to be there. Les was the first speaker at the three-day event.*

The group was restless and doubtful about a "motivator." The clincher came as we were walking out of the breakfast, heading for the auditorium where Les would speak: A very accomplished woman entrepreneur walked up to me and said, "Why did you schedule a motivational speaker? I don't need to be motivated. I'm already motivated. I came here to get information, and contacts." The next thing I knew, I was introducing Les.

To say that his speech was a magnificent triumph would be a great understatement. The excitement he injected into the occasion lasted for all three days. At the end of the entire event, the woman who had made the negative comment made a point of seeking me out: "Les Brown's presentation opened up my mind, I learned more from the other sessions because I was so motivated. But even more importantly, he opened up my heart."

Les brings people to the brink of tears, or perhaps over the brink, then gets them all laughing. He motivates you to take on whatever challenges you're facing. While speaking is of course an art, everything about Les comes across as genuine, sincere, and honest—and totally without self-importance. No wonder people love him.

—SCOTT DEGARMO, FORMER PUBLISHER
OF *SUCCESS* MAGAZINE

Turning Points for Les Brown

Les began life with the greatest possible rejection. His birth mother became pregnant by another man while her husband was overseas in the military service. She gave Les and his fraternal twin brother up for adoption.

Les was adopted by a woman who has a great spirit. She raised the two boys all alone and became his magnificent inspiration.

However, for years Les hated his birth parents. He says it was a lot of work to hold that grudge. He finally dropped the heavy load of hate with the help of a quote from Kahlil Gibran: "Our children come through us, not from us."

Les says he realized that we are responsible for what we become. His adopted mama, Mrs. Mamie Brown, chose him by love.

Les explains that he has forgiven his birth parents. He plays with the hand life has dealt him and will not allow himself to be burdened with anger, resentment, regret, and guilt.

—DOTTIE WALTERS

Les Brown epitomizes the image of a self-made man. His life has been the quintessential tale of struggle and overcoming adversity to reach self-actualization.

Born on the filthy floor of an abandoned building, in low-income Liberty City in Miami, Florida, Les and his twin brother, Wes, were adopted when they were six weeks old by Mrs. Mamie Brown, a single woman who had very little education and financial means but a very big heart. He refers to himself more often as Mamie Brown's baby boy than Les Brown, and quotes Abraham Lincoln in saying that "all that I am and all that I ever hope to be, I owe to my mother."

As a child his inattention to school work, his restless energy, and the failure of his teachers to recognize his real potential resulted in his being mislabeled "educable mentally retarded." The label and the stigma stayed with Les, damaging his self-esteem, and took several years to overcome.

> *I met a speech teacher in high school, Mr. Leroy Washington. I saw in this man's character a person who did not allow his circumstances to define who he was. He lived his life with a sense of destiny, of "I'm going to impact the planet." Even in this stage of my life at 53, I don't call him Washington, or Leroy, I refer to him as Mr. Washington.*
>
> *In his presence he made you feel, without uttering a word, that you had greatness within you. That man triggered something in me that reminds me of what Goethe[1] said, "Look at a man the way that he is, he only becomes worse, but look at him as if he were what he could be, then he becomes what he should be."*
> —**LES BROWN**

Mr. Washington believed in him and taught him that while we are not always able to control what life puts in our path, we can always control who we are and what we will become. He instructed him after school in the principles that would affect his life:

- You don't get in life what you want, you get in life what you are.
- There is noting as powerful as a made-up mind, determined to succeed.
- Work to develop your communication skills: Once you open your mouth you tell the world who you are.
- Practice the OQP—associate with *only quality people*. If you run around with losers, you will end up a loser.

> *As a youngster I listened to the most colorful radio personalities of the day, from Milton Butterball Smith to the legendary Paul Harvey. They fascinated me.*

[1]Johann Wolfgang von Goethe, 1749–1832, German poet, dramatist, and novelist.

> *I started as a go-fer at a Miami station. My goal was to be behind the microphone, "spinning the platter an' giving the chatter!" With perseverance, hard work, and hunger for my goal, I positioned myself to be in the right place at the right time.*
> —LES BROWN

> *I remember going to see the motivational speakers Dr. Norman Vincent Peale and Zig Ziglar decades ago and I said to myself, I can do that! But when I started going to the parking lot my inner conversation activated itself and said, "Les Brown, you can't do that. What makes you think corporations like AT&T, Procter & Gamble, McDonald's Corporation, General Electric, IBM, Xerox [clients I have now] what makes you think you can do that?" So for 13 years, I didn't do what I am doing now, because I doubted myself. There is an old African proverb which says, "If there is no enemy within, the enemy outside can do us no harm." I finally conquered the enemy called fear, and set out to persue my dream of speaking to touch people's lives.*
> —LES BROWN

Les began speaking and was a tremendous success. Soon he was asked to do the *The Les Brown TV Show*. It was a nationally syndicated daily talk show focused on solutions rather than problems. It made Les famous; then it was dropped!

> *I look back on my TV show as one of my greatest experiences. I learned as much from losing that show as I learned from winning anything in my life.*
> *I fought trash talk TV and I lost that fight. But I learned that you can fall down for anything, as long as you stand up for what you believe in. I may not have made the millions that others have made, but you can't put a price tag on integrity and peace of mind.*
> —LES BROWN[2]

[2] *Sharing Ideas*, newsmagazine for professional speakers, Dec/Jan 1996.

Les Brown told the story of how he was fired, how depressed he was. Well, I was depressed at that time because I had just been fired from my job as a radio personality. I went from working 60 hours a week, to 6 . . . I had to do something, quick.

After hearing his story, it made me realize that being fired, was really a blessing in disguise. The Universe was pushing me to do something else, and being fired was the way to push me into doing it. His next few words were like stingers from a bumblebee. He said, "Any idiot can sit behind a microphone and talk. You're bigger and better than that. You were put here on this earth to do more than what you're doing now. You were made to do great things!"

I sat up in my chair. Thoughts were running wild, like a stampede of wild horses. I knew he was talking to me.

Now I am a certified training consultant. I speak and train groups of people, and I am back in radio, at the number one urban station in Chicago, WGCI-AM 1390, Sounds of Gospel (where I was told I would never get a job).

—ZELDA ROBINSON, INTERNATIONAL SPEAKER, TRAINING CONSULTANT, AUTHOR, RADIO PERSONALITY

In 1995 Les fell in love with the woman of his dreams, legendary singer Gladys Knight, of The Pips, and became, he would laughingly tell his audiences, the conductor of "The Midnight Train!" Two years later, he filed for a divorce.

My greatest failure, my deepest regret, is that of my marriage with Gladys Knight. If you want to give God a good laugh, just make him think you've got life figured out! That's when you really get caught! I thought I had this whole issue of relationships figured out. I did not. It caught me by surprise. I know how to make millions of dollars, I know how to be a good parent, I know how to handle many challenges of life, how to motivate and inspire people. As I look into my future, I am learning what it is I have to do to reinvent myself to make a marriage work.

—LES BROWN

That same year he lost Gladys, 1997, he was diagnosed with prostate cancer.

> *1997 was a year I was glad to see go!*
>
> *Sometimes God has to stop a life in order for Him to step in. Prior to these challenges I was traveling across the country, in five or six cities a week and my life was a big blur. But when my health challenge showed up I HAD to get off the road.*
>
> *It was as if Life said to me, "You've got to PROVE your stuff— you've got to LIVE the message you give!"*
>
> *I immediately sought medical treatment and saw my PSA level (which indicates the presence of cancer, 1 to 4 is normal), jump from 6.1 to 7.5 after medical procedures. I realized then I had to take this to a higher source.*
>
> *Through prayer, meditation, and visualization; through other people praying for me continuously; by radically changing my diet to include organically grown live fruits and vegetables, and by focusing on being centered and calm, my PSA is now down to 3 and is going down to 0!*
>
> *Once you are confronted with a life and death situation, life takes on a greater level of intensity. You value every moment. You speak the spirit of who you are, and how you have changed comes through even more so.*
> —LES BROWN

In 1998 Les took his message to music. He delivers it to millions from the platform of a classic Soul radio show, featuring songs from the seventies, eighties, and nineties. Radio station WMMJ's programming is syndicated nationally throughout the country. It allowed him to give people motivational Motown music, and in-between records, "Hi! This is Les Brown at 8:15 a.m. Stand up for what you believe in, because you can fall for anything. We'll be right back!"

Special Wisdom of Les Brown

> *I tell Les's life story as one of my signature stories. The main message I tell from Les's life is that no matter what society labels you, you can do*

it. Also, "I'm hungry, I'm persistent, I'll do whatever it takes." He lives that, he personifies that, now he is an extremely well paid speaker.
—JACK CANFIELD

- You can fall down for anything, as long as you stand up for what you believe in.
- When life gets you down, fall on your back because if you can see up you can get up!
- Don't let nobody turn you around. Go after your dreams as if your life depends on it, because it does.
- If I want to be different, to stand out, then I have to be willing to do the things that others won't do, in order to have the things tomorrow others won't have.
- Act the way you want to be and soon you'll be the way you act.
- Practice doesn't make perfect, it makes improvement.
- In order to do something you have never done, you've got to be someone you have never been.
- You learn from experiences. Grow through it, rather than just go through it.
- It ain't over until I win!

Jack Canfield

The thing that impresses me most about Jack is his humble, loving attitude. He seems to me to be the personification of his own favorite quote by Leo Buscaglia: "Love is life. And if you miss love, you miss life." Jack Canfield reminds me of one of my favorite quotes by my friend of the mind, Albert Einstein: "Try not to become a person of success, but rather, try to become a person of value."
—DOTTIE WALTERS

Jack Canfield, a brimming cup of Mega-success. Co-creator of the, let me say it again, Mega-success *Chicken Soup for the Soul*® series, which has had at least one book on the *New York Times* best-seller list every week for the last three years. Sometimes as many as eight *Chicken Soup* titles have been on the best-seller lists at one time!

The *Chicken Soup* product line is the publishing phenomenon of the decade, possibly of the century. In addition, Jack says, "Everyone and their uncle has come at us for licensing agreements." In the works: calendars, screensavers, tee-shirts, personal planners, a series of children's books, posters, a possible animated television series for kids, a set of CD compilations of music with Rhino Records, a syndicated weekly newspaper column, a possible radio show, and a TV show on PAXTV.

Jack Canfield is the CEO of Chicken Soup for the Soul Enterprises, president of Self-Esteem Seminars in Santa Barbara, California, and chairman of the board of the Foundation for Self-Esteem in Culver City, California. Jack has conducted intensive personal and professional development seminars for over 750,000 people worldwide. He has spoken to hundreds of thousands of others at numerous conferences and conventions, and he has been seen by millions on television shows such as *Oprah Winfrey, The Today Show, America's Talking AM, The Caryl and Marilyn Show, 20/20, Rosanne, Eye to Eye,* CNN's *Talk Back Live! The New Hard Copy, The John Bradshaw Show, Home Team with Terry Bradshaw,* PBS, the BBC, QVC, Home Shopping Network and the NBC and CBS nightly news shows. He created and starred in a 90-minute PBS special entitled "Living Your Dream," which was used nationwide as a PBS fund-raising show.

He has published 21 books, including the best-selling *Chicken Soup for the Soul* series. He is very proud of having won the ABBY (the American Booksellers Book of the Year) award, which is given for the book that booksellers most loved recommending to potential readers. His other titles are *The Aladdin Factor, Dare to Win, Heart at Work,* and *101 Ways to Develop Self-Esteem and Personal Responsibility in the Classroom.* Jack has 17 audio programs, including Career Track's six-cassette *Self-Esteem and Peak Performance,* with over 360,000 albums sold, and Nightingale-Conant's *How to Build High Self-Esteem,* with over 100,000 albums sold. He developed a video training program for California welfare recipients entitled *The GOALS Program.* Over 2,000,000 welfare recipients and people-at-risk in 25 states have participated in this motivational success program over the last eight years. His *STAR (Success Through Action and Responsibility) Program,* a three-day video-based training program, has been purchased by numerous *Fortune* 500 Companies and is also offered regularly by the American Management Association.

Jack is a graduate of Harvard; he has a master's in education from the University of Massachusetts and several honorary doctorates in psychology.

He inspires with his spirituality and kindness, and he quantifies information with his vast knowledge. He has a relaxed, matter-of-fact approach. Audiences feel his genuine love for them.

Turning Points for Jack Canfield

After teaching history in Chicago in an all-black inner-city school, Jack went to work in a Job Corps Center in Clinton, Iowa. The mission of Job Corps was to take kids who had dropped out of school and give them a second chance to learn basic education and job skills so that they could become independent and self-sufficient wage earners. During that period of time he took a workshop that was offered by the W. Clement and Jesse V. Stone Foundation, called "The Achievement Motivation Program." At that time W. Clement Stone was the publisher of *SUCCESS* magazine, which was edited by Og Mandino.

That weekend workshop changed my life forever. I learned about the power of keeping a positive focus in life, the importance of setting measurable goals, and the basic underpinnings of a science of personal success. I started applying Stone's principles of success in my teaching and suddenly my students really started learning.

I started coming to work as an assistant at Stone's seminars on every free weekend I had just so I could learn more about his ideas and how to apply them to my life and the lives of my students.

Then due to politics, the Center was closed. I was out of a job. The Stone Foundation asked me to come work for them. "We need, someone who has experience in the inner city." I went and became a trainer.

> *Over the next two years I learned a great deal about motivation, self-esteem, values, goals, and perseverance, all of the basic building blocks of "success." After two years, I grew restless. I knew that everything I was teaching was working, but I didn't know why, and my mind wanted to figure out why. So, when I had the opportunity, I enrolled in a doctoral program in psychological education at the University of Massachusetts. This was when I took the somewhat pop-psychology approach of W. Clement Stone and was able to deepen it with the latest information about adult learning theory and psychology. After two years in that program I started giving talks and workshops to teachers in school systems all over New England. By then I had a viable speaking career.*
> —JACK CANFIELD

What launched Jack from a successful, brilliant speaker, into a brilliantly, successfully business phenomenon, was his love of beautiful "heart stories," and his friendship with another great motivational speaker, Mark Victor Hansen. (See Mark's story on pages 31–36.)

Special Wisdom of Jack Canfield

- Even though your heart gets broken, it is better to love and be vulnerable, to share your feelings, say "I love you," and give appreciation—even to people who don't appreciate being appreciated.

- Believe in your dreams. Believe that the dreams that were put in your heart were put there by God and it's part of your purpose to fulfill them, and in doing that, you serve others. By having a loving relationship, you serve others by modeling that relationship. It's not selfish to love yourself. To care about others, to be involved in making a difference, in serving others. When you contribute, you feel better about yourself.

- We have a culture that seems to think if you can't solve a problem in 30 minutes—about how long a TV show lasts—give up. I think most people don't push through the hard times, they throw in the towel too early.

- There is a God. He's behind you, believes in you, cares about you. He wouldn't have created you, then left you alone. Just tune in, meditate, pray, ask for guidance, and give back through tithing and making a difference and reaching out in love.

Deepak Chopra

Deepak Chopra, M.D., is perhaps the highest profiled embodiment of the "technological miracles of the West meets the wisdom of the East" movement. His wisdom has inspired countless people to experience the inner journey into self-awareness. His spirit has moved Debra Winger, Martin Sheen, Goldie Hawn, Madonna, Laura Day, Demi Moore, and many others.

He is the son of a cardiologist and himself an American-trained endocrinologist turned Ayurvedic expert; endocrinology being the branch of medicine dealing with the endocrine glands and the various internal secretions. Ayurveda is a 5,000-year-old healing tradition initiated in the East, which incorporates the connection between mind, body, and spirit as the crucial element to healing and wellness.

Dr. Chopra is the author of 23 books, and more than 30 audio, video, and CD-ROM programs. He has been published on every continent and in dozens of languages. Nearly 10 million copies of his books have been sold in English alone. His best-selling books include *Ageless Body, Timeless Mind: The Quantum Alternative to Growing Old; The Seven Spiritual Laws of Success; The Return of Merlin;* and *The Path to Love.* His popular audio and CD-ROMs include *Magical Mind, Magical Body; The Higher Self; Journey to the Boundless;* and *The Wisdom Within.* In conjunction with PBS, he has produced a number of television and video programs. Among them are *Body, Mind and Soul: The Mystery and the Magic,* one of the most highly viewed and successful fund-raisers in the history of the network, as well as *The Way of the Wizard, Alchemy,* and *The Crystal Cave.*

He appeared as a keynote speaker at the inauguration of the State of the World Forum and the Peace and Human Progress Foundation, founded by the former President of Costa Rica and Nobel Peace Prize winner, Oscar Arias, as well as at the Orient Foundation. *Esquire* magazine has designated him as one of the top 10 motivational speakers. In the distinguished company of President Nelson Mandela, Congress-woman Barbara Jordan, Tom Peters, and Garrison Keillor, Toastmasters International awarded him highest honors for communication excellence and leadership, as one of the five outstanding speakers of 1995. He was also the recipient of the 1997 Toastmasters Golden Gavel Award. For his constant dialogue to further peace and international collaboration, Dr. Chopra was awarded the Medal of the Presidency of the Italian Republic by the Pio Manzu Centre, chaired by Mikhail Gorbachev.

Formerly chief of staff at the Boston Regional Medical Center, Dr. Chopra also taught at Tufts University and Boston University Schools of Medicine and built a successful endocrinology practice in Boston. In 1992, he served on the National Institutes of Health Ad Hoc Panel on Alternative Medicine.

In 1995, Dr. Chopra established The Chopra Center for Well Being in California, where he serves as chairman. The center offers a wide variety of individual and group programs in mind/body medicine and personal development, integrating the best of Western medicine and natural healing traditions to provide a fresh approach to modern health needs. Under the auspices of Infinite Possibilities Seminars and Infinite Possibilities Knowledge, Dr. Chopra and his colleagues conduct public seminars and workshops and provide training for health-care professionals in the principles and practices of mind/body medicine throughout the world.

Dr. Chopra's techniques emphasize meditation, a balanced lifestyle, health-promoting foods and herbs, rejuvenating body therapies, and personal empowerment. Together, they promote longevity and maximize human potential and success, while increasing personal balance, happiness, and fulfillment.

Turning Point for Deepak Chopra

While in strictly traditional medicine I was frustrated with the limited way that I was affecting patients. It was the realization that mechanisms of illness are not the origin of illness. You can try to interfere with the mechanisms of illness and cause a temporary alleviation of illness, but not unless you go into the origins of illness,

you're not going to bring about curing or healing anyone. I came to the realization that although medicine has made great technological advancements, doctors like myself needed to become better healers.
—Dr. Deepak Chopra

Dr. Deepak Chopra has established the fundamental principle that perfect health is not just the absence of disease but a lively state of balance and integration of body, mind, and spirit. He is widely credited with melding modern theories of quantum physics with the timeless wisdom of ancient cultures. Simply put, his message is that we are in total control of our bodies and our ability to heal ourselves within, by healing our minds.

This entire concept is being more accepted and less faddish. According to a scientific survey, more than 50 percent of Americans are seeing alternative practitioners.

Special Wisdom of Deepak Chopra

There's a whole grassroots movement in the United States that is dissatisfied with our prevailing system of medicine where doctors have become superb technicians who know everything about the human body and really lousy healers because they know nothing about the human soul.

Western medicine looks at mechanisms of disease and knows how to interfere with them and get rid of disease frequently. But Western medicine is not involved at the moment in the alleviation of suffering. Suffering is more than just pain. Suffering occurs in another realm where Western medicine can't peer through its microscopes. You can be completely cured of an illness and still be suffering—suffering from the anguish of the treatment, from the fear of mortality, from the fact that it has disrupted your whole life. And so we begin to see that people want healing.
—Dr. Deepak Chopra

- It all starts with the self. When you change yourself, then you can change the world a little bit. By expanding your self-awareness, becoming more familiar and intimate with the field of infinite possibilities that exists within you. Once you've become that, then you begin to change the world.

- Meditation is a great technique to learn to quiet the mind and access your inner silence. It is a very important tool for those seeking enlightenment.

- Nutrition is also extremely important. When you are feeling bad, every other part of your life is affected so you need to maintain a balanced diet, with exercise and restful sleep.

- I think it is important to not take yourself too seriously. Life is a joyous, magical experience, and laughter is an essential element to happiness and fulfillment.

Stephen Covey

Stephen Covey is author of *The Seven Habits of Highly Effective People,* one of the best-selling books of all time. It's been on the *New York Times* best-seller list over 270 weeks, and has sold more than 12 million copies in 32 languages and 70 countries. The *Seven Habits* book was recently chosen by readers of *Chief Executive* magazine as the number one most influential book of the twentieth century. In South Korea the *Seven Habits* book is the best-selling foreign nonfiction book of all time. Besides the *Seven Habits* book, published in 1989, he has several other best-selling books including, *Principle-Centered Leadership, First Things First,* and *The Seven Habits of Highly Effective Families.*

Covey and his associates have also produced legions of resource materials, training programs and videotapes, time management tools including the Franklin Day Planner, audiotapes, manuals, videos, lecture series, and satellite-based training programs. Covey's training program is being used in 3,500 school districts and universities nationwide and through statewide initiatives with education leaders in 27 states. Last year Covey gave lectures, in person and via satellite, to a total of over 170,000 people.

I heard Stephen Covey at the Points of Light Convention, in San Francisco, in 1996, where he presented two thoughts that stay with me:

1. The Seven Habits are not a set of separate psyche-up formulas. They express the natural laws which create habits from three areas; knowledge, desire, and skills.

2. Everyone can be in a win-win approach, if we change our paradigms of thinking.

From his inspiring presence and powerful words, I was motivated to start my speaking business and work on writing two books. His example of passion, helped me to understand the magic of words to move people.

—MARY LAKE, THE LOVELADY

Covey was the founder and chairman of Covey Leadership Center (1984 to 1997). Since 1997, he has been cochairman of Franklin Covey Co., headquartered in Salt Lake City, Utah. The firm provides leadership development programs for 82 of the *Fortune* 100 companies, more than two-thirds of the *Fortune* 500 companies, and thousands of small and mid-size companies, educational institutions, communities, and all levels of government.

Covey was awarded the the Toastmasters International Top Speaker Award, Ernst & Young and *Inc.* magazine's National Entrepreneur of the Year Lifetime Achievement Award for Entrepreneurial Leadership, and several honorary doctorates. He has also been recognized as one of "America's 25 Most Influential People" by *Time* magazine. He also makes numerous guest appearances on various local, regional, and national television and radio news broadcasts.

He is a retired professor of management and organizational behavior at the Marriott School of Management, Brigham Young University, Provo, Utah. His has a doctorate from Brigham Young University, an M.B.A. from Harvard University, and a B.A. from the University of Utah.

. . . although I had read his book The Seven Habits of Highly Effective People, *seeing him in person made a profound impact on my life. I find he is one of the most, if not the most influential motivational speaker in the last 50 years. In that speech, he gave lots of emphasis to habit 5, seek to understand and then be under-*

stood. Since that day, I have always had that habit engraved in my mind, and it has served me faithfully over the years.

When I came back from that session, I bought his tapes and gave them to my daughter to listen to. Of course, I listened to them as well. A few years later, Stephen was invited to speak at the National Speakers Association. My daughter and I always go to the NSA convention and I wanted her to meet Stephen. While I was speaking to him, I saw my daughter at a distance and waved at her to come and say hello. When I introduced her to him, my daughter said "Mr. Covey, my dad gave me your tapes when I was a little girl a few years ago. I must confess that I found you the most boring speaker I had ever heard!"

At that point I almost fainted and gave my daughter one of those looks she will never forget. Then Stephen said, "My wife feels the same way," and we all laughed.

My daughter then fixed it by saying, "However, I heard you today and you were great." That little girl of mine is very smart.

—JOACHIM DE POSADA, INTERNATIONAL MANAGE-
MENT CONSULTANT, BUSINESS AND SALES SPEAKER

Covey is considered one of the best motivators of all time. But it is not for a highly entertaining speaking style. As both Covey and his critics are quick to point out, it is his character and his content that create change in the listener.

He does not have the oratorical style of a Martin Luther King, or the mesmerizing magic of Maya Angelou. What Stephen Covey has is a clearly defined purpose, sincere passion for the subject, and loving compassion for the audience. All three qualities have combined to help him develop superior materials and content that are extremely appropriate to what people are searching for in this last part of the twentieth century.

Despite his superstar status, he lives a comparatively quiet lifestyle. He and his wife Sandra live in Utah, have 9 children, and 31 grandkids.

Turning Points for Stephen Covey

Stephen Covey, author of *The Seven Habits of Highly Effective People,* suffered as a teenager from a terrible degradation of the thighbones, which caused him to spend three painful years on crutches with long steel pins implanted in his legs.

Many hear his voice and read his words and assume he is a giant of a man. But this sickness very possibly stunted his physical growth and was a turning point, redirecting him towards his present work.

> *I was a pretty good athlete, I really was. But this shifted me totally into academics, and also into forensics. I got into debate and speaking, and I got turned on by that.*
> —STEPHEN COVEY

Another turning point for Covey occurred during his two-year term as a Mormon missionary. He was sent off to serve in England. After only a few months he was reassigned from the field and told to go to Nottingham to train "branch presidents" (lay leaders in the church) of new congregations.

> *I had no idea at all I could train leaders. I was totally over-whelmed and nonplussed, and my mission president just said, "You can do it." That was very significant. I told the grandson of my mission president just the other day: "Your grandfather probably got me into this business of training leaders."*
> —STEPHEN COVEY

Special Wisdom of Stephen Covey

> *To do well you must do good, and to do good you must first be good.*
> —STEPHEN COVEY

His seven habits of highly effective people, briefly, are these:

1. Be proactive. Take the initiative and be responsible.
2. Begin with the end in mind. Start any endeavor—a meeting, a day at the office, your adult life—with a mental image of an outcome conforming to values you cherish.
3. Put first things first. Discipline yourself to subordinate feelings, impulses, and moods to your values.
4. Think win-win. Seek mutual benefit.

5. Seek first to understand, then to be understood. Listen with the intent to empathize, not with the intent to reply.

6. Synergize. Value the differences. Create wholes that are greater than the sum of their parts.

7. Sharpen the saw. Take time to cultivate the four essential dimensions of your character: physical, mental, social/emotional, and spiritual.

Here are some more of Covey's profound statements:

- Private victories precede public victories.

- More important than being successful is being significant. Significance means making a contribution to others.

Sir Winston Leonard Spencer Churchill

History will be kind to me for I intend to write it.
   —SIR WINSTON CHURCHILL

Sir Winston Leonard Spencer Churchill, 1874–1965, British states-man, soldier, orator, journalist, politician, biographer, historian, and scholar. There are legion and colossal volumes written by and about Churchill, so I will be brief here about who he was, and try to explain throughout this book why his words, more than many speakers in history, are still remembered and repeated today. For all kinds of interesting information about him, go to http://www.winstonchurchill.org.

Son of Lord Randolph Churchill of England and Jennie Jerome Churchill of the United States. Educated at Harrow and Sandhurst. I remember with fondness the movie, *Young Winston,* which tells of his flamboyant stint as a reporter, and his coverage of the Boer War. He had been hired by *The Morning Post* to cover the war in South Africa (1899). His accounts of his capture and imprisonment by the Boers and his escape raised him to the forefront of English journalists.

He held many offices in British politics, colored with brilliant triumphs and miserable failures. During one of his less-favored, and out-of-office periods, he was one of the few who bellowed, unheeded, forewarning to the world: Nazi Germany was rising. A warning which went mostly ignored by the world. When World War II broke out (September, 1939), Neville Chamberlain appointed him First Lord of the Admiralty. The following May, when Chamberlain was forced to resign, Churchill became Prime Minister.

Although he was elected as Prime Minister again in 1951, he is most remembered for his terms from 1940 to 1945, when he became Prime Minister and Minister of Defense. When the Fascist forces in Europe and Japan threatened the rest of the free world, he was the mobilizing force for Britain, the heart of England in "her finest hour."

Arguably, the greatest statesman of the twentieth century. He was the first honorary citizen of the United States. He coined the term "iron curtain."

> *In the dark days and darker nights when England stood alone— and most men save Englishmen despaired of England's life—he mobilized the English language and sent it into battle.*
> —PRESIDENT JOHN F. KENNEDY, APRIL 9, 1963,
> UPON PROCLAIMING CHURCHILL AN HONORARY
> US CITIZEN[3]

His biographical and autobiographical works include *Lord Randolph Churchill* (1906); *My Early Life: A Roving Commission* (1930), a four volume study of his ancestor Marlborough (1933–1938); and *World Crisis* (4 vols., 1923–1929), his account of World War I. *The Second World War* (6 vols., 1948–1953) was followed by *A History of the English-Speaking Peoples* (4 vols., 1956–1958). For much more on Churchill, see his speeches, edited by R. R. James, and *Blood, Toil, Tears and Sweat,* edited by David Cannadine; the multivolume study by his son Randolph Churchill and Martin Gilbert; and a biography by Martin Gilbert.

He was loved and hated with equal power. On Churchill's fiftieth birthday, A.G. Gardiner reflected that Churchill's life was "one long speech. He does not talk: he orates."[4] His gift with words won him the

---

[3]Quoted in *The Churchill Years 1874–1965,* intro. Lord Butler of Saffron Walden (New York: The Viking Press, 1965), p. 231.

[4]A. G. Gardiner, "Genius without Judgment: Churchill at Fifty," in A. G. Gardiner (ed.), *Portraits and Portents* (New York: Harper & Row, 1926), p. 63.

Nobel Prize in Literature for his writing and oratory. It brought a world hope in despair and brought fear to our enemies.

At Thanksgiving my father, Thomas Munro, Jr., would take out an old red book with a dark, dry red rose pressed into it. It was a copy of Churchill's early war speeches, Blood, Sweat and Tears *that my father's British mother, who was to die before war's end, gave to my father before he went overseas in WWII. My father carried this book—and the red rose—with him throughout his war experiences.*

My father's favorite part of the book was Churchill's speech on the Battle of Britain. I was six or seven as Dad read those speeches to us around the table, but I knew who Hitler was and knew he was very bad indeed.

My father said "Churchill was Shakespeare, Shaw and St. George all in one. He was a great author, orator, and he was a great soldier of freedom as well." Never was there a man better placed to create a union among democratic nations and the English-speaking peoples.
> —RICHARD "RICARDO" MUNRO, TEACHER AND
> AUTHOR FEATURED IN *Calliope*, WORLD HISTORY
> MAGAZINE FOR YOUTH

Turning Points for Winston Churchill

Winston Churchill failed sixth grade. By his early 20s, his mother despaired of his ever becoming a success.

You seem to have no real purpose in life and won't realize at the age of twenty-two that for a man life means work, and hard work if you mean to succeed.
> —JENNIE JEROME CHURCHILL (1854–1921),
> ANGLO-AMERICAN MOTHER OF WINSTON
> CHURCHILL. LETTER, FEBRUARY 26, 1897, TO
> WINSTON CHURCHILL [PUBLISHED IN RALPH G.
> MARTIN (ED.), *Jennie*, VOL. 2, 1971].

At the turn of the century he switched political parties from the Conservative Party to the Liberal. A good move, as they were on the rise.

With typical Churchillian gusto, he went all the way over and became a "raging liberal." He flirted with socialism and he tried to create state-run monopolies in forestries and nationalized steel production.

> *The personal exhilaration he felt in these moral crusades helped change his character. He was at 33 a confirmed irascible, unattractive bachelor. But then during this period of time he married Miss Clementine Hozier, a lifelong liberal, who did much to stabilize his impetuous nature, his boozing, his arrogance, and rudeness to subordinates. She was a civilizing influence to him and introduced him to many liberals and socialists who later became his wartime allies.*
> —RICHARD "RICARDO" MUNRO, TEACHER, AUTHOR,
> AND CHURCHILL HISTORIAN

Later he rejected socialism, recognizing it a sly enemy of freedom with totalitarian propensities.

During World War I (1914–1918) the Allies (principally the British and the Australian and New Zealand forces) unsuccessfully attempted a massive prototypical sea and land invasion of Turkey in the Gallipoli Campaign (April 25, 1915–January 8, 1916).

Frustrated in his political ambitions Churchill, already a successful author, turned to painting, journalism, and a veritable flood of serious, brilliant writing. He wrote the splendid historical narrative *The World Crisis* (six volumes), began his *History of the English-Speaking Peoples,* and wrote his biography of Marlborough.

> *Now approaching 60 he seemed a pot-bellied balding has-been. But to the astonishment of many and to the great wonder of the democratic world Churchill would once again be electrified by a cause: the survival of Britain itself and indeed Western Democracy itself what was arguably the greatest challenge to free institutions since the Persian Wars. Churchill rose to the challenge to become an orator of the rank of Pericles[5] or Lincoln.*
> —RICHARD "RICARDO" MUNRO, TEACHER, AUTHOR
> AND CHURCHILL HISTORIAN

[5]Died 429 B.C. Athenian leader noted for advancing democracy in Athens and for ordering the construction of the Parthenon.

Despite all his amazing successes in WWII, he was thrown out of office immediately after it was over, in 1945. But he turned this disaster into a triumph of art and diplomacy with his address at Westminster College, Fulton, Missouri.

> *When Sir Winston reminded President Truman and the Western World that "an iron curtain has descended across the continent," it could be said that he laid the seeds of a NATO, the EEC, and the ultimate defeat of the last great totalitarian threat to the democracies.*
> —RICHARD "RICARDO" MUNRO, TEACHER, AUTHOR, AND CHURCHILL HISTORIAN

He went on with his writing and topped his political success with a Nobel Prize for literature. John F. Kennedy hailed Churchill for his inspiration and his leadership of all the democracies. Few persons have achieved so many great and varied honors! 1999 saw the launching of the USS *Winston Churchill.*

> *Success consists of going from failure to failure without loss of enthusiasm.*
> —SIR WINSTON CHURCHILL

Special Wisdom of Winston Churchill

- It is a good thing for an uneducated man to read books of quotations.
- I have nothing to offer but blood, toil, tears, and sweat.
- It has been said that democracy is the worst form of government except all the others that have been tried.
- The greatest lesson in life is to know that even fools are right sometimes.

Elizabeth Dole

Elizabeth Hanford Dole has served five U.S. presidents. She held Cabinet positions under Ronald Reagan and George Bush.

According to a Gallup poll that was done for *Ladies Home Journal,* she was number three on the poll's List of Most Admired Women in America for 1998. She was a Presidential candidate for 2000, perhaps the first viable female Republican nominee in the history of the United States, and had an impressive eight-year tenure as president of the American Red Cross.

As president of the American Red Cross, Elizabeth Dole received numerous awards for her humanitarian efforts and leadership among women. She directed more than 32,000 paid and 1.3 million volunteer staff. She is a manager of great strengths and broad vision, competently leading this charity with $2 billion a year in revenue and missions as diverse as a *Fortune* 500 company.

Turning Points for Elizabeth Dole

I would say one of the biggest turning points in Mrs. Dole's life was her decision to move to New England upon her graduation from Duke. Her brother had offered her a job in the family floral wholesaling business in North Carolina, and this was an era where young women were expected to stay close to home.

　Instead, Mrs. Dole chose to travel to Boston, where she accepted a job in the Harvard Law Library. A few years later she went from working in the law library to studying in the law library—as one of only 24 women in a class of 550.

　　—JOAN MUENCHEN, GROUP TOUR DIRECTOR
　　　IN FLORIDA

Following graduate school, she accepted a position with the Department of Health, Education, and Welfare, where she prepared a conference on education for the deaf. She began practicing law as a public defender in Washington, D.C., in 1967.

I decided from almost my first day in Washington that I would bypass the full-time practice of law, and instead seek a career in government service. Like many others of my generation, I regarded public service as a noble calling—as a chance to make a difference in the issues of our time.

> *Some said back then that I had "stars in my eyes" when it came to my desire to work in government. And perhaps I did. But my years as a servant of the public were everything I had hoped for and more. And that's a message I share as often as I can with America's young people.*
>
> *I share it because over the years Americans have grown increasingly disenchanted with our government. I believe many qualified people are being discouraged from entering government service. The words, "I'm from the government, and I'm here to help," are guaranteed to get laughs. And that was not the case when I started out.*
>
> —ELIZABETH DOLE

During the mid-1960s, as a registered Democrat, she held several posts in the administration of President Lyndon Johnson. Then, much as Churchill did, she changed parties. After becoming a Republican, Dole served under President Richard Nixon and President Gerald R. Ford.

A major turning point in her personal life, and one thoroughly endorsed by her family was in 1975, when she married Senator Robert Joseph "Bob" Dole.

> *They first met when she went to lobby him for the inclusion of a consumer protection plank in the 1972 Republican platform. At a reception for Mrs. Dole at the 1996 Republican Convention, Senator Dole surprised her by giving her something very special he had framed—his "schedule card" from the day they met.*
>
> —KERRY TYMCHUK, SPEECHWRITER
> FOR ELIZABETH DOLE AND COAUTHOR
> OF *Unlimited Partners*

Elizabeth Dole also feels a profound turning point when she realized all was not what it should be in her life.

> *In my case, my career became of paramount importance. I worked very hard, to excel, to achieve, my goal was to do my best, which is all fine and well. But I'm inclined to be a perfectionist. And it's very hard, you know, to try to control everything, surmount every difficulty, foresee every problem, realize every opportunity. That*

can be pretty tough on your family, your friends, your fellow work-
ers and on yourself.

   I was blessed with a beautiful marriage, a challenging
career . . . and yet . . . only gradually, over many years, did I real-
ize what was missing—my life was threatened with spiritual star-
vation.

   I knew it as time to cease living life backwards, time to strive to
put Christ first, preeminent—with no competition, at the very
center of my life . . . it was time to submit my resignation as
Master of my own little universe . . . and . . . God accepted my
resignation.

   —ELIZABETH DOLE, SECRETARY OF
   TRANSPORTATION, NATIONAL PRAYER BREAKFAST,
   WASHINGTON, D.C., FEBRUARY 5, 1987

In 1983, Dole was appointed America's first female Secretary of Transportation, and she was made famous by introducing the stop lights that sit on the rear windows of American cars. During Dole's four and a half years at the Department of Transportation, the United States enjoyed the safest period to date in all three major transportation areas—rail, air, and highway. She led the civilian government in the initiation of random drug testing and the national effort to raise the drinking age to 21.

President Bush made her the nation's twentieth Secretary of Labor in January, 1989. There her priority was America's human resources—improving the skills of our work force, helping to resolve a bitter coal strike.

In 1991, she became president of the Red Cross. She rescued a critically injured blood program and delivered "real-life miracles" to victims of natural disasters around the world. At a time when the Red Cross, like many charities, had seen its United Way funding plunge, Dole not only made up the difference, but used her own tenacity and persuasive charm to increase public donations by 9 percent.

She undertook a seven-year, $287 million transformation of the way the organization collects, tests, and distributes half of the nation's blood supply. The system is now considered by many the best in the world.

The Red Cross was built by volunteers. And our tradition of trust was built from the grassroots, in communities across the country. Our assistance is not delivered by strangers or faceless bureaucrats; rather, it's given by friends and neighbors. The Red Cross patch can be found on the arm of the merchant on Main Street or the retired teacher, two houses down.

I've thought a lot about that patch, and the over one million volunteers who wear it today. I've thought about how I wanted to get the message out that it is the volunteers who are the heart and soul of the Red Cross. And I decided that the best way I can let volunteers know of their importance is to be one of them—to earn the patch on my sleeve. Therefore, during my first year as president, I will accept no salary. I, too, will be a volunteer.

—ELIZABETH DOLE, FROM HER RED CROSS
INAUGURAL SPEECH

After her very successful time with the Red Cross, Elizabeth took a leave of absence in 1996 to campaign for her husband's Presidential bid. Although famous before the campaign, her speech at the Republican National Convention of 1996 is one of the main reasons she is considered a Superstar.

The occasion was the Republican National Convention of 1996. With her husband, Robert Dole, about to be named as the Presidential candidate in the upcoming campaign, Elizabeth Dole took the floor to speak on his behalf.

It wasn't her words that had me sitting before the TV in tears. It was the person speaking to the convention and the country that so moved me then and still "speaks" to me today.

Ever since that evening, I have been rejecting the temptation to fulfill the world's female "image." There is no substitute or counterfeit for class and dignity. It has to be earned and learned. Elizabeth Dole continues to be a role model for me in this pursuit; not for what she says, but for what she is!

—JOAN MUENCHEN, GROUP TOUR DIRECTOR
IN FLORIDA

She returned to the Red Cross in January 1997. She left in 1999 to make her own Presidential bid, as the first viable female candidate for President of the United States of America!

> *God forbid that someday I look back and realize I was too distracted by things of this world, too busy, too driven . . . and my work was given to another.*
>
> *Each of us has a unique assignment in this world given to us by a sovereign God—to love and to serve those within our own sphere of influence. We've been blessed to be a blessing; we've received that we might give.*
>
> —ELIZABETH DOLE, SECRETARY OF
> TRANSPORTATION, NATIONAL PRAYER BREAKFAST,
> WASHINGTON, D.C., FEBRUARY 5, 1987

Special Wisdom of Elizabeth Dole

Mrs. Dole appreciates good quotes. Two of her favorites:

> *To live fully is to be engaged in the passions of one's time.*
> —OLIVER WENDELL HOLMES

> *We are face to face with our destiny, and we must meet it with a high and resolute courage. For ours is the life of action, of vigorous performance of duty. We must live in the harness, striving mightily. We must run the risk of wearing out, rather than rusting out.*
> —TEDDY ROOSEVELT

More of the common sense of Elizabeth Dole:

- We must rekindle a spirit in our hearts, something . . . buried beneath a thickening layer of skepticism, doubt, and loss of faith in our institutions.

- But let us never forget that the true heroes of our society are not to be found on a movie screen or a football field. They are to be found in our classrooms.

- When you look back on your life, I sincerely believe what really matters won't be how much money you make, how many titles you held, or how much prestige you amassed. Instead, you'll be asking, "What did I stand for?" Did I make a difference—a positive difference—in the lives of others.

- Life is much more than the sum total of your possessions. For material resources will rust away, wear away, or depreciate. But your inner resources—your character—must never tarnish.

- Life is not just a few years to spend on self-indulgence and career advancement. It's a privilege, a responsibility, a steward-ship to be lived according to a much higher calling—God's calling. This alone gives true meaning to life.

Mark Victor Hansen

He is called "America's master motivator" and for good reason. In more than 2,500 presentations since 1974, his message has reached over 2,000,000 people in 35 countries and virtually every major city across America.

His credentials include a lifetime of entrepreneurial successes, in addition to an extensive academic background. Mark Victor Hansen is also the co-creator (with Jack Canfield, see page 12) of the astonishingly successful *Chicken Soup for the Soul*® series. The series *Time* magazine calls "the publishing phenomenon of the decade" has collectively sold over 40 million copies in North America alone, making it one of the most successful publishing franchises in America today.

He has been seen by millions on television shows such as *Oprah*, CNN, *Eye to Eye*, QVC, *The Today Show*, *Hard Copy*, PBS, The People's Network, and has had his autobiography produced and aired on *Nostalgia*, Good TV. He has been featured or appeared on the cover of dozens of national magazines and newspapers such as *Entrepreneur*, *SUCCESS*, *Time*, *U.S. News and World Report*, *USA Today*, *The New York Times*, *The Washington Post*, *Dallas Morning News*, *Chicago Tribune*, and *The Los Angeles Times*.

Everything with Mark is done "totally." Sounds just a bit like left-over slang from his childhood. Then you get to realize, it's not slang with Mark. He does it *totally* involved or he doesn't do it.

Mark is delightful. Delightful! Full of light, full of life, full of laughter. He makes silly jokes and laughs so hard you are just carried away in merriment. He uses your name often in conversations, making you feel important. He makes quotes about people that are wildly loose and wonderful exaggerated.

His trick is that it's not a trick. He laughs, and cries repeatedly in any presentation, from the heart. He will hear someone tell a sad story in a hallway and cry. You will hear laughter from someplace in a crowd, and you can bet it's Mark. He feels life, and passes the feelings onto his listeners, both on and off the platform.

Every time I hear Mark speak, I cry. He is gifted at touching the heart.

> *I want to talk to people who care—about things that matter.*
> *They are going to make a life-changing difference in their lives.*
> —MARK VICTOR HANSEN

Turning Points for Mark Victor Hansen

But how did Mark Victor Hansen get to be the speaker/publishing phenomenon of the century? Many turning points made him the man he is today.

> *I learned to be an entrepreneur at an early age.*
>
> *My father was a Danish immigrant who had the guts to come to America with the trade of a baker and a limited education. He had no choice but to suck it in and tough it out. As he prospered and matured, he wanted to take my mother, my brothers and me to Denmark so we could see where he was born. In addition to getting a flavor for the language and culture, I was introduced to low handlebar racing bicycles, I was addicted. They were not available in America, for the most part, and my desire turned into obsession. I wanted one with my heart of hearts. I said, "Dad can I have it?" Dad replied, "You can have it when you are 21." I was immediately immune to his negativity and rejection.*
>
> *To Dad, free enterprise meant the more enterprising you are the freer you are. So, I asked him if I could have it sooner if I earned it myself. He said, "Sure, go for it!" So I did.*

While reading Boy's Life magazine, I came across an ad offering an opportunity to sell greeting cards on consignment. I said to myself, "I can do this!" I went to work right away going from neighbor to neighbor. I rang the doorbells, the woman of the house would come to the door, and there I was, with a red cold face, with my little furry mittens. They would always invite me in and say, "Here young man, we need to blow your nose!" And I knew I was home free. My closing line was, "Would you like to buy one box of Christmas cards, or two?" In a very short time, I became the number one greeting card salesman, at nine years old.

At an early age my daddy encouraged me to earn, but he also taught me something far more valuable, how to save. He took half of everything I earned and saved it for me. This became immensely helpful later on in life. I am now a master saver.

—**Mark Victor Hansen**

I have cried and laughed more hearing Mark speak than any other speaker besides my mother. He is a master storyteller, inspired by *his* mother.

My mother was a divine sweetheart of a mommy. But the thing that really got me the most was she was a great storyteller. Our family would go on these outrageous family vacations. Later we would sit at her feet while she was on the phone telling a friend all about it. She could take incidents, problems, travail, and reframe it with such enthusiasm! She went on a different trip than we did. I don't know where she went, but it was so exciting that I wanted to go where she had been because it was so different from where I had been. I think I learned from her that when you take a problem and reframe it and change your perspective, it gives you a change in life.

—**Mark Victor Hansen**

Very early on he knew he was supposed to speak.

When I was 16 years old, God came in and gave me a revelation that I was supposed to be in front of 80,000 people at a time. So

> *far I have had the great honor of talking to 38,000 at a time—*
> *which sends you so much energy that is blows you over.*
> —MARK VICTOR HANSEN

Mark went to Southern Illinois University. He wanted to be there the rest of his life. It was his Camelot.

At Southern Illinois University Mark meet a man who shaped his life and became his mentor, R. Buckminster Fuller.[6] Mark soon became one of Fuller's research assistants and one of his best students.

> *Fuller was my great inspiring intellectual teacher. He taught at*
> *Harvard, got kicked out when he was 65 for being too old, and*
> *was hired on at Southern Illinois University as chairman emeritus*
> *of the Design Department where I was a student.*
>
> *Super bright, blind at birth. Bucky thought in triangles, when*
> *everyone else was seeing squares. Ultimately he invented the*
> *geodesic dome. He was an artist, writer, thinker, scientist, mathe-*
> *matician, synergist, anticipatory design scientist, cartographer,*
> *game theorist, comprehensive cosmogonist,[7] cosmologist, philoso-*
> *pher, Charles Elliot Norton Poet Laureate at Harvard, an inven-*
> *tor, student of Albert Einstein, the Leonardo da Vinci of our time.*
> *He could speak 15 different technical languages, wrote 40 books.*
> —MARK VICTOR HANSEN

Mark, inspired by Fuller, went to New York to start his own business. One of the things Bucky got his 2,000 major patents for was geodesic domes, which are spherical structures built out of triangles.

> *I ultimately get to New York and started selling them. I'm having a*
> *really good time. I built the Wall Street Racket Club, and the*
> *Botanical Gardens Aviaries. I am eating at the Top the Sixes. I was*
> *in heaven. I'm convinced this time nothing can go wrong.*
>
> *I didn't see it coming. We had the oil embargo. The Arabs said*

---

[6]R(ichard) Buckminster Fuller (1895–1983).

[7]One who studies the astrophysical origin and evolution of the universe.

this time we can cash checks so big your banks will bounce! I went straight down the tubes. I went down so fast that I had to check a book out of the library, How to Go Bankrupt by Yourself! *It was amazing. I was upside down. I was sleeping outside of another guy's bedroom in his sleeping bag for six months. I was driving around in this permanently pitted, poorly air-conditioned Volkswagen. It was so bad, that when I went into get gas, the guy would say, "Fill it up?" I'd say, "No, 25 cents will do just fine. Thanks!"*

But it was one of those experiences that really 'sourced' me. It got me out of what I shouldn't be doing and into what I should be doing, which is what I am doing today.

Every one of us has a right livelihood, and I am now in my right livelihood. I said, "Boy, if I could do what I really want, I'd like to be a speaker." This time allowed me to think right, talk right, act right, live right, so that I could teach it right.

Being upside down I found my calling. I was going through that "place." That place you don't want as a destination but that everyone of us has hit. Everyone gets to go there at sometime during their lives: the pits.

—**MARK VICTOR HANSEN**

Mark is another of those up from the ashes stories. When he began his business, he had money for a tiny office, but none for an apartment. So he slept on the floor by his desk. He never gave up.

Luckily, as an undergraduate, someone had given Mark a tape by Cavett Robert (a Superstar I will profile in a future volume), the founder of the National Speakers Association, called *Are You the Cause, or Are You the Effect?* He never thought that it was important . . . until his life was in serious trouble.

But now, I start listening to this thing, and it really tuned me in. I caught on that in my heart of hearts I wanted to be a speaker. The trouble for me was everyone who was speaking had a ton more experience than me! They were an attorney, or a celebrity, or a medical doctor. How does somebody, just 26 years old, get into this speaking business?

What I did is what I teach everybody, ask! Ask everybody. Ask, ask, ask, ask, ask. Someone said to check out this guy, Chip Collins who was speaking in Melville, Long Island, New York. This guy is charismatic, he does a mental dance, he's on top of them, he's funny, he's light, he's enlightening. Afterwards I say to him, "Here, I'll buy you lunch." I picked his brain. I said, "Here is what I want to do." He said, "You stay out of the real estate market that's mine, you go into life insurance." He gave me four magic questions to ask prospects, how to close, good work habits.

So I go out to try to sell this. He told me all I needed to do was make 10 calls a day. Remember, I am going into a business that I know zero about. I didn't even own any life insurance. I didn't know what a commission in terms of premium of life insurance was, and I didn't know what a CLU meant.

I only had that beat-up old Volkswagen and one suit the bankruptcy courts haven't taken from me.

It's 4:30 in the afternoon when I make another cold call. I'm feeling emotionally beat up, everybody's been saying, "What the hell do I want a motivational speaker for?!" Then I get this lovely guy at Metropolitan. His name was Tony. A guy of great size and substance. He says just the opposite, "I'll take your seminar." I said, "You mean it!?"

"Better than that, I'll give you a directory and you tell everybody that Tony sent you, and you'll get everywhere."

By the time my friend Chip got back, I had more talks booked than he did! I had four a day at $25 an hour, and I was sky-rocketing!

—MARK VICTOR HANSEN

Today you would need to think in terms of $20,000 to have Mark talk to your group for that same hour. That is mainly because a few years ago at a conference Mark Victor Hansen heard his friend Jack Canfield say he intended to put stories in a book. "Without all the philosophical and theatrical crap in between," Hansen replied, "I want to do that with you." They compiled signature stories they had come across in their many years as motivational speakers and seminar leaders. Simple stories of faith, hope, and affirmation. It was a very difficult sell, 33 publishers turned down their idea. But "Who's Sorry Now?" is their theme song because this series is currently the best-selling series of all time!

One week in 1998, 5 of the top-10 slots on the paperback best-seller list at *Publishers Weekly* were filled by *Chicken Soup* titles. Jack and Mark have seen total sales of more than 44 million books. The original book is in 29 languages. There are 23 others in print. Six more books a year are planned for the next five years.

Special Wisdom of Mark Victor Hansen

Mark Victor Hanson's mission is reshaping the vision of what is possible in our lives. His presentations focus on engaging our human imagination. Mark's words make you *think big*. Many say it, but Mark makes *think big* work in your heart.

- Think big! Most people don't dream big enough, think big enough, achieve big enough, and strive high enough.
- Figure out what you want if you had what you want in your heart of hearts.
- Visualizing is realizing. What you impress, you express.
- What do you want? Write it down and *ask, ask, ask.*
- Get your team together to get your dream together (1 + 1 actually = 11).

Lou Holtz

Lou Holtz never inherited a winning college team. But he managed to turn all of these teams of macho football playing kids into winners within two seasons!

He was at the helm of the Fighting Irish of Notre Dame during the school's longest winning streak (23 games), and his teams were invited to a major bowl game in 9 of his last 10 seasons. Holtz compiled seven seasons with 10 or more victories, an accomplishment bettered by only eight coaches in college football history.

After his departure from Notre Dame following the 1996 season, he joined CBS Sports as a studio football analyst. As most suspected,

Holtz could not stay away for long, and soon became the head coach of the South Carolina Gamecocks.

Lou Holtz is author of *Winning Everyday; The Fighting Spirit: A Championship Season at Notre Dame* (with John Heisler); *The Offensive Side of Lou Holtz; The Grass Is Greener;* and *Kitchen Quarterback* (a book for football beginners). He is also creator of three of the best-selling motivational videos of all time, *Do Right, Do Right II,* and *If Enough People Care,* and the audiotape *Teens' Gameplan for Life.*

The Lou Holtz Hall of Fame is located in Holtz's hometown of East Liverpool, Ohio.

Holtz has championed countless charitable and educational causes. Among the current beneficiaries of the Lou Holtz Foundation are the Juvenile Diabetes Foundation and The American Cancer Society.

His success as a man is just as impressive as his coaching career. From humble beginnings, he has fashioned a life that inspires everyone who hears him to a greater sense of purpose and the strength to fulfill that purpose. Lou's answers to almost every question I asked dealt with responsibility, commitment, family, wife, and children.

As a legendary team leader, Lou Holtz is the perfect speaker on achievement and overcoming seemingly impossible challenges, and setting goals. His main speech is called, a "Game Plan for Success." Lou's message transcends athletics. It resonates—even to those who aren't sports-minded. The focus is on people and the values that make relationships (and organizations) excel. A very dynamic mix of God, common sense, humor, success, and sports analogies. Like Stephen Covey, he isn't a great "orator," but he is unpretentious, committed, believes in helping people with his heart, and it all shows on the platform. He's funny because he laughs at himself, and at the same time he is a person of great personal integrity.

*I have a philosophy and a belief. That's why a guy that's 5' 10",
152 pounds, wears glasses, has a lisp, very limited intelligence—
lower half of his high school class—not a good athlete, not impressive, yet was able to marry a lovely woman and stay married for
38 years and have four children who all graduated from college
and who still say, "I love you," and call me Dad. I think that's a
pretty good accomplishment for a guy like me!*
—**Lou Holtz**

Turning Points for Lou Holtz

A short man with several physical handicaps, including a speech imped-
iment. No snappy dresser. So how did he become one of the top coaches
in college football history?

> *I had something to prove. I think it comes from insecurity. I didn't
> come from a broken home, but during those formative years we
> lived with my grandmother. My dad was in the service, all my
> uncles were in the service, and there was just the uncertainty of it
> all, dealing with loved ones who may not come back. I was small
> of frame, a poor athlete, and a poor student in high school. I
> wanted to prove something.*
> —Lou Holtz

It is odd to imagine that someone whose name is synonymous with
sports, was never a great athlete as a child.

> *I wasn't very big to start with. I played on some teams that got beat
> pretty badly, where the other team was frolicking on the other side.
> It wasn't fun. The pain of losing goes away. The pain of embar-
> rassment lasts longer. Those kinds of things happen, and they give
> you that fervent desire to excel at everything you do. If you don't
> want to do something at maximum ability, you're in the wrong
> society.*
> —Lou Holtz

In 1966 Lou went to South Carolina as an assistant coach. His wife was
eight months pregnant with their third child and they had spent every
cent they had as a down payment on a home.

> *It wasn't easy to hang in there back then. My wife was very posi-
> tive. She supported me in every way, including going to work while
> I watched the kids.*
> *You need to look at the situation. Don't take responsibility for
> the things you have no control over. Look at it realistically. Ask
> yourself, "What could I have changed?" This was not a case of my*

not being good enough. They just didn't know me, and they were tight on money. So I made up my mind to just do it. It was a great experience.
  —Lou Holtz

He started out coaching at William and Mary, moved on to North Carolina State, spent seven years at Arkansas, moved on to Minnesota.

We think of Lou as being "the" college football guy. But in 1976, he joined professional football with the New York Jets. He says that's where he learned about commitment.

It was a tremendous opportunity, but I didn't really understand the intricacies of it and I probably wasn't adequately prepared for it. I didn't go there with a commitment—I went to work every day thinking, "Well, if this doesn't work out, I can always go back to college football." I wasn't happy and I wasn't helping. There wasn't anything wrong with the New York Jets or professional football. It was Lou Holtz. I didn't do a very good job and I'm not happy to stand up and tell people that—but that's the way it is.
  —Lou Holtz

Well, he obviously took the lesson to heart. He joined Notre Dame in November 1985 as the twenty-seventh head football coach in Irish history. In only three seasons, he transformed a struggling program into one that captured a national championship (a 1988 team that went 12–0).

We always have a strong faith in God. God is going to control my life. I have a faith in Him and He has a plan for me. So, if I do the best I can and try to do what's right, and be the best I can be and care about others, it will work out.
  —Lou Holtz

Special Wisdom of Lou Holtz

In High School I was often asked about Dad's philosophy: "Can such simple philosophy 'to do right' work in the tough world we all

face?" I often answered yes back then because I thought that was what the microphone wanted to hear. But, now as an adult, when I face challenges and choices, his words, "Is it the right thing to do? If you have any doubt, take out the Bible. Do the right thing" guide me, and yes, it does work!
> —KEVIN HOLTZ, LOU HOLTZ'S YOUNGEST SON

- I can't believe that God put us on this earth to be ordinary.

- How you respond to the challenge in the second half will determine what you become after the game, whether you are a winner or a loser.

- If you teach them to handle the ball well, you can always fall back on that.

- The only thing that can change you from where you are now to where you'll be five years from now are the books you read, the people you meet, and the dreams you dream.

- I use these criteria in my family life, in raising children, in coaching, and in living a life. It is my belief politically and socially. (1) Get rid of excuses; (2) take pride in making sacrifices; (3) stay focused on what you want; (4) dream great things; (5) build-up (by asking): Can I trust you? Are you committed? Do you care?

- These are the only three basic rules I had on our football team: (1) Do what is right; (2) do your very best; (3) treat others as you'd like to be treated.

Vince Lombardi, Sr., and Vince Lombardi, Jr.

He spoke of striving for the perfectly disciplined will. Coach had that fire that gives that great energy! He said one time, He had "a burning incandescence in his gut." He had a fire about him.
> —JERRY KRAMER, CHAMPIONSHIP GREEN BAY
> PACKER GUARD FOR LOMBARDI FOR NINE YEARS

The name Vince Lombardi is arguably one of the most famous in coaching history. Late in his life, in the 1960s, Lombardi, Sr., finally got his shot as a head coach. He led the Green Bay Packers to five NFL championships. At his side his young son was watching, listening, and learning.

That young man, also named Vince Lombardi, whom I will inaccurately, but for the sake of clarity, call Vince Lombardi, Jr.,[8] in this book, earned a law degree and maintained a practice while serving in the Minnesota legislature. He went on to work with management for many NFL teams and associated organizations. With careers in banking and law, he is a speaker I have often booked. He is the author of the book *Coaching for Teamwork: Winning Concepts for Business in the 21st Century* and co-author of *Baby Steps to Success.*

There are many books about Coach Vince Lombardi, including: *When Pride Still Mattered: A Life of Vince Lombardi* by David Maraniss (Simon & Schuster); *Winning Is a Habit: Vince Lombardi on Winning, Success, and the Pursuit of Excellence,* edited by Gary R. George (HarperCollins); *Strive to Excel: The Will and Wisdom of Vince Lombardi,* compiled by Jennifer Briggs (Rutledge Hill Press); *Vince: A Personal Biography of Vince Lombardi* by Michael O'Brien Press (Morrow); *Vince Lombardi: His Life and Times* by Robert W. Wells (Prairie Classics).

Turning Points for Vince Lombardi, Sr.

Dad was a very successful high school coach in New Jersey. He won five or six state championships; they won 36 games in row. He went on to be an assistant for Army, then for the Giants.
— VINCE LOMBARDI, JR.

Leadership is based on a spiritual quality; the power to inspire, the power to inspire others to follow.
— VINCE LOMBARDI, SR.

---

[8]The elder Lombardi is actually Vincent T. Lombardi, while his son, the speaker, is Vincent H. Lombardi.

*My father had a strong faith in God. In his formative years the
Jesuits and the military were big influences. He was in the seminary
until his senior year in high school. He went to mass and communion just about every day of his life. He went to Fordham University
which was a Jesuit institution. That had a profound effect on him.
He spent a number of years at West Point. That is where he gained
much of his technique as a coach and his approach to life.*
                                        —VINCE LOMBARDI, JR.

The "military way" can be seen in all of Lombardi's approaches and
ways. Those cadets had so little time to practice, they had to have discipline to get the job done. He learned how to give it to them.

*By now he was 47, generally a time that is acknowledged you have
made it as a head coach, or you are not going to make it. He felt one
reason he didn't advance was that he was an Italian Catholic; in the
50s, that was a problem in some areas of the country. Forty-seven is
pretty late in life in anybody's line of work to make it to the top.*

*He saw a lot of people who were equally talented, or not as tal-
ented get the head coaching jobs that he wanted. He had to sit
back and wait for quite a while. He knew when his time came, he
would only have one opportunity. He planned and worked; when
it came, he was ready. He watched how others did it, he planned
how he could do it better. When his opportunity came, he knew
two things: Exactly what he wanted to do and that this would be
his only shot. But he knew that if he blew it, it would be because
he did it his way.*
                                        —VINCE LOMBARDI, JR.

The Green Pay Packers had a record of one win, ten losses, and a tie
run in 1958. Not good. The management decided to try an assistant
coach from the New York Giants. It is no exaggeration to say Vince
Lombardi saved the Packers.

After hearing this new coach speak to his ragtag team for the first time,
a young quarterback from Alabama ran to the phone and called his wife.
Bart Starr told her, "Honey, we're going to win!" And win they did.

I had a really bad day and Lombardi chewed my ass out good. Gave me the "concentration talk." Proved to me I didn't have any!

I'm in the locker room, head in my hands, looking at the floor, thinking maybe it's time for me to move on and find another career or another team. I sat there for 30 minutes. Lombardi came into the locker room and saw me. He knew I was down. He came right over and put his hand on my shoulder, "Son, one of these days, you're going to be the best guard in football."

That 10 seconds changed my life. From that point on my motor was started. He never bitched at me again. Didn't need to.

—JERRY KRAMER, CHAMPIONSHIP GREEN BAY
PACKER GUARD FOR LOMBARDI FOR NINE YEARS

Lombardi, Sr., is perhaps most famous for saying, "Winning isn't everything, it's the only thing." His son told me his father didn't originate the phrase, and actually was frustrated at the way it was interpreted by his critics. Faultfinders would hold that up and say Lombardi was telling his team to win, regardless of ethics or morality. Jerry Kramer, a Green Bay Packers guard with Lombardi for nine years, is also one of Lombardi's main biographers.[9] He told me that he loved that quote of Lombardi's, but not the way it was abused.

I hate the way it has been abused. Making the effort to improve as a human being is what Coach Lombardi was all about. He was able to see the gap between where we were and what we could become—both as football players and as people. And he felt it was his God-given responsibility to close that gap.

—JERRY KRAMER, GUARD ON LOMBARDI'S PACKERS
AND AUTHOR OF MANY LOMBARDI BIOGRAPHIES

Lombardi's son felt his father picked up the saying from the 1953 movie *Trouble Along the Way*, the story of Steve Williams, played by John Wayne, a hard-bitten football coach at a small Catholic college.

[9]Jerry Kramer is the author of *Lombardi* and *Distant Replay*, a look-back at the impact of Lombardi coaching, editor of *Winning Is the Only Thing*, and other books.

Winning is not a sometime thing: it's an all the time thing. You don't win once in a while; you don't do the things right once in a while; you do them right all the time.

Dad got a lot of criticism! The sixties, the Vietnam war, was a time in of upheaval in this country. He was out there talking about "Winning is a habit. Winning isn't everything, it's the only thing." He talked about doing things the "right way. You don't do things right once in a while, you do it right all the time."

I think he said those things because he felt as a country we had a vacuum of leadership at the time, and these things needed to be said. But that vacuum caused him to be criticized for what he said, what he did, and the way he drove his players. He was criticized in all the major magazines and newspapers. And it hurt. It really hurt. He felt it was not justified.

But he believed in what he was doing. It didn't dissuade him or change his course. Mainly he dealt with it by talking to those of a similar frame of mind, to confirm he was on the right track.

     —VINCE LOMBARDI, JR.

In 1969 after nine years with the Packers, and after winning their first two Super Bowls, for the 1966 and 1967 seasons, he became tired of coaching. They were still winning, but not by the previous amazing margins.

His fire was not diminished, but it was harder to stoke.

To generate that kind of energy week in and week out, to play the game at those kinds of high levels, is extremely difficult. The older you get, the harder it is. He was responsible for bringing not only himself but every one of us up to that peak performance level, and we were all getting older. Sometimes he would stay up to 4 a.m. with the coaching staff to prepare strategy for the next game. Eight a.m. he'd be back at it again. His complexion was turning gray. If he could have just taken a two week break in the middle of a season, he could have made it. But the game doesn't allow for fatigue.

     —JERRY KRAMER, GUARD ON LOMBARDI'S PACKERS,
       AND AUTHOR OF MANY LOMBARDI BIOGRAPHIES

He stepped out of coaching and went on to be the general manager of the Packers. After only a year he knew he missed it. He needed to get back into coaching. He had already appointed someone else to coach the Packers, so Lombardi asked to be released from his contract as general manager. He went back to Washington to coach again.

He died of cancer after one season at Washington, on September 3, 1970.

Green Bay would go through almost 30 years of misery until, 1997, when they were able to achieve a shadow of the excellence they had obtained under the leadership of Vince Lombardi, Sr., and make it back to a Superbowl. Vince Lombardi, Jr., told me his father would be pleased with the Packers' return, with only one reservation: "He would have said, 'What . . . took so long!?' "

Special Wisdom of the Lombardis

A great disciplinarian, my father always knew how to get the best out of his players. He focused on teamwork and understood that if you treat people with respect and treat them like winners, they will perform as winners.

The cornerstone of Vince Lombardi's teaching methods were commitment, sacrifice, and mental toughness, three attributes which continue to be stressed by many of today's successful coaches and by many successful business people as well.

—Vince Lombardi, Jr.

Vince Lombardi, Sr.

- Winning isn't everything, it's the only thing.
- There is no room for second place. There is only one place in my game and that is first place. I have finished second twice in my time at Green Bay and I never want to finish second again.
- To accomplish anything worthwhile, you must pay the price.
- Once you learn to quit, it becomes a habit.
- Dictionary is the only place that success comes before work. Hard work is the price we must pay for success.
- Inches make champions.

Vince Lombardi, Jr.

- We can orchestrate high performance.
- Winning is choosing to change.

    Winning is choosing to grow.

    Winning is choosing to improve our performance.

Earl Nightingale

Earl Nightingale, the 1940s radio action hero Sky King, can reasonably be credited for kicking off the entire audio self-improvement industry as the co-founder of The Nightingale-Conant Corporation. His first recording, *The Strangest Secret,* became the largest nonentertainment recording in the record industry and was awarded a Gold Record.

His definition of *success* is perhaps the most quoted in motivational literature: "Success is the progressive realization of a worthy ideal."

Earl became one of the most highly recognized voices and names, throughout the United States. He created and narrated more than 7,000 daily broadcasts of his daily radio program *Our Changing World.* It was the world's most widely sponsored radio program. It was heard daily across the United States, Canada, Mexico, Australia, Bahamas, Guam, New Zealand, Puerto Rico, Armed Forces Radio, and thirty other countries.

He wrote and starred in many television programs, was inducted into the Radio Hall of Fame and the International Speakers Hall of Fame. He received the Napolean Hill Foundation Gold Medal Award for Literary Excellence.

He is the author of many books and audio products, including: *The Strangest Secret: Earl Nightingale's Library of Little Gems,* with his wife Diana Nightingale; *The Essence of Success: 163 Life Lessons from the Dean of Self-Development; The Strangest Secret for Succeeding in the World Today; Earl Nightingale's Greatest Discovery; The Essence of Success: The Earl Nightingale Library; What Every Young Person Should Know;* and *Lead The Field,* which may be the largest-selling audio program of all time.

*In May of 1986 I finally reached the apex of my childhood
dreams as a member of the 1986 World Champion New York
Mets. . . . ticker tape parade, a visit with the President of the
United States at the White House.*

*Shortly thereafter I was felled by a shoulder injury. I spent the
next three years attempting a comeback from this severe injury. But
in the Spring of 1991, it became obvious there would be no more
opportunities for me in baseball.*

*Three short months after I began my new career in the business
world, I was diagnosed with three very serious and potentially life-
threatening illnesses which made my shoulder injury pale by com-
parison. I had gone from being a big, strong professional athlete to
a man who was too weak to get out of bed without assistance. At
one point, I found myself alone in my basement with a loaded
.357 Magnum pistol, contemplating whether or not I wanted to
continue swinging at life's curves.*

I had to do something.

I became a cassette-tape junkie.

*Earl Nightingale was the first professional speaker I listened to.
If it were not for the inspiration I received from this man's work, I
probably would not have continued to pursue other speakers and
their materials, all of which were so important in literally saving
my life, turning it around, and eventually leading me to the
opportunity I now have to positively impact others' lives through
my speaking and writing.*

—ED HEARN, MOTIVATIONAL SPEAKER AND AUTHOR
OF *CONQUERING LIFE'S CURVES: BASEBALL, BATTLES,
AND BEYOND*

Turning Point for Earl Nightingale

Earl Nightingale was born in Los Angeles in the early 1920s during
economically depressed times. He and his family struggled for the very
basics of life. His father left them when Earl was only 12.

*The old man never gave my mother a penny for the upkeep of our
house or the livelihood of her three boys. I was the oldest, and I*

> *helped out by selling newspapers. My mother worked in a WPA*
> *sewing factory for $55 a month.[10]*
> —EARL NIGHTINGALE

As a child Earl desperately wanted to know why some people grow up to enjoy prosperity, while others struggle merely to survive.

A very inquisitive child, the kind neighbors think of as a pest with all their questions, he began to find the answers he was thirsting for while in high school. He discovered books and the Long Beach Public Library. He loved to read almost anything.

Knowing college would be out of their financial reach, in 1938 he joined the Marines. He was thrilled that he would get to see far-off lands like China. Well, he made it as far as Hawaii. On the morning of December 7, 1941, he was on a lookout tower of the battleship Arizona. He was 1 of 100 of the 1100 aboard the Arizona who survived the attack on Pearl Harbor that day.

He was discharged in 1946 and got a job with KTAR radio in Phoenix. But he dreamed of the "big time," which in those days meant Chicago!

He became the voice of Sky King, the flying cowboy turned rancher, an ex-F.B.I. agent, and Navy pilot, as he battled the forces of evil in the West, one of radio's most famous action heroes! Mike Wallace announced the first broadcast in 1946, which became the basis for a television series of the same title. That wonderful commanding voice had listeners around the United States glued to their cavernous console radios.

By the time he was 30, in 1952, he was pulling in an amazing $98,000, the top in his field in earning power. He had made a special deal which allowed him to sell advertising for his own commentary program and keep 40 percent.

> *I would do the program in the morning, after writing half the*
> *night, and then I'd spend the rest of the day making sales calls.*
>
> *I ran like that for seven years, for four of these years I was play-*
> *ing Sky King as well. I was going 18 hours day, six and seven days*
> *a week.*
> **—EARL NIGHTINGALE**

[10]*SUCCESS* magazine, June 1983.

To add more challenge for himself, at the height of his broadcasting career he bought an insurance agency. In 1957 he announced his retirement from radio for the comparative quiet of running the insurance company full-time. He worked hard at building and motivating his sales force. His input was so valuable that in 1956, when he planned to take a short vacation, where he would be unavailable, his manager got panicky.

> *He asked me to record some messages the guys could listen to on Saturday mornings in place of coming down and giving them a pep talk. It seemed important to him.*
>
> *I woke up at four o'clock one morning and literally cried, "Eureka!" It was there in my mind. I jumped up and threw on a pot of coffee, went out to my little study, and started hammering away on the typewriter. By about seven o'clock, I had it written. I showered and shaved and went down to the studio and recorded it. I was finished before noon.*
> —EARL NIGHTINGALE

Earl called the message *The Strangest Secret*. He arranged with Columbia Records to duplicate the record and it began to sell. He soon met Lloyd Conant, a successful, local businessman and direct-mail expert. Lloyd helped Earl market *The Strangest Secret* and eventually became his life-long business partner. *The Strangest Secret* is the largest-selling nonentertainment recording *ever* in the record industry.

> *When I heard Earl Nightingale on his LP* The Strangest Secret *in 1967, he said, "You become what you think about."*
>
> *After hearing that, I was able to focus on what I wanted to do, and I remember those words motivated me to place the first ad (that cost me $5) and set me on the way to producing a Wild West Show. Because of those words, I was fortunate enough to carry out my dream of taking a Wild West Show around the world, and have so far performed in 26 countries, and will present Buffalo Bill's Wild West at the base of the pyramids in Cairo, Egypt, in 2000.*
> —MONTIE MONTANA, JR., PROFESSIONAL COWBOY
> PERFORMER AND SPEAKER

Because of the overwhelming success of *Strangest Secret,* in 1960 Earl and Lloyd formed Nightingale-Conant Corporation. They called this new stuff they were doing "electronic publishing." They started with phonograph records, and did well.

To help their coverage, Earl and Vic created five-minute radio spots, with Earl doing social commentary and philosophical musing, *Our Changing World.* It sustained them through their lean growing years. Conant got the idea to syndicate the show to the untapped radio market of smaller communities around the United States. *Our Changing World* is said to be the longest-running, most widely syndicated show in the history of radio. Some schools even made it required listening!

A huge turning point was the advent of audio cassettes; they created the idea of turning your car into a learning center, and Nightingale-Conant took off! Today they are still the leader in the audio publishing industry.

In 1972 Earl developed a chronic condition brought on by a tumor on the pituitary gland that changed his features so much, friends from years past would hardly recognize him. But it didn't slow him down. He was actively involved in creating programs for Nightingale-Conant for many more years, until he developed complications after heart surgery. On March 28, 1989, Paul Harvey broke the news to the country on his radio program that, "The sonorous voice of the nightingale was stilled." But not forgotten.[11]

> *I have no idea what tomorrow will bring, but I'm looking forward to it, because I've always got another program to write![12]*
> —EARL NIGHTINGALE

Special Wisdom of Earl Nightingale

Early in my life I was given a record of Earl Nightingale's The Strangest Secret. *He said, "The mind is like rich fertile soil. It*

---

[11]All of Earl's classic programs are still available through Nightingale-Conant, 800-572-2770.

[12]*Success* magazine, June 1983.

returns what we plant." Being raised on a sandy-land farm in Central Texas, I understood that you couldn't plant corn and get okra. The law of the soil is so exact it will return to us what we plant or what seeds blow there. Our responsibility is to keep watch on what we allow to grow in our consciousness.
        —BOBBI SIMS, EXPERT IN SELF-RESPONSIBILITY
        TRAINING AND AUTHOR OF *Don't Let 'Em Crumble Your Cookies*

- You become what you think about.
- Success is the progressive realization of a worthy ideal.
- Your world is a living expression of how you are using and have used your mind.
- A person needs to chip away everything that doesn't look like the person he or she most wants to become.
- For every action, there is an equal and opposite reaction, as Sir Isaac Newton taught us in physics. And the same rule operates unfailingly in our lives.
- Life doesn't care whether we are rich or poor, sick or well, strong or weak. It is impartial and rigidly fair. We have, we will always have, exactly what we earn; no more, no less.
- Our attitude toward life determines life's attitude toward us.

Norman Vincent Peale

There are a good many discouraged people out there. They are coming to hear you speak. You must fill them up so when they go out into the world they can solve their problems.
        —DR. NORMAN VINCENT PEALE[13]

Often called "the father of the power of positive thinking." Dr. Norman Vincent Peale was perhaps one of the most influential motiva-

[13]Quoted in Lilly Walters, *Secrets of Successful Speakers: How You Can Motivate, Captivate, and Persuade* (New York, McGraw-Hill, 1993).

tional speakers and authors in the world. Dr. Peale was perhaps the person most responsible for bringing business psychology into the segments of the Christian church and Christianity into business psychology, merging theology and psychology.

Author of 46 books, including the inspirational best-seller of all time, *The Power of Positive Thinking*. Other than the Bible, this book is perhaps the most successful single book ever published. It has been translated into 42 languages, with a sale of over 20 million copies. It was the model for the thousands of self-help books that have followed. The title itself has become a catch phrase in English and in many languages.

He was also a motivational speaker on countless platforms; his message took him on a global journey. He spoke to an average of a hundred groups a year until he was 93, an estimated live audience of 20 million.

Dr. Peale received 22 honorary doctoral degrees. He traveled to Vietnam at the request of President Nixon and was awarded the Presidential Medal of Freedom by Ronald Reagan.

We cannot talk about Dr. Peale without talking about the organizer of much of his success, his wife, Ruth Stafford Peale. Ruth worked closely with her husband in all aspects of his ministry and established a separate identity as a religious leader, public speaker, and author. Both of their stories are more fully told in the biography by Arthur Gordon, *One Man's Way*.

In 1945 Dr. Peale and Ruth founded the organization now called Peale Center for Christian Living, in Pawling, New York, and *Guideposts* magazine. The Peale Center circulated Peale's precepts around the globe through publications, audio- and videotapes, seminars, and conferences. *Guideposts* circulation has grown to the 1999 figure of 4,190,000. According to the Magazine Publisher's Association, this ranks *Guideposts* among the top 15 largest publications in the country, with the largest circulation of any religious magazine.

Dr. Peale's dreams continue to be achieved. Every year, *Guideposts* and the Peale Center (now merged as one company) touch over 48 million lives with its programs and products.

As the outreach division of *Guideposts*, Peale Center conducts many additional projects: See more at the Guideposts Web site: www .guideposts.org.

As Dr. Peale spoke, your heart and mind pumped with the awe-some adrenaline power of positive thought. I first heard him over 25 years ago and I can honestly say, he never missed a beat in a quarter century. He literally lifted the human spirit of millions the world over. In my book, Dr. Norman Vincent Peale should be declared an international treasure.

> —HARVEY MACKAY, CHAIRMAN OF THE BOARD AND
> CEO OF MACKAY ENVELOPE CORPORATION

Turning Points for Norman Vincent Peale

Born in the Ohio hamlet of Bowersville on May 31, 1898, Norman Vincent Peale was the son of a physician turned Methodist minister. Peale grew up helping support his family by delivering newspapers, working in a grocery store, and like Zig Ziglar, selling pots and pans door to door.

Peale confessed that as a youth he had "the worst inferiority complex of all," and developed his positive thinking/positive confession philosophy just to help himself.

Perhaps his most significant turning point was in a summer vacation in 1921; he went to a church meeting with his father where the music and the sermon moved him deeply. Later that year, he enrolled at the Boston University School of Theology.

Following ordination, Dr. Peale gained a reputation as a dynamic pastor whose churches grew. At University Methodist Church in Syracuse, New York, he met and married Ruth Stafford, who became his life partner for 63 years. They were the perfect complement—he energetic and creative, she organized and managerial.

At age 34 he accepted a call to Marble Collegiate Church in New York City (a Protestant Dutch Reformed church founded in 1628). It had 600 members when he arrived to pastor in 1932; it had over 5,000 by the time he retired in 1984. A common sight on Sundays was tourists lined up around the block to hear him.

With Marble Collegiate Church as a base, Dr. Peale launched far-reaching innovations in the decades of the 1930s, 1940s, and 1950s. In 1933, he began a weekly radio broadcast, *The Art of Living,* on NBC that was to continue for a record-setting 54 years.

Then *Guideposts* was founded in March 1945 as an interfaith forum for people—both celebrities and ordinary folk—to relate their inspirational stories; stories intended to provide a "spiritual lift" to all readers. The brainchild of Dr. Peale, Ruth, and Raymond Thornburg, a Pawling, New York, businessman.

Armed with only their vision, they gained support, and raised $1,200, from such people as Frank Gannett, founder of the Gannett newspaper chain; J. Howard Pew, the Philadelphia industrialist; and Branch Rickey of the Brooklyn Dodgers.

Working out of a rented room over a grocery store in Pawling, they produced the first issue of *Guideposts:* a four-page leaflet containing a single story by World War II flying ace, Captain Eddie Rickenbacker, entitled "I Believe in Prayer." Some 10,000 copies of this issue were distributed and readers were invited to subscribe at a cost of one dollar a year.

In 1947 disaster struck that should have destroyed *Guideposts* had it been the average business. A fire engulfed the magazine's Pawling headquarters, destroying not only the office but the only list of *Guideposts'* subscribers, who at the time numbered 35,000.

Norman, Ruth, and the *Guideposts'* staff, armed with only the power of positive thinking, started over. Friends rallied to the cause: A radio broadcast by Lowell Thomas and an article in *Reader's Digest* alerted *Guideposts* subscribers as well as potential readers to the magazine's difficulties, and the recovery accelerated. In only a few months, there were enough subscribers to resume publication. What began as a four-page leaflet mailed at irregular intervals became a 48-page, full-color monthly publication reaching more than 15 million people throughout the United States and the world.

In 1951 hotelier Conrad Hilton, impressed by *Guideposts'* philosophy and content, began providing copies in the rooms of all his hotels. Meanwhile, DeWitt and Lila Acheson Wallace, founders and publishers of *Reader's Digest,* had taken an interest in the new inspirational magazine. Grace Perkins Oursler, wife of the celebrated author and *Reader's Digest* editor Fulton Oursler, joined *Guideposts* as executive director, and the size and stature of *Guideposts'* staff began to grow.

Dr. Peale's fourth book, *The Power of Positive Thinking,* was published in 1952 and become one of the best-sellers of all time.

> *The original transcript for* The Power of Positive Thinking *was initially turned down; he was really depressed about that, and threw it in the waste basket. His wife, Ruth took it out and brought it to another publisher. This publisher looked at the work, then titled "The Power of Positive Faith," and said, "What keeps coming up here is the power of positive thinking; that should be the title of the book." The rest is history.*
> —LES BROWN

By the sixties his fame had grown so that his life was even the subject of a 1964 movie entitled *One Man's Way.*

In May of 1992, in the last speech he ever gave, Dr. Norman Vincent Peale looked out at the graduating class of his old alma mater at Ohio Wesleyan University and said, "Shoot for the moon! Even if you miss it, you will land among the stars!" At exactly that moment the bells in the tower rang, as if God was giving tribute to this man, these words, and his impact on the world.

One of the last forewords he wrote was for the prequel to this book, *Secrets of Successful Speakers: How You Can Motivate, Captivate, and Persuade* (McGraw-Hill, 1993). He was so busy with his other projects that he had stopped becoming involved with outside projects, like my book. I was honored and humbled that he made an exception for me. There is no doubt that my book is such a success because of Dr. Peale's witty and insightful remarks to those who would take up the gauntlet and go forth to "motivate, captivate, and persuade" in a confusing and complicated world. His contribution helped push my book to be a favorite and began those bells ringing for me.

On Christmas Eve 1993 at 95 years young, his light passed up into those stars. It caused millions around the world to pause and to reflect on the infinite thoughts and dreams this man's words have ignited.

Do you hear the bells ringing?

I do.

Special Wisdom of Norman Vincent Peale

Although business tycoons, kings, and politicians sought him out, he never lost his basic humble shyness. He was not interested in the mass audience; he wanted to help each solitary individual who was overwhelmed by life. His formula was simple: "Picturize, prayerize, and actualize solutions."

Here are quotes and concepts for which he is most famous.

- What you see and believe in, you can achieve.
- Change your thoughts and you change your world.
- Life's blows cannot break a person whose spirit is warmed at the fire of enthusiasm.
- Those who are fired with an enthusiastic idea and who allow it to take hold and dominate their thoughts find that new worlds open for them. As long as enthusiasm holds out, so will new opportunities.
- Practice hope. As hopefulness becomes a habit, you can achieve a permanently happy spirit.

Once I heard Dr. Norman Vincent Peale tell about a friend whose business and personal life had gone from good to bad and from bad to terrible. This friend, formerly a dynamic man, had lost all confidence and was filled with self-blame and self-pity. Dr. Peale gave him a five-point formula for a comeback:

1. *Stop running yourself down. Empty your mind of your mistakes and failures.*
2. *Eliminate self-pity. Think of what you have left instead of what you have lost.*
3. *Quit thinking only of yourself. Start thinking of ways to help others.*
4. *Have a goal and put a timetable on it.*
5. *Every morning speak these words out loud to yourself: "I can do all things through Christ who strengthens me."*

His friend took the advice and rebuilt his life (better than ever) based on that formula.

After I heard that story, I was motivated to bounce back from my own problems and self-doubt using the five-points. I have since progressed as a speaker and writer and have compiled two books in a Bounce Back series, with a third book in progress.

I am happy to share this "bounce back" formula from Dr. Peale's talk because I have proved in my own life that it really works!

—DIANA L. JAMES, AUTHOR/EDITOR/COMPILER
OF THE "BOUNCE BACK" SERIES

Christopher Reeve

Christopher Reeve has spoken for us (The Peter Lowe Success Seminars) 25 times, to crowds of 20,000.

We get incredible audience response from his talks. The fact that he is able to live such a positive life, considering the challenges he faces, puts life in perspective for all of us.

We use an interview format with Christopher on stage with either my wife Tamara or me. Everyone is transfixed by his answers. You see a lot of tears in the eyes of the audience.

Once, he spoke for us when he had pneumonia. I can't think of any other speaker who would speak when they have pneumonia. But he was committed to be there, no matter what. Amazing!

—PETER LOWE, PRESIDENT AND CHIEF EXECUTIVE
OF PETER LOWE INTERNATIONAL

Christopher Reeve performed in 18 movies, 15 television shows, and 31 plays, ranging from Shakespeare to *The Music Man. Somewhere in Time* and *Deathtrap* are two of my favorite Reeve movies. He gained outstanding fame as the star of *Superman.* He walked up to the mike at the Academy Awards in 1978 and humbly told the world with a Boy Scout grin that he had gained stardom, only because he looked like a cartoon character!

But at the Academy Awards in 1996 he gained Superstar status as one of the greatest motivators of all time when he made a surprise appearance in a wheelchair. Just the sight of him created a crescendo of startled applause which swept through the Dorothy Chandler Pavilion and continued around the world. Christopher Reeve can no longer move freely in the beautiful landscape near his home in New York, but he can, and does, take audiences on an exhilarating journey across the landscape of our minds. His example certifies in our hearts that courage and determination can help a person fly higher than any Hollywood special effects.

> *While lying in bed with serious injuries of my own and feeling desperate, a TV was brought into my room with the intention to take my mind off my pain. There he was, this Superman of the past crippled and unable to breathe without assistance. His future was bleak; there is no cure for his particular injury, yet he was smiling and talking about how he is handling it. He even joked during his interview about his fear of the ventilator not working. He had determined to live—through the love of his wife, his faith, and the experts handling his machinery.*
>
> *I thought, through my tears: "What an incredible man—what irony for the superbly active Superman. He is more Superman today than he ever was on celluloid. How small my injuries are. I shall walk tomorrow: when will he?*
>
> —ROSEMARY HOWELL, CREATIVE WRITER, I CHING
> PRACTITIONER AND TEACHER, SOUTH AFRICA

Today he is a much more popular speaker than before the accident. Speaking has become his main source of income. He has been featured in the famous Peter Lowe Success Seminars with such Superstars as Barbara Bush, Margaret Thatcher, Elizabeth Dole, General Colin Powell, Charlton Heston, Mary Lou Retton, and Hank Aaron.

Besides being a speaker, he is keeping very busy with projects such as his debut as a director in *The Gloaming*, which won four cable ACE awards. It is a beautiful HBO minimovie about a young man dying of AIDS. Christopher was the voice of King Arthur in an animated feature called *The Quest for Camelot*. His name and endorsement are on a line of polo shirts.

He is the author of his wildly successful autobiography, *Still Me*, with writer Roger Rosenblatt, for which Random House reportedly paid him $3 million. Brave, funny, and deeply moving, it is the story of how he kept going with a life he thought was utterly ruined and found that there was still much in it worth having. He reads the three-hour audio version of *Still Me* (Random House Audiobooks). It's no overstatement to say that Reeve's autobiography is among the most life-affirming books ever published.

Turning Points for Christopher Reeve

Christopher Reeve was rolled out in his wheelchair to give the commencement address at the University of Virginia. The last time he was at the U. of V., he nearly lost his life after a riding accident that has left him paralyzed from the neck down and still unable to breathe on his own.

"I regard my visit here in three stages. This is the second stage. The first time I came lying down. I was strapped on a board in a helicopter. This time, I'm sitting. The next time, I'll walk here," he said to a cheering crowd of graduates.

At their young age, they were witnessing how you reinvent yourself in the midst of tragedy, how you pick up the pieces, fashion a life, focus on the good things in your life when times are bad and maintain your sense of humor in the process. He told this group of eager young men and women to take time to explore, to find what they have passion for and follow it.

"And you want to do something fun." He had also spoken about failure; the many rejections of his screenplays, the parts he did not get, and what sustained him in the process. It was the love of doing the work, the fun. "Fun is not about partying or just about enjoying life or just relaxing into some kind of complacency. Fun is about hard work, and the rewards are tremendous. It's about taking something that may be difficult, that will challenge you, that will require self-discipline, that will make you angry and frustrated, where achievement will be difficult, but if you pull through all of that, you look back and say, 'It was all worth it. It was fun.' "

I'll never forget as I watched him give this speech, the twinkle in his eye. Life could take away his limbs, his ability to breathe on his own, but it could not take away the three things most important: his heart, mind, and spirit. And that has made all the difference.

— CHERYL MCLAUGHLIN, PROFESSIONAL COACH, SPEAKER, AUTHOR, MCLAUGHLIN SPORTS PERFORMANCE

Being chosen as the star for the 1977 blockbuster *Superman* was a major turning point for the struggling actor. Another for this Princeton native was trying to move *beyond* the role! He wanted roles that were more creative and fulfilling, like the beautiful *Somewhere in Time* in which he starred with Jane Seymore rather than just being the "action flick" hero.

But on Memorial Day of 1995 he was thrown from his horse and hit a turning point of catastrophic magnitude. He became a C2 vent-dependent quadriplegic. From that point on he had to learn to live with a body he can scarcely move or even feel. Immobile below the shoulders, he cannot sweat, control his bladder or feed himself; his respirator tube must be cleared frequently, and his body must be shifted every two hours to keep his muscles and joints flexible.

Reeve married Dana Morosini, an actress, in 1992. In his book and speeches he tells of the few dark moments right after the accident, while he was at the University of Virginia Medical Center in Charlottesville. He wondered whether it would be better to die.

When I heard Christopher Reeve speak, he told about the equestrian accident that severed his spinal cord and life as he had known it. His life would be drastically changed. During the long battle that ensued, there were many dark days of depression.

Both he and his mother considered pulling the plug. His loving wife, Dana, persuaded him to fight back by saying "You're still you, and I love you." She vowed to stay by him all the days of her life.

— LAURA LAGANA, REGISTERED NURSE, PRESIDENT OF SUCCESS SOLUTIONS

I heard Christopher Reeve say that he felt lucky because many people in his situation have to face it from much worse circumstances.

He was thankful that he is able to deal with it from such a supportive environment.

After I went home, those words reminded me of what I used to say when I was bringing up two small children, "If this is so hard for me living in an advantaged environment with enough money and space, how hard it must be for those who face economic difficulties."

The inspiration for me was twofold. One, that we must count every blessing love, comfort, and circumstance that we have. Two, that we must work as hard as we can to get improved conditions for all of our fellow men. I use these words constantly when problems come up. Now I see the problem as being lodged in my world of advantage and then find support in working through the situation.

—DR. SALLY GOLDBERG, PROFESSOR OF EARLY CHILDHOOD EDUCATION, AUTHOR, SPEAKER

Christopher Reeve refused to let tragedy turn him into a martyr. He is now an enthusiastic crusader for spinal cord injuries, and speaks to the world about courage, optimism, how to eliminate self-defeating emotions, how to live with joy and purpose, and how to make a difference in the world. He is a living testament to knowing how to live beyond your limitations—something we should all emulate.

The following is a quote from this superb and courageous man that I shall always remember: "I believe we all have more potential inside of us than we have any knowledge of. And when a crisis happens, you can find out what you're made of."

After his speech, his story inspired and motivated me to begin writing my book, tentatively entitled "Touched by an Angel of Mercy." Because of Christopher Reeve's courage and optimism, his focus on eliminating self-defeating emotions and making a difference in the world, I decided it was finally time for me to learn how to live beyond my limitations.

—LAURA LAGANA, REGISTERED NURSE, PRESIDENT OF SUCCESS SOLUTIONS

Reeve says he doesn't believe he was in this position for any God-appointed reason. Instead, he saw his new role in life as yet another challenge and he saw his celebrity status as a tool to move research ahead, so he and others could regain their mobility without relying on anyone else.

It was clearly difficult for him to speak for long periods, but he remained the calm, powerful, energetic man that we had come to love in the movies. He stayed until he said what needed to be said, and he has made thousands of people vividly aware of what can happen to instantly alter their lives. We all need to work together to find cures for paralysis and other medical mysteries.

I watch him every chance I get because I never grow tired of his uplifting message.

—BRENDAN TOBIN, THE TOBIN GROUP, A PERSONAL AND BUSINESS DEVELOPMENT FIRM

In most cases of spinal injury, it is extremely rare for patients to continue improving after the first two months. In 1997, he confounded his doctors by reporting that sensation was returning to his arms, hands, and back. Apparently through sheer force of will he is gaining some ground and has some feeling all the way down to the base of his spine, which is really a breakthrough because six months ago he couldn't feel down there at all. How? Perhaps through the extraordinary fortitude associated with his alter ego.

For the first time since my injury, I can feel the touch of my five-year-old son, Will. My greatest wish is to be able to cuddle him. I can feel his arm on mine. The thing I want more, though, is to be able to put my arms around him. That's what he is entitled to. And I believe that day is coming.

—CHRISTOPHER REEVE[14]

Special Wisdom of Christopher Reeve

- I've become president of a club I wouldn't want to join.
- I don't believe in fate. I go on at the level that I'm on . . . I'm working to change things.

[14]Quoted in Jeremy Laurance, *Cape of Good Hope*, Independent, May 15, 1997, pp. 2, 3.

- I believe we all have more potential inside of us than we have any knowledge of. And when a crisis happens, you can find out what you're made of.
- You have to focus on what remains, not on what you've lost.

Anita Roddick

Anita Roddick is heralded as a pioneer of naturally based skin and hair products and creator of one of the premier international models of a socially responsible business. This 5 ft., 2 in., bundle of organic dynamite is Great Britain's best-known—and one of its richest—businesswoman. She presides over a multinational corporation catering to men, women, and children, with 1,600 stores in 47 countries, trading in 24 languages across 9 times zones, via more than 40 distribution centers.

Committed to the idea of fully integrating values and business, Anita Roddick's success story comes with the ideals of honest trade, environmental awareness, and campaigning for social change. She is often seen as a female version of Richard Branson, presenting the caring face of capitalism.

In 1976, she opened her first shop in Brighton, on England's south coast. Since then, she has overseen her company's rapid global expansion. In 1998 she became co-chair along with her husband, Gordon, pulling away from the day-to-day operation to concentrate on the creative aspects of the business.

Anita Roddick has been called the "queen of green," but The Body Shop has never been just a manufacturer and retailer of environmentally aware cosmetics. Anita's dream was bigger. The Body Shop has focused on human and civil rights, animal and environmental protection, social justice, equality, poverty, and the problems caused by globalization. The commitment of The Body Shop is: "to dedicate the business to the pursuit of social and environmental change." She is another of those speakers who motivate by who they are.

I am mystified by the fact that the business world is apparently proud to be seen as hard and uncaring and detached from human

> *values . . . the word "love" was as threatening in business as talking about a loss on the balance sheet. Perhaps that is why using words like "love" and "care" is so difficult in today's extraordinarily macho business world. No one seems to know how to put the concept into practice. . . . I think all business practices would improve immeasurably if they were guided by "feminine" principles—qualities like love and care and intuition.*
> —ANITA RODDICK

Anita often visits remote tribal communities around the world searching for ingredients. She then brings them back to her research and development department in England to see if a product can be created that will not only help customers in the West feel better about themselves, but also generate income for economically marginalized peoples.

Instead of paying for expensive advertising, she has created in herself an outspoken, high-profile media icon. She calculates it has saved her company an estimated £2 million a year in advertising costs!

> *I'm always looking for new and outrageous ways to make this work!*
> —ANITA RODDICK

Like the time she traveled by elephant while handing out condoms to truckers entering red-light districts in India and the time she clinched a deal with a group of tribal women by dropping her drawers to show them her pubic hair.

Anita follows her heart and honors her sense of humor. She also loves to break the rules, even when Queen Elizabeth II bestowed upon her the Order of the British Empire medallion in 1988 in a very formal ceremony.

> *Here's the Queen, right? I'm coming toward her, and there's music from* My Fair Lady *coming from somewhere. My hair is wild. I walk up and curtsey, she hooks on the medal and says, "It's going well in America, is it?" And that was her fatal mistake! Because I never stopped talking! I even left the bloody medal at Buckingham Palace!*
> —ANITA RODDICK

Turning Points for Anita Roddick

She was born Anita Lucia Perella, one of four children of first-generation Italian immigrants, in the town of Littlehampton, West Sussex.

But her character was shaped by an early sense of the injustice in the world. She vividly remembers the first photographs she ever saw of the Holocaust. Later, the time she spent on a kibbutz showed her the real power of community. In the 1960s, she marched against hunger and nuclear weapons. In later life, her experience of poverty in parts of the United States had a huge effect on her, as did her visit to the orphanages of Eastern Europe.

Anita had already bounced around the globe, getting into various scrapes and adventures when she met the equally adventurous Gordon Roddick in 1968. Gordon also was a wanderer. He'd canoed the Amazon and mined for tin in Africa, though his formal training was actually as a farmer. But, like Anita, his spirit roamed. They wed in 1971.

In 1976 Gordon decided to fill a life's dream to travel on horseback through the Americas, a trip that would take two years! Ever the one to dream big dreams and support them in others, Anita gave him her blessing and off he went.

To help "keep the wolf from the door," Anita decided to open a business. Her exotic travels had given her the idea of selling naturally based cosmetics. She found a herbalist in the Yellow Pages, and together they conjured up soaps and lotions using the herbal ingredients she remembered from her globe-trotting.

> *In Polynesia I had seen women rubbing cocoa butter on their breasts and bellies and buns. Their skin was like velvet.*
>
> *It wasn't only economic necessity that inspired the birth of The Body Shop. Women, when they want to earn a livelihood, usually earn it through what they are interested in or what they are knowledgeable about. I had a wealth of experience to draw on. I traveled, and I spent time in farming and fishing communities with preindustrial peoples. My travels exposed me to body rituals of women from all over the world.*
>
> *Also the frugality that my mother exercised during the war years made me question retail conventions. Why waste a container when*

> *you can refill it? And why buy more of something than you can use? We behaved as she did in the Second World War, we reused everything, we refilled everything and we recycled all we could. The foundation of The Body Shop's environmental activism was born out of ideas like these.*
>
> *The Body Shop arrived just as Europe was going "green." The Body Shop has always been recognizable by its green color, the only color that we could find to cover the damp, moldy walls of my first shop.*
> —ANITA RODDICK

The commitment of The Body Shop is: to dedicate the business to the pursuit of social and environmental change. If you dream these big dreams, you are going to have big accomplishments . . . and big problems.

One of Anita's first endeavors into community trade was with the Kayapo Indians, natives of the Amazon rainforest. Their lands were being manipulated out from under them by loggers and miners, then being destroyed for quick profits. They were desperately in need of help.

Anita thought of a way to help make the rainforest profitable for the Kayapo Indians, without their having to sell logging rights. The Body Shop agreed to buy Brazil nut oil from two Kayapo villages for a new hair product, Brazil Nut Conditioner. The union of an activist mentality with commercial reality in a third world country soon taught her some very difficult lessons about helping indigenous peoples.

Today The Body Shop still works with the Kayapo, but the company has sharpened its system of choosing, assessing, and developing trade links with the development of the community trade program. There are now strict guidelines for choosing communities, one of which is that the group, co-operative, women's association, or tribal council should already exist, and have a product to sell. The Body Shop puts hard cash in the hands of those making the products, enabling them to make their own decisions and help their own communities.

Special Wisdom of Anita Roddick

In her presentations, Anita Roddick reveals how "the double bottom line"—creation of a profitable venture that works as a force for positive

social change—reaps unimaginable rewards, both personally and professionally. Anita Roddick's success story comes with the ideals of honest trade, environmental awareness, and campaigning for social change.

- It is impossible to separate the company values from my own
  personal values and issues that I care passionately about: social
  responsiveness, respect for human rights, the environment, and
  animal protection.

- What are The Body Shop's values? To have fun, put love where
  our labor is, and go in the opposite direction to everyone else.

- Entrepreneurs must always have their head in the clouds, feet
  on the ground and heart in the business.

- Travel is a journey of discovery, much like a university without
  walls.

- I wake up every day and say "This is my last day." And I jam
  everything into it. There's no time for mediocrity. This is no
  damned dress rehearsal.

*Anita Roddick is a no-nonsense speaker with a terrific sense of
humor. She walks her talk—she actively supports what she believes
in with her energy, her mouth, her money, and her power.*

*I last saw her speak at an annual dinner for National
Association of Women Business Owners—she stayed behind the
lectern, brought slides from her travels and had the audience mesmerized. She is a real person who is very approachable, charming,
and fun to have in your presence.*

*When she shared how she started her company—including how
she chose the name and how she could only afford the plastic jars that
urine samples were used for—she had her audience hooked. She
shared that she strongly believed in giving back. Her travels have
taken her to remote areas where she would seek out women who were
making herbs, fabrics, and products. Anita sought ways that she
could buy things—almost anything from these women—that would
create money for them. . . . and a way to feed their families.*

*I went home and those words inspired me to commit to use her
products (and tell others) so that women all over the world would*

have a better life because of her support of them. Every time I'm in an airport (which is approximately 150 times a year), there isn't a time that I don't think of her comments when I pass The Body Shop.

> —JUDITH BRILES, AUTHOR OF
> *WOMAN TO WOMAN 2000*

Tony Robbins

It's hard to believe that it was only eight years ago that I sat in the audience of the Tony Robbins seminar not knowing that the information and ideas I was experiencing would change my life forever.

Tony was sharing his experience and relating stories about how he raised himself from the depths of poverty to become a successful writer and speaker, and he was having more fun than anyone else! I thought to myself, "I have a lot of similar experiences."

I decided that evening to follow my heart and began writing a newsletter. Over time, my little newsletter grew into a book which has gone on to become an international best-seller.

> —JIM DONOVAN, AUTHOR AND SPEAKER

Anthony "Tony" Robbins has become a brand-name leader in the personal and professional development industry. He was overwhelmingly voted number one in our survey to find the world's greatest motivational speakers.

Tony had accomplished more by his early thirties than most people do in their entire lives. He became a millionaire by the age of 24. He has built and controls an empire entirely on his own thoughts and words, through books, tapes, and seminars. In 1998, his seminars grossed around $22 million, and his tapes, sold via the "Personal Power" infomercial, took in another $30 million or so.

Anthony Robbins is a best-selling author with three titles published in 16 languages around the world: *Unlimited Power, Awaken the Giant Within,* and *Giant Steps.* He has produced the best-selling personal development audio series of all time, *Personal Power,* with 30 million educational audio tapes sold in less than 10 years. At Robbins' headquarters, two dozen operators take about a thousand calls a day concerning reservations at his resort in Fiji, his live events, his brand-new coaching program, and his latest audio series, *The Time of Your Life*.

Tony conducts more than 80 days of seminars a year in eight nations globally. More than two million people have attended Robbins' seminars, and he is the founder and dean of Mastery University, a yearlong educational experience, which he facilitates along with a faculty of experts in such fields as life management, physical health, emotions, and relationships. Past instructors for this three-part program have included General Norman Schwarzkopf on leadership, Dr. Deepak Chopra on health, Anita Roddick on socially conscious entrepreneurship, and Peter Lynch and Sir John Templeton on finance. The University has been attended by over 15,000 individuals representing 70 nations.

Robbins was the first American since Ronald Reagan to speak at Parliament before members of both the House of Commons and the House of Lords. Further, he was a featured speaker on regenerating government at Vice President Al Gore's Putting Customers First conference, attended by hundreds of U.S. government department heads in November 1993. Princess Diana also sought a private consultation with him.

A&E's signature show, *Biography*, featured Tony. His work has also been covered in *Esquire, Time, Newsweek, Life,* and *Success* magazines, the *CBS Evening News* with Dan Rather, *NBC News,* and *PrimeTime Live,* as well as newspapers and radio programs worldwide. Robbins is also a regular contributor to CNN's *Larry King Live.*

The only thing greater than Robbins' size is his charisma. Robbins stands a powerful six feet, seven inches tall, but what really sets him apart is his commanding presence. When Tony Robbins walks into a room, people listen.

A Tony Robbins presentation seems like part rock concert, part late-night talk show. Listening to Tony Robbins speak, the first thing you'll notice is his command of language, speech patterns, and tonality. His voice is bassoon-like, his face animated. His eyes have a laser intensity. His speaking style is conversational, lighthearted, and his sincerity radiates through the room—any room. Tony has been described as part religious leader, part carnival barker, dash of cheerleader thrown in. He has the athleticism of a basketball player, the comedy of Jim Carrey.

Today Tony and his wife of 10 years, Becky, live in La Jolla, California, with a bedroom that looks out over the pristine beaches of San Diego. He is the proud father of four children.

Turning Points for Tony Robbins

Robbins grew up on "the other side of the tracks." His dad was a parking lot attendant. His parents split up when he was about seven. His mother married four times, and was extremely dependent on having Tony in the house and attached to her. Tony was an honors student and entrepreneur at an early age. In high school he started a sports column, went after major sports celebrities to interview (including the inimitable Howard Cosell) and got them to agree! His success was detailed in the major newspapers. His mother, uncomfortable with his success, forced him to quit.

Finally on Christmas Eve, 1978, at only 17 years of age, frustrated at not being allowed to advance, Tony left home. He rode his bicycle to a movie theater, sat alone inside, depressed. He started sleeping in self-service laundries, at friends' houses, then in his Volkswagen Baja bug. He worked for an uncle, until his mother found out, and had the uncle fire him. She said, "If Tony wants to make it on his own, let him find out what on his own means."

Not long after, Tony was invited to attend a seminar presented by Jim Rohn. He spent his entire week's pay on the ticket.

I was blown away. Jim Rohn talked about all the books I had read. I got so excited! I wanted to make a difference in the world.

From that night on I began to set goals. I used the Rohn technique to write a plan. Then I went back to the Jim Rohn seminar and convinced him I could do a job for him selling tickets to his seminars. I pulled up to the South Coast Plaza Hotel in my '69 bug, wearing a blue leisure suit I got at a thrift store. The wind hit you and you looked like you were flying. I had minestrone-soup acne and a fake-gold chain. I turned the car off, and it exploded. The valet came out, and I said, "Take care of this baby." I ran up to Rohn and told him I wanted to work for him. I told him that he changed my whole life and I was on my own now, becoming a salesperson. I went to work for Rohn, and I sold every human being I sat down with. I was the youngest guy who sold tickets for Jim Rohn's seminars, but I became their top salesman in a month. It is still like a legend with those people.

I slept in my Volkswagen and convinced the bank to lend me $1200 to live on, more than the car was worth.

I'd read a book about conditioning my mind and I'd drive the freeway, screaming my affirmation. People would look over at me. I'd crack up seeing their faces.

I studied every sales tape there was; I listened to J. David Evers while I was sleeping. I'd sell cassettes, workbooks, a speed-reading course. I was like a laser beam. I would ask questions—that was my secret.

I made 125 phone calls a day. I booked myself to speak three times a day to anybody who would listen. I became the best speaker anybody had ever seen. I made $20,000 in one day—I was 19 years old.

—**TONY ROBBINS**

Soon he was promoting other speakers, like Harvey and Marilyn Diamond, authors of the popular Diamond Method diet. Before long, he and the Diamonds parted company. Robbins now says, "I was too intense and hard to get along with." He went broke, moved into a dinky apartment where he washed dishes in the bathtub. He soon gained 38 pounds.

One day he was listening to the Neil Diamond song "I Am, I Said;" the lyrics lament how no one heard him at all, not even the chair, and the fire ignited Tony.

I felt like hell, I looked like shit. I was eating everything I could get my hands on. My big thing was fishburgers. I was more than a big guy, I was jumbo. I was impossible to be around. I had no direction. And that is why I know the power of physiology.

> *You asked me the moment of my change? I went for this run on
> the beach. I ran from Venice Beach to the Marina Del Rey pier, a
> couple of miles. I don't know if you've ever run so hard you feel
> like spitting up blood—that intensity—pushing beyond every mus-
> cle in my body I was in such a state of physical intensity. I sat
> down and wrote every damn thing I wouldn't stand for anymore,
> physically, emotionally.*
>
> *Then I started pursuing neurolinguistic programming with even
> more intensity. I was on a mission to create change.*
>
> —TONY ROBBINS

Tony's fame came in part with his successful use of the firewalk. He
learned it from a California man, Tolly Burkan. By teaching the atten-
dees what to think and how to hold their bodies, he showed them how
to walk barefoot through a bed of coals burning at 2,000 degrees
Fahrenheit. He called his firewalk "The Mind Revolution." In any
given seminar of 2,000 people, only about 20 get blisters.

Robbins' infomercial is the most successful motivational infomercial
ever. It has sold $200 million worth of tapes via TV.

Robbins got into infomercials by doing an endorsement in an
infomercial for Napoleon Hill's audio program based on Hill's, *Think
and Grow Rich.* Robbins was deeply inspired by this classic work, and
very, very familiar with its message. The focus groups cited Tony Robbins
conviction to the product as a main reason they bought Hill's tapes. The
producers, knowing a good thing when they saw it, asked Tony to make
his own infomercial. Robbins developed and produced a series of five
television infomercials that have continuously aired every 30 minutes, 24
hours a day, somewhere in North America since their introduction in
April, 1989. Nearly one-third of America has now seen him on TV.

Special Wisdom of Tony Robbins

> *He is in his private life what he teaches in his public life. He is
> driven by his desire to make a lasting contribution. He is also
> moved emotionally by "average" people who overcome incredible
> odds.*

He has a deep love for children (probably because he is such a big kid himself).

I have met few people who are as motivated as he is. He keeps himself motivated by doing what he preaches (i.e., belief system, modeling, never-ending improvement, asking quality questions). He is a big believer in finding masters in the major areas of life (i.e., financial, emotional, physical, relationships) and modeling their behavior. He often travels with a personal physician, chiropractor, and massage therapist to keep his health at its peak.

—ART BERG, MOTIVATIONAL SPEAKER WHO HAS
WORKED WITH ROBBINS AT HIS PROGRAMS

Tony first began to move into the realm of Superstar with the use of a little-known therapeutic technique, called *neurolinguistic programming* (NLP). Even though his endorsement made NLP famous, today he has shifted away from NLP and toward neuroassociative conditioning (NAC). The main cores of his message are:

- Find models of excellence. Find the best and do what they do.
- Live with passion!
- The past does not equal the future.
- It's in your moments of decision that your destiny is shaped.
- Put yourself in a state of mind where you say to yourself, Here is an opportunity for me to celebrate like never before, my own power, my own ability to get myself to do whatever is necessary.
- If we want to discover the unlimited possibilities within us, we must find a goal big enough and grand enough to challenge us to push beyond our limits and discover our true potential.

He is the kind of person you go into a one-hour meeting with, then go home and take a two-hour nap! His passion is created from his intense desire to make a huge difference in the world.

He is compassionate. On dozens of occasions, I've seen Tony stay with an audience or with a person hours longer than he "should"

have. Why does he do this day in and day out? Because he truly
cares about people and wants to help them create the life they desire
and deserve.
                    —NATE BOOTH, LEAD TRAINER FOR TONY
                    AT ROBBINS RESEARCH

Brian Tracy

One of America's leading authorities on the development of human
potential and personal effectiveness. Brian has traveled and worked in
over 80 countries on six continents and speaks four languages. He is an
avid reader in management, psychology, economics, metaphysics, and
history and he brings a unique perspective and style to his talks. He has
the remarkable ability to capture and hold audience attention with a
fast-moving combination of stories, examples, humor, and concrete,
practical ideas that get results—fast.

He is the author/narrator of best-selling audiocassette programs,
including: *The Psychology of Achievement, Fast Track to Business Success,*
The Psychology of Selling, Peak Performance Woman, The Psychology of
Success, and *24 Techniques for Closing the Sale.* Brian is the author of
Maximum Achievement and Advanced Selling Strategies, published by
Simon & Schuster.

Brian Tracy has produced over 300 different audio and video learning programs covering the entire spectrum of human and corporate
performance. These programs, researched and developed for more than
25 years, are some of the most effective learning tools in the world.

He addresses thousands of men and women each year on the subjects
of personal and professional development, including the executives and
staff of IBM, Arthur Andersen, McDonnell Douglas, and The Million
Dollar Round Table. His exciting talks and seminars on leadership, self-
esteem, goals and strategy, creativity, and success psychology bring
about immediate changes and long-term results. Brian has a bachelor of
commerce degree from the University of Alberta and a master of administration and management degree from Columbia Pacific University. He
is the chairman of Brian Tracy International, a human resource company based in California, with affiliates throughout America and in 31
countries worldwide.

Prior to founding Brian Tracy International, Brian was the chief operating officer of a development company with $265 million in assets and $75 million in annual sales. He has had successful careers in sales and marketing, investments, real estate development and syndication, importation, distribution, and management consulting. He has had high-level consulting assignments with several billion-dollar-plus corporations in strategic planning and organizational development.

Brian is a master at uncovering and sharing the "recipes of success." He is very precise and methodical.

> *Brian is the encyclopedia of our business. There is nobody with a better work ethic than Brian. He is the creative mogul of our business. He creates over one new six-cassette album package per month! That's incredible.*
> **—MARK VICTOR HANSEN**

Turning Points for Brian Tracy

At 28, Brian Tracy packed everything he owned in the back of his little car and moved from Vancouver, British Columbia, to Edmonton, Alberta. He had almost no money, only one or two contacts, no education to speak of, and no great future to look forward to. He created his own turning point.

> *I was working at laboring jobs, drifting from place to place and sleeping in my car, I had so little money for so many years that I could tell you at any time, within a dollar, how much I had in my pocket. Comparing myself with others doing better than I, led me to my lifelong search for the answer to the question "Why is it that some people are more successful than others?"*
>
> *In looking back, a major factor that shaped my early life was my upbringing which had instilled in me a deep belief in the importance of honesty and truthfulness. I have found over the years that many problems in life begin when a person deviates from these qualities, especially in the area of lying to themselves or attempting to believe things about themselves or their situations which are simply not true.*
> **—BRIAN TRACY**

In the middle of a minus-35-degree freezing winter, Brian sat down and developed a personal blueprint for success. This blueprint included goals, plans, timelines, and daily activities.

> *One of my goals was to work with one of the most respected business people in Canada, Dr. Charles Allard. One year later, I had studied and learned the profession of real estate development, optioned and then bought a piece of property, developed and built a three million dollar shopping center and then sold three-quarters of the shopping center to Allarco Developments, owned by Dr. Charles Allard. This venture began a mentor/mentee relationship that lasted for several years.*
> —**BRIAN TRACY**

In 1978, Dr. Allard was asked if he would be interested in distributing the Suzuki four-wheel-drive vehicles in Western Canada, and he asked Brian to join him.

Within two years, they built what the Japanese had described as the fastest and most successful vehicle distributorship in their history in 120 countries. He set up a $2 million line of credit, imported hundreds, and then thousands, of Suzuki vehicles, set up 65 dealerships through the four western provinces, and sold $25 million worth of the vehicles. The Suzuki four-wheel-drive vehicle on the roads in the United States was essentially the vehicle that he worked with the Japanese engineers to develop for the American market.

A student of professional development, one day he decided that he could put together a seminar that was superior to some of those he had attended on the subject.

> *This was arrogant of me at the time. I knew nothing whatsoever about professional speaking. I did not have the advantage of reading* Sharing Ideas.[15]
>
> *In my first three years, I had to liquidate all of my savings, sell my house, borrow from my friends and relatives, and move into rented premises with my young family in order to continue giving*

---

[15]*Sharing Ideas,* newsmagazine for professional speakers. Royal Publishing, Phone 626-335-8069; Fax 626-335-6127; http://www.walters-intl.com

seminars. Gradually, like a plane in a nose dive, I managed to pull up, level off, and begin to climb.
—BRIAN TRACY

Special Wisdom of Brian Tracy

His universal laws of success covers many things of value, including the law of cause and effect and that everything counts.

- The same wind blows on all of us . . . it's how we set our sail.
- The potential of the average person is like a huge ocean unsailed, a new continent unexplored, a world of possibilities waiting to be released and channeled toward some great good.
- Be careful whom you let near your mind, it's very contagious!
- You are responsible for your own life and you cannot change until you accept that.
- Read a book a week for five years.

When I heard Brian Tracy say that "the same wind blows on all of us, it's how you set your sail," it made me realize that we all have opportunities. Some of us see life as obstacles and some see the opportunities.

I immediately came home and set my sail, and I'm now on course for success. Brian also said that "failure is not an option." Every time my inner voice even considers a negative thought or failure I say aloud, "No thanks, failure is not an option." It has changed my entire way of thinking and I now enjoy life in a happy, positive vein.
—JUDIE SINCLAIR, AUTHOR AND SPEAKER,
PRESIDENT OF POSITIVE IMPACT

Dottie Walters

Dottie Walters, how does it feel to have blown a handful of stardust to the world?
—NAPOLEON HILL (LETTER TO DOTTIE AFTER HER
APPEARANCE ON *TO TELL THE TRUTH*)

My mother, the most magical speaker I have ever known, is a world premier sales and motivational speaker, author, and consultant.

Dottie is former president and founder of Hospitality Hostess Service, the largest newcomer welcoming agency and advertising company on the West Coast. She sold that business about 15 years ago to concentrate on her own speaking, giving seminars, writing, and publishing her news-magazine *Sharing Ideas,* a resource for professional speakers, which is today the largest publication in the world for paid speakers.

She is perhaps most famous as the author of *Never Underestimate the Selling Power of a Woman* (Wilshire Book Co.), the first book ever written by a woman for saleswomen. *Speak and Grow Rich* (Prentice Hall-Simon Schuster), which she and I co-authored, was selected in an industrywide survey—by an overwhelming majority—as *the* most valuable book ever written for professional speakers. We also authored *101 Simple Things to Grow Your Business and Yourself: Easy Ideas to Improve Sales, Productivity and Service!* (Crisp Publishers).

She also has authored several outstanding audiotapes and albums about sales and professional speaking.

She is the author of numerous articles in publications around the world. She is constantly being interviewed on the radio. You might have seen her interviewed on TV by CNN, ABC, *Good Morning Australia, Good Morning South Africa,* and many other TV shows. She was featured on American Air Lines Business Channel on all domestic and international flights, and on Sky radio broadcast to major cities and to United and Delta Air Lines passengers. She was radio program host for National Business Radio Network on the subject of great business ideas, heard in 75 major cities in the United States.

She is the president of Walters Speakers Services, the premier source for information on speakers, speaking, seminar leaders, humorists, and experts. We help speakers and those who wish to hire speakers.

She is the founder of the professional association for speakers bureaus, International Group of Agencies and Bureaus (IGAB). She is the recipient of IGAB's John Palmer Award for outstanding contributions to the bureau industry. She is also a founding member of the National Speakers Association, past national board member, and founder of the Los Angeles chapter NSA, life board member.

*I love Dottie's stories. She changed my life after a two-day confer-
ence with her. I love the way she taught me to say "Tell me more"
to business colleagues. I love the confidence she gave me.*
I started a completely new direction after those two days.
        —Martha Campbell Pullen, Ph.D., national
        TV host and international magazine pub-
        lisher of Sew Beautiful

Turning Points for Dottie Walters

Mom had a very difficult childhood. One she overcame with a love of
words and stories, writing, and reading. Her father would not have been
awarded "Father of the Year" . . . of any year. Grandmother couldn't
afford babysitters, and she needed a safe and cheap place to leave Mom,
so she chose the public library, next door to the grocery store. Rather
than feeling afraid and lonely, Mom found a refuge of friends-of-the-
mind who call to her: Benjamin Franklin, Ralph Waldo Emerson, Albert
Payson Terhune, even the fictional detective girl Nancy Drew! She read
her way around the shelves of that old library, and she has continued to
read about six books a week ever since.

By the time Mom entered high school, her father had, thank good-
ness, left them permanently. She had some pretty big emotional blocks
to overcome. Mom had survived her father through reading; now she
fell in love with writing.

She went to work in a midnight bakery every day after school and
weekends. After Mom washed the bakery cases and mopped the floors,
she took out paper bakery bags, leaned on the counter, and wrote
poems, editorials, stories, articles, for her beloved *Alhambra High
School Moor Newsletter.*

Shortly after finishing high school, she married her first and only
sweetheart, my dad. He survived WWII with honors, no doubt carried
through by the words she wrote to him daily. They had two babies, my
older brother and sister. Life looked great until that massive recession
hit. One night in 1948, dad brought home devastating news.

*The dry cleaning business had seemed so right for Bob. But I could
see what had happened. With his happy-go-lucky disposition, Bob*

hadn't told me the bad news because he was so long recognizing it himself.

We talked all through dinner, searching for a way out. The worst part was my aunt. We'd borrowed $5,000 from her to buy the business, and this obligation had to be repaid.

After putting the kids to bed, I took a look at myself too. Twenty-three years old, just a high school education, no special training or talents. There was nothing someone with no talent like me could do!

—DOTTIE WALTERS

Mom started to look for work, but met with many closed signs. "Sorry, no help needed." Finally she talked a coffee shop into letting her wash dishes for them during their lunch hour. But after one day the owner said he couldn't use her for another week. She set a goal for herself— their house payment. Doing dishes once a week was not going to get that paid!

That night I couldn't sleep. If only I could do one thing well.

Suddenly I remembered Miss Pettifer, my high school English teacher, who'd had so much faith in my writing ability that I'd become feature editor and advertising manager of The Alhambra-Moor.

But all this had been many years ago, I told myself that night, with housework and babies filling every moment since. No, I'd have to think of something else.

—DOTTIE WALTERS

And quickly too because their creditors were beginning to use frightening words like *foreclosure* and *repossession.*

I turned to prayer. I simply asked God, "What can I do?"

And then, quite suddenly and quite sharply, two Biblical stories came back to me.

The first was the story of the widow in II Kings who when despairing of losing her two sons into slavery, asked the prophet

Elisha, "What can I do?" She didn't ask him what he could do for her.

Elisha questioned her, "Tell me, what hast thou in the house?"

And she said, "Thine handmaid hath not any thing in the house, save a pot of oil." She might have said, "I have nothing," but no one has nothing. She scored on two points: first, she was ready to help herself and second, she recognized something of value which was already hers—little though it was.

Elisha told her to go out, borrow vessels from her neighbors and fill them with her oil.

She didn't stop to doubt but filled up so many vessels her son couldn't find any more to bring her. Then she went back to the prophet and he said, "Go, sell the oil, and pay thy debt and live thou and thy children off the rest."

I asked myself, "What do I have in the house to sell?"

The other biblical story that came to me was the story of the talents in the Book of Matthew. The men who had been given many talents went out into the world and multiplied them, but the poor man who'd been given only one talent had hidden it in the earth. And God took that talent away and gave it to a man who already had 10 talents.

Matthew ends the parable by saying, "For unto every one that hath shall be given, and he shall have abundance; but from him that hath not shall be taken away, even that which he hath."

I slipped into my robe, tiptoed into the kitchen and turned on the old, faithful coffee pot again.

In the wastebasket beside the stove was a copy of the Baldwin Park Bulletin, *our weekly newspaper. I pulled it out, spread it open on the kitchen table and carefully read every advertisement.*

Painstakingly I wrote up a sample shopper's column—making it just as eye-catching as I could. I finished at dawn.

—DOTTIE WALTERS

That morning after dad left for work, mom dressed up in her best clothes, dressed the children in their best, put them in a stroller—Jeanine riding in the seat, Mike hanging on behind—and walked two miles downtown to the newspaper office. (I came along 10 years later.)

An older, important-looking, gray-haired woman glanced up from her desk. "Yes?"

> *I swallowed and blurted out, "I would like to work for your news-paper."*
>
> *The lady laughed. "My dear child, we don't need any help here. You haven't a chance." With that she turned back to the papers on her desk.*
>
> *Suddenly I felt as if a white light was shinning on me, illuminating me.*
>
> *A small, thin, worried-looking man came through the inner door of the office.*
>
> *"Sir," I blurted out, "are you the publisher? Because if you are, I want to buy an ad!"*
>
> *I poured out my plan. I'd buy their space for my "Window Wishing" shopper's column on wholesale at a regular basis and then resell it for a little more than I paid for it—the difference would be my profit.*
>   —Dottie Walters

And she got him to sell her the first week *on credit!*

Dad's business improved. Mom worked hard, always walking into town. With only one pair of shoes, she was soon putting cardboard soles in to increase her mileage. Many times she would bring my older brother and sister along in a rickety, dilapidated stroller, meant for one child. The wheel kept coming off! She would take off her shoe and whack it back on.

Dad couldn't take that for long; he scraped together enough to surprise Mom with a battle-scarred old car.

> *. . . a beautiful two-door Model A Ford, just for me!*
>
> *"The back seat is so big the kids can't fall out," he said with a twinkle in his eyes, "and this'll get the cardboard out of your shoes."*
>
> *"Oh, Bob, we really can't afford it."*

"We can't afford not to," he said firmly. "You're going to get sick if you keep this up. Besides, think how you can sell more ads if you aren't spending so much time walking."
—DOTTIE WALTERS

The magic words! Which of course sold it to Mom!

One day I asked Mr. Heacock, the publisher at the paper for more work. Every little bit helped.

"Okay Dottie, I'll pay you $1,000 if you sell 1,000 new newspaper subscriptions for me."

"You mean $1 per?"

"Sure!"

I grabbed up a stack of newspapers to use as samples.

That very afternoon I was out calling on the new houses in town, the new tract developments, wherever I knew I'd find newcomers who wouldn't have had a chance to subscribe to the paper.

Mr. Staples, one of my regular ad customers, heard about what I was doing. He asked me to sell the newcomers on signing up for his trash pickup service. Then a fence man asked me to pick up sales leads for him.

Soon I was too busy and talked my neighbor Virginia into being my business partner. Hospitality Hostess Service, a newcomer welcoming agency, like Welcome Wagon, was born. We were a hit!
—DOTTIE WALTERS

For 20 years Hospitality Hostess Service was the largest newcomer welcoming agency on the West Coast. She built that business into four offices, 285 employees, and 4,000 continuous contract advertising accounts.

She began speaking to the service clubs to promote her sales. Her subject was, "What Does Your Customer Really Want?" Then one day the owner of a department store chain came up to her and asked, "How much would you *charge* to do that talk for my employees?" Charge? Soon after Dottie Walters, professional speaker, stepped onto the speaking platform.

As she researched information to use in developing her team of saleswomen, mom read every book she could find on sales technique. However, she noticed the authors never seemed to be speaking to her, "Take your prospect to a bar, buy him a drink, offer him a cigarette. . . ." Not techniques she felt comfortable with.

When she asked the librarian where the books were for women in sales, she was assured, "There are no women in sales, so there are no books for them!"

But that very night, in an empty slot on the library shelf, Dottie saw a new book—not yet produced! She visualized the title *Never Underestimate the Selling Power of a Woman!* and felt a great tug at her heart. She must write it. As she worked on it, she had no idea that it would be the first book ever written for women in sales by a saleswoman.

In 1962, before it first hit the shelves, Tupperware bought out the entire first printing for their team, including a front section with a letter and picture of their president. They booked Dottie to speak at their big rallies around the country. Many other direct sales companies followed suit.

One section in the book was pulled out by the publisher. The subject "Men Selling to Women." The day that chapter arrived back on Dottie's desk, the same mail contained an ad from SMI (Success Motivation Institute) in Texas. They were creating a line of talking records on business topics. She felt that "call" in her heart again. She picked up the phone immediately and called SMI. "Have you thought of producing an audio product on selling to women?"

"Odd that you should ask!" they answered. "We were planning one on that subject, but the woman we were after just turned us down. Send us the manuscript!"

She did, they loved it. The product was a best-seller for years. It was translated into several languages.

Soon W. Clement Stone, of *SUCCESS* magazine heard about her and asked her to create *The Selling Power of a Woman* audio album. *SUCCESS* did sales rallies around the country. They used Dottie on the platform with Dr. Norman Vincent Peale, Zig Ziglar, and many other noted speakers.

> *Dottie has that special talent to put her thoughts into words so that the words go out and move the people.*
> —EARL NIGHTENGALE

When the National Speakers Association was formed, the founder, Cavett Robert, called mom and asked her to attend the first meeting. While there she noticed there was a scarcity of women. All of the "girls" sat at one little table at the event and wondered how they could best support each other. For her part, mom said she would start a little newsletter. In October 1978, *Sharing Ideas Among Women Speakers and Their Friends* was launched. Before many months the male speakers were saying, "We want to subscribe!" So, she changed it to *Sharing Ideas Among Professional Speakers*. Today it is the largest publication in the world for paid speakers, with all the issues, news, tips, and trends.

As she was more and more often asked to speak, her customers would ask for help in finding additional speakers. Soon Walters International Speakers Bureau came into existence. In 1985 she asked me to come on board and run it.

Walters Speakers Services has become the premier source for information on speakers and speaking, seminar leaders, humorists, and experts. We help speakers and those who wish to hire speakers. We created the top products available on how to market yourself as a speaker, including the entire line of "Speak and Grow Rich" products. For more, see http://www.walters-intl.com.

Special Wisdom of Dottie Walters

- When in doubt, take a survey.
- Listen to the great conversation of mankind.
- Never sell one when you can sell two, three, or four or a subscription
- When the angel knocks and yells at the door of your heart, open it! The bolt is on your side. Then arise and go forth!
- Bill Marriott told me, "Failure? I never encountered it. I just stumbled over a few temporary setbacks."

- Earl Nightingale told me when I was feeling low: "Arrogance is Gods' gift to shallow people. Move on!"
- No one else knows what you are capable of. Put your fingers on your wrist and feel the beat of your own heart.

I have wanted to give up and let the whole project drop numerous times, but remembering Dottie's story of perseverance helped me get to this wonderful point in my life. Now I am in the early stages of self-publishing, and the whole project is going great. It just takes perseverance.
                    —AMY W. BERGER, PRESIDENT,
                       MOTIVATIONAL MAGIC PRESS

Zig Ziglar

When I heard Zig Ziglar say, "You don't pay the price of success, you pay the price of failure." I knew that I had been paying the price of failure. It was at that moment that I decided to change my life by changing the way I thought. I went from an overweight, depressed housewife, sleeping 18 hours a day, to vice president of Disney's radio and TV stations in three years.
                    —PAM LONTOS, FORMER RADIO ADVERTISING EXECU-
                       TIVE, AUTHOR, AND SPEAKER

Zig Ziglar is the antithesis of one of the old golden rules of speaking, "Do not bring your religion to the platform!" Yet in our survey, Zig, who does just that, was overwhelming at the top as one of the greatest motivators— *ever.* Yet he not only brings his Christian faith and the results of his frequent chats with God to his talk, but all of his work strongly resonates the beliefs of a born-again Southern Baptist. In his best-selling *See You at the Top* he is totally *un*-politically correct. He cautions things like "horoscopes are Satan's daily bulletin, published in Hell." Did I mention that he (with Tony Robbins and Les Brown) were *overwhelming* at the top of our survey? Why? Because even if you disagree with the presenter's doctrine, you will respect the person and listen if the message is passionately given from the heart, with compassion, with a well-defined purpose. Purpose with passion and compassion is the secret of superstar speakers.

A talented author and speaker, Zig Ziglar has an appeal that transcends barriers of religion, age, culture, and occupation. Since 1970, he has traveled over five million miles across the world, delivering life improvement programs with messages that are psychologically, theologically, and physiologically sound.

Prior to his career in the speaking and training field, Zig Ziglar was a sales champion. He is now the chairman of the board of the Zig Ziglar Corporation and instructs his Born to Win seminar.

He has shared the platform with such distinguished Americans as Presidents Ford, Reagan and Bush, Generals Norman Schwarzkopf and Colin Powell, Dr. Norman Vincent Peale, Paul Harvey, Dr. Robert Schuller, plus numerous U.S. congressmen and governors. A well-known authority on the science of human potential, Zig Ziglar has been recognized three times in the Congressional Record of the United States for his work with youth in the drug war and for his dedication to America and the free enterprise system.

Zig Ziglar has a client list that includes thousands of small and mid-sized businesses, *Fortune* 500 Companies, U.S. Government agencies, churches, schools, and nonprofit associations. In addition, Mr. Ziglar has written 15 celebrated books on personal growth, leadership, sales, faith, family, and success, including *See You at the Top, Raising Positive Kids in a Negative World, Top Performance, Courtship After Marriage, Over the Top,* and *Secrets of Closing the Sale.* Nine titles have been on the best-seller lists; his books and tapes have been translated into over 32 languages and dialects.

He and his wife, Jean, whom he refers to as "the redhead," live in Dallas. He is an exercise buff and enthusiastic golfer.

I love Zig Ziglar just because he is such an inspirational man. I love his energy and his stories. My life was enhanced and enriched by his dynamic Christian presence on and off the platform. I would love to go to his Sunday School class. I rode on a elevator

once with him. He took the time to tell me, "I love redheads I am
married to "the redhead." Since I have red hair, he got to be my
friend immediately.

> —MARTHA CAMPBELL PULLEN, NATIONAL TV HOST
> AND INTERNATIONAL MAGAZINE PUBLISHER OF
> *SEW BEAUTIFUL*

Turning Points for Zig Ziglar

Born Hilary Hinton Ziglar in rural Coffee County, Alabama. One of
12 children, Ziglar graduated from high school in Yazoo City, Mississippi. He attended Millsaps College in Jackson, Mississippi, and the
University of South Carolina in Columbia. Ziglar was dubbed "Zig
Ziglar" not long after he began speaking, and the nickname stuck.

After a discharge from the Navy in 1946, Ziglar studied at the
University of South Carolina. However he soon abandoned his studies
and began selling aluminum cookware door-to-door for the Wearever
Aluminum Company.

During the first two and a half years all I did was prove they
had been right not to hire me in the first place. It was really a
question of survival. When our first baby was born, I had to lit-
erally go out and sell two sets of cookware in order to get her out
of the hospital.

> —ZIG ZIGLAR

For two and a half years Zig was a less than successful salesperson for
Wearever (heavy duty waterless cookware), an unknown person of little accomplishment. Ziglar's turning point came during a regional sales
meeting. An executive pulled him aside for a chat, which surprised him
because of his dismal sales record. The executive told Zig he had been
wasting his time; if he'd only recognize his ability and work on a regular schedule he could become "a great one."

If it wasn't for some words of encouragement from P. C. Merrell, I
would have probably found another job. Merrell said, "Ziglar, you

have real ability, you're champion caliber." Those words inspired me to become the number two salesman in a company of 7,000 in one year.
—ZIG ZIGLAR

After years as a cookware salesman in South Carolina, in 1955, Ziglar began his teaching career as an instructor at the Dale Carnegie Institute in New York City.

The most profound turning point for Ziglar was his acceptance of God in his life. Thanks to an elderly African-American lady from Tullahoma, Tennessee, who spent the July fourth week in his home, he became a born-again Christian. Floating in his trademark arrow-shaped swimming pool of his lovely Dallas home, he said to himself, "Lord, I know you put this whole big universe together, and I know that someday you're going to take it down." A shooting star passed through the sky, Ziglar heard: "That's right, boy, and don't you ever forget it!" He never has, as you hear from his words on the page and on the platform. Another time Zig was on a telephone call in a difficult conversation when the Lord told him to leave it simply up to Him. He would take care of the little things. A lesson for us all.

Special Wisdom of Zig Ziglar

I heard Zig Ziglar tell the story of how he was broke, with no money, and a family to support, he got a job as a salesman, and decided to turn his life around. I decided to go back to school to complete my degree in broadcast journalism, and become a radio personality. Because of his story, I knew that even though everyone said I would never find a job in radio because I was a woman, I knew I would.

As long as I kept the words of Zig (See you at the top!) within my soul, I knew that one day, I would get a job in radio. It's been 25 years since I first heard Zig, and I have been in radio for only five years, but his words still ring in my ears today. When someone tells me I can't do something, I quietly affirm his words, See you at the top!

—ZELDA ROBINSON, INTERNATIONAL SPEAKER, TRAINING CONSULTANT, AUTHOR, AND RADIO PERSONALITY

- I believe that persistent effort, supported by a character-based foundation, will enable you to get more of the things money will buy and all of the things money won't buy.
- The world's most deadly disease is "hardening of the attitudes."
- The weatherman on TV says that we have a 20 percent chance of rain or that it will be partly cloudy. Why doesn't he tell us that we have an 80 percent chance of sunshine and that it will be mostly fair?
- Be careful of your associates. You acquire much of the thinking, mannerisms, and characteristics of the people you are around.
- What you get by achieving your goals is not as important as what you become by achieving your goals.
- You can get whatever you want, if you help enough people get whatever they want.
- It's not what you've got, it's what you use that makes a difference.
- Success is the maximum utilization of the ability that you have.

Zig said if we don't put something into life, we will never get anything out. He called his program, "Biscuits, Pump Handles, and Fleas." The first edition of his book had the same name; then his new publisher changed it to See You at the Top. *I love Zig's description of himself: "I fit people with new glasses—not rose-colored, but magnifying glasses."*
—DOTTIE WALTERS

About 18 years ago, my wife, Jocelyn, and I were at a "trash and treasure" sale in the public carpark of Toukley, a little town north of Sydney (Australia). Among the "junk" was an oldish-looking cassette album, minus a couple of cassettes, of a U.S. salesmasters convention hosted by Hal Krause. Many of the tapes were seized up, but there was a Zig Ziglar tape which was in good working order. I paid a dollar for the album.

On his tape, called "Five Steps Up," Zig tells about a cook named Maude who made biscuits that did not rise. She says "They squatted to rise but they just got cooked in the squat" and Zig used this to introduce the breed of people known as "gonna do-ers" or "want-er-do-ers" who actually are the "never do-ers."

He also said "every tub sits on its own bottom" which, to me, translates to "whose bottom were you sitting on when the world passed you by?"

He carried an old water pump which he used to demonstrate the power of persistence in that, sometimes, the water is so far down that you have to pump for a long time but, when the water finally comes, it is abundant and sweet. Likewise, in life, we must persist, despite setbacks along the way, and, when the rewards ultimately come, they will be abundant and sweet.

Of course, says Zig, we have to put something in before we can get anything out. Often we have to put in a great deal of effort which is where the persistence comes in. We have to "keep on pumpin'," despite setbacks along the way, and the rewards come but often only after "an awful lot of pumpin'."

Zig even tells us how to get out of bed in the morning. That is, to jump out of bed, slap the hands together, and say out loud "Oh Boy! It's a great day to go out and do whatever it is that I do!" If nothing else, it starts the day on a positive note and usually creates a little amusement in the household! I made a copy of this for my friend Laurie and, to this day, whenever I see him, one of us will say "Oh Boy . . . . etc.!" and it sparks up both of us.

Zig talks about people who tell us what cannot be done—what is "impossible" for one reason or other. He says scientists have proved that it is aerodynamically impossible for a bumble bee to fly but, because it does not read the scientific reports, the bee flies beautifully. I am often told that "this cannot be done" or "that is impossible" and I usually find that it is simply not true. One needs to "have a go" and apply oneself and most of life's obstacles can be overcome.

I still have Zig's tape in my car and I play it every month or so or when I feel that I need a lift. I've applied his principles in lots of ways especially the persistence part because almost everything that has come to me in life has been as a result of persistent effort.

Finally, Zig has a catch-cry which translates to "If I help others, I'll achieve whatever I want." This is important to me. Although I've achieved financial success, the application of these principles in personal affairs has been more rewarding. By sharing my experience, strength, and hope with others I may have helped them and, in the process, I've received great benefits. I've found that, in business and personal life, whatever I give away, I get back tenfold in other areas. Whatever I have is a gift that is not mine to keep. If I share with others, I experience the joy of living with peace of mind and serenity.

Over the years, I've heard many motivational speakers, but I must say that if I had only one cassette to keep for the rest of my life, it would be Zig's.

      —TREVOR HOUSLEY, HOUSLEY COMMUNICATION
      (SYDNEY, AUSTRALIA)

2

How the Motivators
Stay Motivated!

What keeps motivators motivated? This chapter covers some of their sources of inspiration, and it explains how they stay motivated in the lean years.

Sources of Their Inspiration

Who influenced them most? What are their sources of inspiration? Their mentors? Why? You become what you think about. Think about what has inspired these Superstars to find the source of your own Superstar inspiration.

> *I get inspired by things that happen every day. In one week, I had over 15 requests to call people who were sick or who were dying, had a stroke, or adversity of some sort. You call those people and talk to them and you see how well they've reacted to tremendous adversity. I put up the phone and say, "I hope I have as much courage as these people have." Then, you realize that there are not any special people, there are just special ways to react to different situations.*
> —Lou Holtz

> *As the child of an Italian immigrant couple in an English seaside town, I was a natural outsider, and I was drawn to other outsiders and rebels. James Dean was my schoolgirl idol. I also had a strong sense of moral outrage, which was awakened when I found a book about the Holocaust at 10 years of age.*

I have been inspired by a number of thinkers: from the philoso-phy of Rousseau to Ralph Nader and Noam Chomsky in modern times. Walt Whitman is my favorite writer, but I am also inspired by visuals: political posters and photojournalism. And, of course, any challenge to globalization appeals to me.
        —ANITA RODDICK

Surround Yourself with Passionate Supporting People and Teachers

When the student is ready, the teacher appears.
        —CHINESE PROVERB

When I saw Dr. Norman Vincent Peale and Zig Ziglar, I saw for the first time outside of Booker T. Washington High School where I was coached, that there were people who were doing what I loved to do and making a difference in others people's lives, and this was their profession. I couldn't believe that.

At the time I was speaking at juvenile detention centers, prisons, church functions, anywhere that I could possibly speak—for the love of speaking. I went to seminars and workshops and saw Dr. Norman Vincent Peale and Zig Ziglar speaking and earning a liv-ing doing what they love to do. It reminded me of something that I once heard, that man was not born to work for a living but to live their making, and to live their making they would make their liv-ing. That I could live my making was to speak, to touch people, to inspire, to empower people and be able to provide for my family and myself, I just could not believe it. It was a dream come true. I followed them, I read all their books, listened to their tapes. Every opportunity when they would come to within a 700 mile radius, I would fly or drive to hear them, just to be near them. I was taken in by their skills, talent, and the message they provided.
        —LES BROWN

In 1952 I heard inspirational speaker Bob Bale from Phoenix. As I watched him on the platform, it was the first time I had seen a man take an obvious delight in what he was doing. It went beyond just being enthusiastic, which is important, but there was a delight in entertaining people and at the same time giving them ideas and concepts that enriched their lives. Seeing him inspired me to want to do the same thing.

— ZIG ZIGLAR

I was a high school teacher in an inner city school in Chicago. A fellow teacher invited me to his church on Sunday. Having grown up a Presbyterian, I had never heard the impassioned preaching of a Baptist preacher. I was mesmerized by the passion, emotion, and deep commitment to love, justice, and harmony—all the values I espoused. The Reverend Jesse Jackson's oratorical skills moved me deeply, as they did everyone else in the congregation. I remember thinking, I want to touch people deeply and move them in the same way. In those days Jesse would always end his sermon by having the audience repeat: "I am somebody! I may be black, but I am somebody. I may be poor, but I am somebody. I may be uneducated, but I am somebody."

— JACK CANFIELD

R. Buckminster Fuller in my imagination, is the ideal speaker because he was an insider on the universe. He was the ideal all high-minded speakers aspire to.[1]

His words, and the man himself have inspired the person I am today. His mission was to make the earth work for 100 percent of humanity. That rings and resonates with my heart and soul. You see he said, was what Christ, 2000 years ago said; we have "fundamental abundance." From a technological point of view, we can feed, house and raise the standard of all six billion people on the planet, right now, and here's the way we do it.

I was one of the guys that caught his Holy Grail, so to speak. I am not saying I'm executing it right, but I am sure that I'm on the board of directors in three companies because of Bucky, one is a global electrical network, which was Bucky's vision. When problems hit at the turn of the century, Bucky's name will be known

---

[1]See more on Buckminster Fuller in the story of Mark Victor Hansen, page 33.

again. Read his material and you think, "Wow! How can someone think so big?"
          —MARK VICTOR HANSEN

My parents were constantly affirming me in everything that I did. Late at night I'd wake up and hear my mother talking over my bed, saying, "You're going to do great on this test. You can do anything you want."

I never did any drinking at all, or smoking, but I had some friends who did, and we went on a trip one time and came home, and they had a fifth of whiskey. They couldn't take it to their home, because they were in trouble with their parents, so I took that fifth, and put it right in the center of my dresser. My parents never asked a question, never said a thing about it, because they knew I wasn't going to do anything with it. It was symbolic, though, of their affirmation.
          —STEPHEN COVEY

My Grandmother, Mom Cathey, who lived within two weeks of her one hundredth birthday, was my role model.

I remember many Sunday afternoons with other neighborhood children in her home—the lemonade and cookies—I think that's what enticed us—the Bible games, listening to Mom Cathey as she read from this Bible—now one of my most cherished possessions.

She practiced what she preached, and lived her life for others. In a tragic accident, Mom Cathey lost a son at the hands of a drunk driver. The insurance policy on his life built a hospital wing in a far-off church mission in Pakistan. Although Mom Cathey was not at all a wealthy woman, almost anything she could share went to the ministers at home and missions abroad.

I love to find her notes in the margin of her Bible, notes written in the middle of the night when she couldn't sleep. For example, I find by Psalm 139, this notation, "May 22, 1952, 1:00 a.m.— my prayer, 'Search me, O God, and know my heart—try me, and know my thoughts. And see if there be any wicked way in me, and lead me in The Way everlasting.' "

> *I can't remember an unkind word escaping Mom Cathey's lips in all the years in which I knew her or an ungracious deed marring her path. My grandmother was an almost perfect role model.*
> —ELIZABETH DOLE, SECRETARY OF
> TRANSPORTATION, NATIONAL PRAYER BREAKFAST,
> WASHINGTON, D.C., FEBRUARY 5, 1987

> *Tony Robbins told me his favorite quote is by Orison Swett Marden, the first publisher of* SUCCESS *magazine: "Deep within us dwell slumbering powers: Powers that would astonish us, that we never dreamed of possessing. Forces that could revolutionize our life, turn it around and put it into action."*
> *When I asked Tony which speaker inspired him, he told me, "Jim Rohn, my first personal development teacher, who always taught me that if you have enough reasons, you can do anything."*
> —DOTTIE WALTERS

Books

These voices of influences are always heard through the filter of the mind. Sometimes we hear them in person, sometimes through books.

> *It was at the library that I met him, my dear friend of the mind, Ben Franklin. In struggling to begin my tiny advertising business with no college education or car, I read all the business books in the small Baldwin Park Public Library.*
> *One was by the popular sales speaker, Frank Bettger,* How I Raised Myself from Failure to Success through Selling. *All through the book, Frank told me about his personal inspiration, Ben Franklin. I took Frank Bettger back to the library, found Ben Franklin's autobiography and fell in love with Ben's great mind, delightful humor, scientific inquiring ideas, and brilliant strategy.*
> *When you come to visit my office in Glendora, California, you will see Ben's pictures, statues, and hundreds of books by and about him which I keep close to me. I have a big life-size photograph of the famous Jean-Antoine Houdon bust where I can see him now. I often think, how would Ben handle this problem? He always gives*

me sound advice, and then he winks at me and grins! Oh yes, it is true. Ben loves women. (We love him back.)

Someone kindly gave me an audiotape recorded by an actor who read Ben Franklin's autobiography. I only listened to it a little while. You see, it was not his voice.
                                    —Dottie Walters

Early on I was inspired by Napoleon Hill's book Think and Grow Rich. *If you want to increase the quality of your life, add to your "profound knowledge information." You will find in a book virtually any answer you ever wanted, or knowledge of any question for which you seek. Books are the greatest treasure that we have.*
                                    —Tony Robbins

I am more inspired by the books, than by hearing the speakers in person. My coach gave a great pep talk when I was playing. I ran down under the opening kickoff and the guy kicked me in the throat, and I couldn't remember a thing he said. It happens all the time, we get all excited and pumped up, then we get a little bit of difficulty and we forget all about what we learned and go into our old trends.

I believe that the only thing that can change you from where you are now to where you'll be five years from now are the books you read, the people you meet, and the dreams you dream. I think Zig Ziglar and Dr. Schuller have been a tremendous influence on so many people. I have enjoyed their books tremendously.
                                    —Lou Holtz

My father, he was very well-read. Considering the hours he spent on football, he still knew what was going on in the world, and could engage in learned conversation on many current issues. Dad taught Latin, chemistry and physics in high school. He would read himself to sleep with Greek and Latin!

One book he was inspired by was Psycho-Cybernetics. *I had his copy, it was underlined in many places. It is one of the first books that stimulated my consciousness in terms of self-help and motivation.*
                                    —Vince Lombardi, Jr.

How Did They Stay Motivated in the Lean Years?

How did these Superstars stay motivated when they were trying to reach that first rung on the ladder of success?

Love What You Do

> *What kept me going was the love of what I do. Even though I had setbacks, even though I had times when I was sleeping on the floor of my office in Detroit. The love of connecting with people, being able to help them see themselves differently, to inspire them to take on challenges, to reach beyond their comfort zones, because it was my passion, the difficulties simply empowered me. In life you will always be faced with a series of God-ordained opportunities, brilliantly disguised problems and challenges.*
>
> *They say the prosperous times you put in your pocket, the lean times you put in your heart.*
> —LES BROWN

Hang in There—No Quick Fix

> *We have instant coffee, instant tea and instant restaurants. Everybody looks for a quick fix. There isn't any. You build it day by day. You don't panic. You don't overreact. You don't change your principles. If you preach the same thing over a period of time, and it doesn't change, one of two things is going to happen. They are going to believe in you or they are going to leave.*
> —LOU HOLTZ

Have Faith and Discipline

> *It's easy to have faith in yourself and have discipline when you're a winner, when you're number one. What you've got to have is faith and discipline when you're not yet a winner.*
> —VINCE LOMBARDI, SR.

> *It is not hard to stay motivated in pro-football. You have a new game every week. Even though he felt he should have been the head*

coach, he stayed motivated because he had a job to do. Pro-sports are easier than other aspects of life to test how you are doing, they put that score up there that tells you. But, in the off-season, I know dad would ask himself why he wasn't being given his chance. He kept thinking it would happen one day and he kept working at it.
—VINCE LOMBARDI, JR.

Program Your Mind

If you want to succeed big, you've to have outstanding goals, build outstanding relationships, and then you'll get outstanding results. When Jack and I first got started, we did two things that really mattered. Number one, we cut out the New York Times, *and we put our names and* Chicken Soup for the Soul *right at the very top. The other thing we do, is carry around a little 3 by 5 card that says, "I'm so happy." The average person does not know if they are happy or depressed. They don't program their minds to be happy. I had a lady come up to me and say, "Don't you ever get depressed?" I say, "Nope, never." She said, "How depressing."*

I'm so happy that I'm going to sell the amount of books I think we are going to sell. I write that amount down, it's signed by Mark and Jack, I look at it four times a day. We've got 74 titles for Chicken Soup for the Soul® *into the future that we know we are going to do. We've had nine of the top 150 on the best seller list simultaneously.*

Can anyone do this? Absolutely. It just takes imagination to realization.
—MARK VICTOR HANSEN

Do What Is Important—
and Know it!

What kept me motivated was knowing that what I said was important, that I was delivering a message that was needed.

I believe strongly in a spiritual message. In so much of education there was the separation of church and state. But in the name of academic intellectual propriety, they had thrown out the baby with the bath water. Out with spirituality were all of the qualities of love, passion, wisdom and perseverance, service, justice, fairness, and kindness. I felt that was a mistake.

One of my big messages was that you have to bring your spirit to work and share that with kids. You can't separate that from your day-to-day life, or you make decisions that are not really healthy for you. Knowing that my message was important sustained me.
        —JACK CANFIELD

But in times of despair, I remember the words of Mother Teresa. Each day for decades she rose and went to work in the ghettos of India. And when asked how she could do such heartbreaking work day after day, with no end in sight, Mother Teresa said, "God did not call me to be successful, he called me to be faithful."
        —ELIZABETH DOLE

Keep Learning Fundamentals

There are those that think with Xs and Os. They sit around and talk all the time, they draw up plays. But when you are trying to win with mirrors and tricks, and just drawing up fancy plays, you have nothing to fall back on. I don't believe you can outsmart people. It isn't what you do theorywise, it's how well you execute. Consequently, they never really have a foundation to fall back upon. If you teach them to handle the ball well, you can always fall back on that.
        —LOU HOLTZ

Learn and Explore

I am constantly learning and exploring. Growing and experiencing new things in my life is my motivation, not success or money or fame.
        —DR. DEEPAK CHOPRA

What strategies do Superstar motivators use to stay motivated that you can apply in your life?

Just surround yourself with passionate supporting people. Look for the teacher to appear. He or she may be someone who has been trying to help you learn for years. Are you now ready to listen? Also look to the wisdom of the ages, just waiting for you in books!

Everyone has lean years. To stay motivated, love what you do! There will be no quick fix—hang in there. Use faith and discipline, and program your mind to achieve what you want. Do what is important— and know it! Keep learning fundamentals, and learn and explore!

3

What Are Their Strategies for Staying on Top?

Many assume the hard part is acheving the dream. They little realize the hardest part is staying on top once you are there!

> *There are some people who say Jack and I are not courteous anymore because we don't answer all their telephone calls. Our offices often get 100 calls and 500 e-mails a day, many from really important people that we want to talk to. It feels bad. Sometimes people call us with wonderful and sincere requests that would be great for us, but we are in the most bizarre state of overwhelm; we are doing 10 books next year. No one has ever done 10 books in a year! We've got 30 products, we expect all to go to number one.*
>
> *You've got to write out your future diary and your plans in detail, because once you start to hit success levels, it tends to hit all at once. It's like an avalanche. There is no question we are riding its crest right now. Based on what everybody else has done, we should have stopped a year or two ago. But it won't stop until I tell it to stop, because it's all in my imagination. I already had the plan written out, so it has to come out. Most people don't dream big enough and think big enough and strive high enough.*
> —MARK VICTOR HANSEN

How do Superstars stay motivated? This chapter gives you the answers!

- How do they keep their ego under control?
- How do they make time for themselves and their families?
- How do they deal the with criticism?
- How do they deal the with rejection?

How Do They Stay Motivated?

> *Success is like anything worthwhile. It has a price. You have to pay the price to win, and you have to pay the price to get to the point where success is possible. Most important, you must pay the price to stay there.*
> —VINCE LOMBARDI, SR.

Take Nothing for Granted (Have an Attitude of Gratitude)

> *I heard Christopher Reeve speak in Auburn Hills, Michigan, in the fall of 1997. As he sat in his wheelchair in front of thousands of awe-struck people, he told the story of how he discovered a purpose to life after his tragic accident.*
>
> *After that day, I was deeply inspired to live with an "attitude of gratitude." Take nothing for granted, and know that I have the ability to rise above any experience I see as negative and to turn it around and use it as a positive springboard for greater things yet to come!*
> —LORI HISSON, PRESIDENT, INSPIRING SPEAKERS
> SPEAKERS BUREAU

Look to Those Higher on the Ladder

> *Oy vey. I wish I could get comfortable and also be a success! I still have inspirational dissatisfaction. The new refined me hasn't shown up yet. I know all the holes I have in me. I am inspired by the people who are way far beyond me, the Richard Branson and*

Ted Turner types that are doing really good thinking for the environment. You know, giving a billion dollars is massively charitable! They are ready to fight the metaphorical windmills. Everyone says you can't win the fight, then they go off and win it.
    —MARK VICTOR HANSEN

Look for Ways to Improve

If you are successful in my business, you become hungrier and hungrier. It is the most amazing thing. For some people, they think the great reward in business will be getting to the point where they won't need to do what they did to get them success!

For me it is doing more of it, and for more people. I am constantly looking for a new and better ways to help more people, better.
    —BRIAN TRACY

Raise the Bar

You have to stay hungry when you are on top. What keeps you staying hungry is to keep on raising the bar for yourself. Keep challenging yourself.

To continue to grow, I still listen to tapes, I still read three to four books a week, just as I did in the beginning.

Oliver Wendell Holmes gave me the idea that "once a man or woman's mind is expanded with an idea or concept, it will never be satisfied to go back where it was."[1] So I am continuously involved in the process of pushing myself to the next level.

Find a way to become fascinated with this thing we call "life." Stretch, and challenge ourselves, do what we ask people to do. Then we are able to make a greater impact, and to create new possibilities for ourselves and the people we are exposed to.
    —LES BROWN

[1]Oliver Wendell Holmes (1809–1894), U.S. physician, poet, and essayist.

Become Addicted to Success

One of the great ideas I use comes from William Glaser. It is the idea of "Positive addiction." Lloyd Conant, the founder of Nightingale Conant Corporation, explained this principle to me many years ago and I never forgot it.

What they both discovered was that you can become positively addicted to activities such as jogging, learning, writing, speaking, surgery or virtually any other field to which you are ideally suited.

When you are doing something that you really enjoy and you are doing it well you actually experience a rush of endorphins in your brain. These endorphins generate an enhanced feeling of well-being and happiness. Your memory of this elevated state will motivate you internally to repeat same actions that gave you the good feeling in the first place. Over time, you can become addicted to positive healthful, constructive, uplifting, and helpful activities that continually motivate you to do them more and more often, and better and better.

  —BRIAN TRACY

How Do They Keep Their Egos under Control?

Arrogance is God's gift to shallow people.
  —EARL NIGHTINGALE

Many people wanted me to ask these Superstars this question about humility. In working with people of remarkable renown for most of my life, I've discovered a secret. The higher up the ladder they are, the less "ego" they flaunt, and the more humble they become.

Churchill was once asked, "Doesn't it thrill you to know that every time you make a speech the hall is packed to overflowing?"

"It's quite flattering," replied Sir Winston. "But whenever I feel that way I always remember that if, instead of making a political speech, I was being hanged, the crowd would be twice as big."

True Greatness Lies in Humility

I asked Vince Lombardi, Jr., if anything made his father humble? He laughed.

In the seminary, until he was a senior in high school, the Jesuit's whole approach was, "true greatness lies in humility." I think he knew his faults, he knew the ideal, and knew he fell short many times. He would lose his temper, he'd blast somebody, he'd be rude, he'd run roughshod over somebody. Then somebody would call him on it, and he'd feel terrible. He would always apologize, he never had any trouble saying he was sorry, and meaning it. He had many opportunities to realize he was less than the ideal he thought he should be. It's paradoxical that the very things that make people great are the very things that lead to their downfall.

Mom kept him humble, he used to say of her, "When I get too big she brings me down, when I get too low she builds me up."
—VINCE LOMBARDI, JR.

My talent is very limited, physically, mentally, every other which way. I didn't want the book to be titled Winning Every Day: Game Plan for Success. *I wanted the book to have a picture of me on the book and call it "You're Better Than This." I want people to look at me and say, "Doggone it! I've got every bit as much talent and ability as that sucker has! If he can do that, I know I can do a heck of a lot better!" That's what I'd like people to draw when I get done speaking.*
—LOU HOLTZ

The more I study, the more I read, and the more I learn, the less certain I am of what I know. I stunned an audience once by telling them, "The only thing I know for certain is that I don't know anything for certain."
—EARL NIGHTINGALE

A Pencil in the Hand of God

> *I don't feel that I have to work at staying humble. The whole process of our success humbles me every day. We have accomplished so much in such a short time that I don't believe we could have possibly have done it without divine guidance and divine intervention.*
> **—JACK CANFIELD**

> *Of myself I can do nothing, I must align myself with this power that's greater than I am to be able to walk into a group of strangers and create a special kind of experience. I love that saying that says, "EGO means 'edging God out.' " To feel part of that process is a humbling experience of itself. These gifts don't come from us, they come from God. As soon as you forget that, you lose the gift.*
> **—LES BROWN**

> *I recognize that any gift I have comes from God. It comes from far beyond me. I don't look upon all the blessings that have come my way as some great personal accomplishment, I believe "from them much is given, much is expected." God gives you gifts in order for you to do something with those gifts that help other people. So I look upon my gifts, such as they are, as things that were given for me to make a contribution to others.*
> **—BRIAN TRACY**

> *I pray, I am a vehicle. I allow God to flow through me to them. Sometimes I'll listen to myself talking and I'll think, "Golly, I don't know any of this stuff!" I mean just that, I don't know the knowledge. I get goose bumps just telling you this. It happened once when I spoke at a church in San Jose. They had three recorders taping me. I wanted that tape so bad. I said stuff that I have never said before, it was all revelation, it was not things that I knew. All the tapes were blank. I know it sounds like, "Come on, Mark, get real." It reminded me of what happened in the movie, "Oh, God!" when God could not be taped. But they were all blank. It has happened a couple of times to me.*
> **—MARK VICTOR HANSEN**

Reality gives me every reason to be humble. At age 45, after a life-time of consistently hard work, a positive attitude, honesty, and enthusiasm, I was broke, in debt, my career was going nowhere, and I was puzzled.

Then I became a Christian. Everything in my career that has been successful occurred after that date, so I have every reason to be humble and profoundly grateful for what God has done in my life.
—ZIG ZIGLAR

How Do They Make Time for Themselves and Their Families?

Being a professional speaker is terrible on your family. You are rarely at home. It takes a serious commitment to keep your time together.

How do you really know if you are spending enough time with them? Try asking them.

If somebody wants great advice, listen to your spouse. Nobody knows you any better, loves you any more, wants to see you succeed more, and who will be more honest.
—LOU HOLTZ

First Seek the Kingdom Inside

You must first seek the kingdom inside before looking outside your-self for love. Indeed only through inner growth will you experience the spiritual rewards of a deep relationship with your family.

You can begin this growth process by devoting time and energy to self-love. Refuse to follow the impulses of anger and fear, and trust that the universe is on your side. Believe that you are enough in and of yourself. Put your attention on positive energies in every situation. And honor your own needs without seeking the approval of others. When you put these concerns foremost in your heart and mind, you will learn self-love and stop expecting love to be con-stantly directed at you.

Given our society, it is likely that your ego is demanding that your life turn out according to certain expectations. You probably feel pressure to be a good provider. These outside pressures can create a chasm between the you and your family, and make it difficult for you to fully participate in your relationship.

And the first thing you need to do to is very practical and simple: Find time for your family. What you do with your time reveals a lot about your priorities. You say you want a deeper relationship? But you are unwilling to take away time from other activities to spend it with your family. (These "other activities" probably revolve around fulfilling ego demands and attaining material success.)

You have a choice. You can decide that your ego demands are more important and forget about deepening the relationships with your family, or you can agree that the relationship is more important.

If you choose the latter, you need to reprioritize your time. Look at all the things you do and eliminate activities you can do without. Arrange to have quality time on weekends, evenings, and even take time together away from work on weekdays. Meet for lunch one day a week no matter what your schedule is like. Take a walk after dinner. Watch the sunset. Do something that brings you together.

—DR. DEEPAK CHOPRA

Recommit to Better and Better

I believe in affirmation and visualization, so I wrote my own marriage vows. Most people get married for better or for worse. I wrote down that I got married for more and more love, for better and better, for healthier and healthier, for happier and happier, for 93 years with options for renewal!

I teach that if you want to stay married to your love, you must get remarried every year. Every 365 days there are a lot of pulsations in a marriage. Patty and I chose early on to get remarried every year. We read our marital vows and recommit each year.

I have two wonderful daughters that live the principles that I teach. They answer our telephone: "Happy Home of the Hansens!"

—MARK VICTOR HANSEN

Incorporate My Family as Merchants of Hope

We find fun things to share with each other along the way. I incorporate my family in the things that I do. I have coached my children on seeing themselves as merchants of hope, that's how I see myself as a speaker. We make it fun, and play together in my work. Most of my children are now using speaking skills in their careers and education. One is working on becoming an attorney, another works with disadvantaged teens, my youngest wants to be a speaker himself.

—LES BROWN

Include Your Family in Your Business

Many Superstars manage to make time for their families by including them in the business. Les Brown takes his son with him to speeches and says the boy is a better natural speaker than he is! From the time I was tiny, mom brought me along to hear her speak and into the advertising company's office to watch the team work, and so I could "help." When she had started her advertising business, 10 years before I was born, she would walk into town to talk to her clients, pushing my older brother and sister along in an old stroller; later they went in the back seat of the old Model A Ford!

Covey also finds time for his family by including them in his business. His son, Stephen M.R., was president of the former Covey Leadership Center and is now president of Franklin Covey's Training and Education business. Stephen M.R. says it wasn't at all strange growing up in a family with a mission statement on the wall.

From my earliest years I remember we would have family councils, where we would discuss our jobs, responsibilities, integrity, courage, fairness, and sportsmanship. I'm sure that many families implicitly do that; this was a more explicit way of doing it.

—STEPHEN M.R. COVEY

In 1998, *The Seven Habits for Highly Effective Teens,* written by Sean Covey, son of company co-chairman Stephen Covey, was released. The new book that teens find they easily relate with is a compilation of stories from actual teenagers and was designed to outline methods for success at home, school, and in the workplace. Sean serves as vice president of Franklin Covey's chain of more than 25 retail stores.

David, Stephen's third son, heads up Franklin Covey's business in Australia and parts of Asia.

Stephen Covey, Sr.'s brother, Dr. John M.R. Covey, who did the majority of the research for *The Seven Habits of Highly Effective Families*, is the company spokesman for the family material, and is director of home and family for the company.

> *People who learn to prioritize their families become more productive at work. When employees' lives are in balance, productivity goes up, creativity goes up, absenteeism goes down.*
>
> *The answer is to look at your life as a whole, determine your multiple priorities such as work, family, and personal life, and then schedule activities you must do to serve each of those. You don't have to quit your job—you just have to know when to end it each day. Work your guts off while at work, then when you're home, be at home.*
> —JOHN COVEY

> *I urge families to draft "mission statements" that say: "We are not just about ourselves. We're about making a difference." For instance, ask your kids to join you in cleaning an elderly neighbor's yard. And don't praise them for it. You don't want them doing it just for your praise. Instead, say, "Look how happy she is!" Focus on the person you're helping. If enough people got involved, we could literally solve our social problems.*
> —STEPHEN COVEY

Put Your Focus Where You Get the Greatest Rewards

> *In the early days of the Reagan Administration, I served as Assistant to the President for Public Liaison. I was charged with rallying support for the President's agenda, and one evening, my staff and I were meeting to divide up the names of senators who*

had not yet taken a public stand on one of the President's legislative initiatives.

The session came to an abrupt end when I said I was going home to cook a candlelight dinner. "That's great, Elizabeth," said my deputy. "But it's only 6 p.m.! Isn't this a bit early for you to be going home? Don't you want to finish targeting those undecided Senators?"

"You don't seem to understand," I said. "Tonight, I'm targeting Bob Dole." And for those of you wondering, I did get Bob's vote. And even though the candlelight dinner was successful, I never tried it out on any other Senator!
    —ELIZABETH DOLE

However, when it comes to getting maintenance things done, I'll tell you my strategy. If you're going to have an extraordinary quality of life, you must put your focus where you get the greatest rewards. If you don't deal with the maintenance aspects of your life, though, they come back to bite you.

My solution is extremely simple. I work incredibly hard to ensure that anything I'm not passionate about doing—anything that doesn't make a difference in the quality of my family, or my friends, or my own life—I do my best to leverage, to hire someone else to do these things.

Unless you get leverage from most of the maintenance things in your life, you'll never achieve the extraordinary goals you're after.
    —TONY ROBBINS

I've only got finite time, and that translates into energy. Since I became a grandmother, I find it easier to make time for myself and my family. I am closer to my own mother. And being Italian, I like nothing better than to bring everyone together round the table. The ritual of food is one of my joys!
    —ANITA RODDICK

Limit My Speaking Engagements

I am constantly striving to create a better balance for my family. What I have done is limit my speaking engagements to three time a

month, decline most weekend engagements, schedule vacations at least four times a year, and long weekends most often. I put my eight-year-old to bed almost every night I am at home. I am also a volunteer for his classroom Cub Scout Troop.
    —JACK CANFIELD

Pick My Kids' Teachers

I pick my kids' teachers. I sit in five to six classes every year to make sure my kids have the best teachers. Yesterday I went and sat in on the first day of the fifth grade. We have the most effervescent teacher there is, and this is in public schools. Nobody will know that this is a woman whose home phone I will have, who will have dinner at our home, and become a friend.
    —MARK VICTOR HANSEN

How Do They Deal with Criticism?

The way *not* to deal with criticism is through reactive anger and revenge.

"Before you embark on a journey of revenge dig two graves."
    —CONFUCIUS

Know Your Critics

I take criticism seriously, but at the same time I feel that, because I am a woman, it is often style rather than content that is being criticized. I am always curious about my critics. What is their agenda? Do I respect their opinions?
    —ANITA RODDICK

The only people who aren't going to be criticized are those who do absolutely nothing.
    I welcome all the suggestions in the world from people who have been involved in doing something . . . but somebody who has never done anything except observe and criticize, I don't weigh that at all.

*But the higher up you go and the more things you try to accom-
plish, the more people try to find fault. There are so many things in
life that are not fair. You work all your life to do something and
people try to tear you down. You can't control it or do anything
about it.*

*When you look at the options of dealing with criticism, there's
really only one option—to pray to God that you have the courage
and the strength that you won't become bitter, and move on with
your life."*
—Lou Holtz

How Do They Deal with Rejection?

These great Superstars got that way because they are also great sales and
marketing people. No one knows rejection better than salespeople!

*Sometimes, even after I have done all I could to make a situation
right, if someone has perceived a fault in me, they are just not
going to be happy. There are some people that have angst and can't
"get it" from you. The fact is, everyone didn't like Christ. You don't
hang a guy on a cross if the crowd is all in agreement.*

*A speaker is supposed to not only be there to cheer them on,
which I hopefully do, but I am also there to be an "evoke-a-tor." I
am there to stab your sprit alive and get you to think some new
thoughts. I hit the people and get them into orbit. Some of those
thoughts you are not going to like.*

*The bigger the audiences, the more chance we have to set off
people for good, but also those few for bad, because they are stuck
in their own karma. As Bill Gove said, "You are responsible to
your audience, not for your audience."*
—Mark Victor Hansen

They Say "No," You Say "Next!"

*Adversity made me strong. Cavett Robert, my motivational inspi-
rational teacher, taught me that "life is a grindstone. It either*

grinds you down, or polishes you up. It's up to you, and you alone. You want to get polished up. Get radiant and shiny."

I teach the next *principle in all my seminars:* When they say "no," just say "next!" *All of us are going to get rejected. We got rejected by 33 publishers who said, "Get out of here! Nobody buys short stories! Besides, it's too much of a nicey, nicey title." And then our agent fired us. He said, "You guys aren't going to make it." Boy, was that a mistake.*

All of us get rejected. My brother told me that somehow when anyone rejected me, what I did was to reject the rejections. I think everyone of us has got to suck it in, tough it out, and reject the rejection. When they say "no," just say "next!"
—MARK VICTOR HANSEN

Ask for What You Want

I don't believe there is anything such as rejection, I think it's a myth. If you asked me to grant you an interview and I said, "no," well, you didn't have me before you asked, and you don't have me after. Your life didn't get worse, it stayed the same. When people get rejected, their life doesn't get worse, it stays the way it was. So I always tell people, if it's not going to get worse, and it has the possibility of getting better, by all means—ask! Mark[2] and I have had to be incredible askers just to get 2000 people to submit and sign off on stories for our books.
—JACK CANFIELD

To summarize, here are the Superstar strategies you can use to stay on top.

To stay motivated, take nothing for granted and develop an attitude of gratitude. Just look to those higher on the ladder to help you set your next goal. Don't be statisfied with where you are now, look for ways to improve, raise the bar, and become addicted to success!

[2]Mark Victor Hansen.

Remember true greatness lies in humility. They greater you become, the more humbling it is to be an instrument in the hand of God, or your Higher Power.

Your success will be very shallow indeed if you don't have your family along with you. Recommit to be better and better and with your family. Incorporate them as merchants of hope in your business. But always, put your focus where you get the greatest rewards, in that emotional bank account: your family.

If you take the platform, you will face criticism and rejection. Remember, most often, you are not the target. Move on. And if they say "no," you say "next!" Always *ask* that next person for just what you want. In the hard times, seek advice and strategies to find that next resource from your own personal dream team.

4

What Are Their Strategies for Achieving Dreams?

There are many ways to achieve your dreams. Here are strategies in the words of the Superstars, and of those who heard the message of a Superstar and achieved their own dreams. These strategies include:

Dreams Are Hard and Worth It

During my early pursuit to be a professional speaker I bought a bunch of products to sell and basically spent my rent money. I thought that just because I was a good speaker people would flock to purchase all that I had. Well, they didn't. I was prepared to pack it in and cut my losses.

The following week I went to see Les Brown speak. He told a story about how he had done the same thing. He spoke about his six concepts. He said, when pursuing your dream, remember this: (1) It's possible (2) It's necessary (3) It's you (4) It's hard (5) It's worth it (6) It's done. I ran home that night and got right to work and never looked back.

Thank you, Les.

— Tony "Books" Avilez, e-book store sales
and speaker

When I heard Christopher Reeve speak, I was sitting in the front row and took his picture. I still keep that picture on my computer to remind me.

He said his accident was like tripping on a shoelace. He'd done that jump hundreds of times. Things happen, just like that, and we must accept the unacceptable. He spoke about how he is committed to walking by the time he is 50 years old (he was 45 then). He said he is working harder now on walking than when he had to get into great physical condition for Superman.

After I went home, those words motivated me: If he can make an incredible commitment and work so hard to walk, what's stopping me?!! That and the photo of him on my computer keep reminding me to be grateful for what I have and to keep on keepin' on!!!
—ROBERT GEDALIAH, AUTHOR, SPEAKER, AND
COMMUNICATIONS COACH

Take Pride in Making Sacrifices

If you're going to be successful you've got to make sacrifices. The losing situations are the ones where everybody sits around and complains about it.

The winning situation, whether it be marriage, children, you are going to make sacrifices. Take pride in the fact you are going to have to make sacrifices to be successful.
—LOU HOLTZ

One of the greatest dishonesties we can indulge in is the idea that there is some kind of shortcut to meaningful accomplishment. Everything good and worthwhile in life takes tremendous time, energy, effort, and commitment. Accepting this as a reality is one of the most important truths that a person can embrace.
—BRIAN TRACY

Go for It!

When I heard Les Brown speak, he told the story of buying his mother a house and was told by the seller that there were no liens against the property. A few months later, after purchasing the house, Les and his mother found out that the seller had lied. They lost the house and learned a valuable lesson in life.

Les went on to explain that these occurrences are all part of the process of living out your dreams. That when you set out to achieve what you want, you will be met by the messenger of misery. He explains that when life gets you down, fall on your back because if you can see up, you can get up. Most importantly though, "Don't let nobody turn you around. Go after your dreams as if your life depends on it, because it does."

That story helped me realize that to be a fully alive human I need to cherish and nurture my deepest inner desires, no matter how difficult the path may be.

Today, after two years of dealing with my own messengers of misery, I'm living out that dream of being a public speaker and living in my dream location in the mountains. I now inspire others to do the same.

> —Dr. Allen Hallada, veterinarian, speaker,
> singer

Write Down Your Goals

After the 1967 season, our entire staff was fired at South Carolina where I was an assistant. My wife bought me a book entitled The Magic of Thinking Big *by David Schwartz. So I sat down and made a list of all the things I still wanted to accomplish in life; there were 107 of them. I broke it down into five categories, things I wanted to do as husband and a father. Things like having all our children graduate from college. Things I wanted to do spiritually, financially, professionally, and things I wanted to do for excitement. Some of them are personal things— like ones pertaining to being a father or those of a financial nature. But my life changed after I made that list. I think I've accomplished 95 of them.*

Just decide what you want to do and then ask the question "What's important now? Now what do I have to do to accomplish

such and such?" And that will tell you the action you have to take. It's not a wish list, it's a set of things I wanted to accomplish, and it really hasn't changed that much.
  —LOU HOLTZ

When I heard Dr. Stephen Covey speak, he told the story of The Seven Habits of Highly Effective People. *That story inspired me to take charge of my career and my life, Dr. Covey showed me that right action follows right thinking and right thinking is based on unchanging principles.*

By applying the first of the seven habits—"Be Proactive"—I changed from reacting to life to setting my own goals and proactively setting my own course of action to achieve them. Now I have the seven habits posted next to my desk where I can refer to them regularly and use a weekly planner to assist in keeping myself on track.
  —LINDA DONAHOE, SPEAKER AND TRAINER

Begin with the End in Mind

Begin with the end in mind. Picture your own funeral, and write what you would want a relative, a friend, a colleague, and someone from another group to say about you. This becomes your definition of success, where you want to be in life, so you can measure each activity by whether it helps. Otherwise, you may work hard at climbing the ladder of success, only to discover that it's leaning against the wrong wall.
  —STEPHEN COVEY

Dream Greater Dreams

The more you lose yourself in something bigger than yourself, the more energy you will have.
  —NORMAN VINCENT PEALE

I defy you to find anything of greatness that ever happened in this world because somebody didn't have a dream. Martin Luther King stood up and said, "I have a dream." Changed the world. What if he were to have stood up and instead said, "I have a strategic plan!"
　—Lou Holtz

I tell everyone I'm going to sell millions of books, have all these products, feed the world. They used be skeptical and say, "Yeah, it's just a 'Mark number.'" But every number I claimed to, where I would take Chicken Soup, *I have made manifest. No one starts off in the world of books and sells one and a half million books in only a year and half, but that is what Jack and I had as a goal. We did it. Now we have sold 40 million books. That was a "Mark number." I predicted it. I am predicting now that we will hit a billion by 2020.*
　—Mark Victor Hansen

All persons have within themselves inexhaustible reserves of potential they have never even come close to realizing; far more intelligence than they have ever used; and more creativity than they ever imagined. The greatest achievements of your life lie ahead of you, the happiest moments of your life are yet to come, the greatest successes you will ever attain are still waiting for you on the road ahead.

Experience joy, which only comes when you first decide what it is that you really love to do and secondly, you throw your whole heart into doing it really, really well. In this way, you will overcome all limits, smash all records, and break through your own success barriers. Think big!
　—Brian Tracy

Develop a larger vision of yourself. You have abilities, talents, and strengths you haven't even begun to reach for—and if you don't, you'll live to regret it. We have always had leaders who say, "I will do this for you." What we have not done is turn people on to themselves, turn people on to the unlimited power they have within themselves.
　—Les Brown

A few years ago, I watched Christopher Reeve on TV as he spoke about spinal cord research, comparing it to our space program and moon landings. He said, "So many of our dreams at first seem impossible, then they seem improbable and finally, when we summon the will, they soon become inevitable."

This has since become my personal and business motto, rallying cry and inspiration. This quote, and this man, continually motivate and inspire me to follow my dreams, believe in my visions, and keep on trying even when things seem shaky and uncertain. If Christopher Reeve can accept himself as he is, and live his life to the fullest of which he is capable, and "still be" himself, then so can I. If Dana and Chris Reeve can still love and cherish and care for and believe in each other, then I can keep on loving and believing in myself, my husband, and our ability to solve our problems and thrive together, no matter how formidable the challenge. If Christopher Reeve believes it is inevitable that he will walk again, then I can certainly hold fast to my vision.

Someday, when he's back on his feet, and I'm ultra successful in achieving my dreams, I'll meet him and his incredible wife Dana, and tell them in person how much I cherish their courage, hope and spirit.

—NANCY GERBER, COACH, TRAINER, SPEAKER,
WRITER, COMMUNICATIONS AND PERSONAL
IMPROVEMENT EXPERT

Learn from the Experts

One of the most important success principles I ever discovered was contained in the four words, "Learn from the experts."

Each person should invest as much time and energy as is necessary to find out how other people have succeeded before them. If you want to be a successful professional speaker, you cannot only become competent, but you can become continuously better, by learning how to speak, by practicing, and by continually studying the craft of speaking.

*If you want to be financially successful and financially indepen-
dent, you must study the rules, laws, and principles of money and
financial accumulation. It is absolutely amazing how many people
worry about money much of the time, yet are extraordinarily resis-
tant to ever studying or learning how money can be acquired and
accumulated in large amounts.*
—BRIAN TRACY

Attitude Is a Choice

*Attitude is critical. Your attitude is going to determine how well
you do something. It's a choice you make every single day.*

*I go to the Jimmy V. Golf Tournament, 40,000 people, I'm sign-
ing autographs, people pulling and tuggin' you, and you know
what? We treat strangers sometimes nicer, more patient, more
understanding than we do the people we live with, love with, or
work with. We think that because we are with them every day it
gives us a prerogative to let our anger, frustrations, or feelings be
vented on them. It's really a shame. Attitude is a choice you make.*
—LOU HOLTZ

In Brian Tracy's Psychology of Selling *program, he told the story
of two salespeople meeting back at the office after a day of sales
calls. The one says, "I had a lot of good sales interviews today." The
other replies, "Yeah, I didn't sell anything either."*

*When I first heard this brief story, I realized that I was also
having "a lot of good sales interviews" without a lot of sales. It
inspired me to take a more proactive, "always be closing" approach
in my selling efforts. Through this shift in attitude, I have been
able to double my sales figures within about one year.*
—HEIDI THORNE, PRESIDENT, TECHNICAL SEMINARS

Fake It 'Till You Make It!

*Act the way you want to be and soon you'll be the way you act. Set
a goal and believe that goal is possible. The key is to work on developing yourself—to develop a personal vision.*

Early in my career, my dream was to be a disc jockey. So I began listening to the radio religiously, practicing techniques, and mimicking announcers. Soon I got a job as a janitor in a radio station in Columbus, Ohio, and worked my way up to become a deejay and eventually a broadcast manager and commentator.

You've got to start thinking of yourself in the future and see yourself there.

—LES BROWN

You Become What You Think About

About six years ago I listened to Earl Nightingale's audiocassette program, The Strangest Secret. *He repeatedly says that "you are and you become what you think about." I wanted to be such a good presenter that I would get a standing ovation.*

Three weeks later I gave my first presentation. Earl Nightingale's magical words, "You are and you become what you think about," were just the medicine I needed. I received a standing ovation and since then many more.

I use Earl's words daily to reaffirm my goals of being a successful businessperson, father, husband, brother, son, friend, and citizen. Through the years I've been interviewed by countless magazines and reporters and they always ask what the secret to my success is and I tell them, "You are and you become what you think about!" Six years ago I never would have thought I could parlay a landscaping company into a $2 million a year operation and travel the country sharing my secrets of success to thousands of people who have paid to hear my story. Today I believe I can do a lot more than this.

—MARTY GRUNDER, FOUNDER AND PRESIDENT OF GRUNDER LANDSCAPING COMPANY

The first time I heard The Strangest Secret *audio by Earl Nightingale, I remember feeling a sense of real understanding about what it takes to be a successful person. Learning that my*

thoughts are what really control my life was a breakthrough revelation. That message motivated me to "take charge" of my life and accomplishments. It inspired me to set lofty goals and test my abilities beyond what I previously thought I could.
—BILLY ARCEMENT, AUTHOR AND SPEAKER

When I first heard Earl Nightingale talk about "the strangest secret," on an old issue of Insight Audio Magazine, *he said, "We become what we think about." This simple message has not stopped inspiring me since that day when I first heard Earl's distinct voice utter those words.*

This has been particularly helpful because when I catch myself "obsessing" over a negative outcome or practically painful lesson, I remember those words. I start thinking of something else! I ask, "What opportunity is presented here?" or "What can I use from this to help others?" Doing this has helped me more effectively manage my emotional states over the long run.
—GEORGE P. KANSAS, SUCCESS COACH, ATTORNEY, AND FATHER

For Every Action There Is an Opposite and Equal Reaction

Right after the war was over, we needed money. I started a little advertising business. I had an old portable battery-run radio I took with me in the very old car we had so that I would not miss listening to Earl Nightingale. His voice, so full of hope and positive ideas, seemed like a life preserver thrown to me as I struggled to stay afloat in a very choppy sea of difficulties.

One dark rainy day, the four ad customers whose ads I had counted on to make the house and car payment all turned me down. "Why?" I asked.

All four told me the same story. "Since the president of the Chamber of Commerce, Mr. Ahlman of the Rexall drugstore, does not buy your shoppers' column ads, the column must not be any good." I was stunned.

Then I remembered Earl Nightingale's words from the radio about the law of physics. "For every action there is an opposite and equal reaction."

If we need to change the reaction, we must go back to the causative action. Mr. Ahlman was always out, or too busy to speak to me. I decided to go immediately and try once more to talk to him. I parked my old car out in front, walked in, and I found him at the back of the small drugstore, filling prescriptions. My heart soared.

"I screwed my courage to the sticking place," as Will Shakespeare advised me, smiled confidently, and held up my shoppers' column in the Baldwin Park Bulletin. I told Mr. Ahlman how much the business people in the community thought of his opinion. I asked him to please look at my work and give me something to tell them when they asked me what he thought of it.

If you have ever been hit hard in the stomach and had all of the air knocked out of you until you could barely stand up, you can imagine how I felt as Mr. Ahlman slowly turned his head from side to side in an emphatic, silent, "No."

I staggered toward the front of the drugstore, to a beautiful old oak soda fountain. I sat down on the nearest stool, thinking I couldn't make it out to the car.

I pulled the last dime out of my purse and ordered a cherry Coke. The tears were very close to the surface as I tried to sip it.

A lady with a very kind face sat next to me. She looked at me and asked, "What's wrong, honey?" I poured out my story about the four businesses who had turned me down that afternoon.

"If Mr. Ahlman would only look at my work!" I choked. "I'm going to lose our home. I don't know where to turn." I bit down hard on my lip, determined to hold back the tears of despair.

"Let me look at that newspaper column!" she said and took it right out of my hand. I wondered why she wanted to read it.

I remember that my Coke was down to the bottom of the glass and the straw gurgled, when she suddenly spun the stool around and jumped down to the floor.

"Reuben Ahlman, you come right out here!" she yelled.

As he came running to the soda fountain, she said to him, "Honey, you buy an ad from this girl." Then she turned back to me and said,

"Give me the names of those four merchants. I'll go and phone them and you can go back and get their ads today." It was Mrs. *Ahlman!*
I had been talking to the wrong person.
Mr. Ahlman was such a sweet man, he bought from everybody. He promised his wife that he would let her handle all of the advertising. Earl Nightingale was right. My action of insisting that I must sell Mr. Ahlman, without finding out how they ran their business, resulted in his negative reaction—"No."
As soon as I understood where my action should have been, my newspaper column filled up with ads. We became best friends with Mr. and Mrs. Ahlman. They arranged for the Chamber of Commerce to honor me with a "Dottie Walters' Banquet" a few years later.
My husband, Bob, bought the soda fountain when Mr. Ahlman took it out of his drugstore. Bob and our son Mike installed it here in my office. We serve visitors cherry Cokes and lots of love.

—DOTTIE WALTERS

When I heard Dottie Walters speak at her California home, she told the story of the old soda fountain that is now in her downstairs office. I attended that seminar during a difficult time in my life, but that story inspired me to take a different path, and not to give up. Listening to her experience, with the actual soda fountain right there, made it much more impacting. I can still see it today, when I think back on that period. I had finished my first book manuscript, but was thinking of not sending it off to the publisher. Frank, a close friend, who had read Dottie's story in Chicken Soup for the Soul, *asked, "Didn't you just meet and attend a seminar with this lady? Didn't you listen to her?"*
I printed out my manuscript and sent it off. A month later my editor told me he was sending a contract. They pulled a book, and my book was moved up in production; seven months after signing the contract my book was for sale on the shelves. That was a learning, and turning point in my life. Things have been going uphill since. Dottie is right, we can all get through temporary setbacks. Just remember to never give up.

—ALAIN BURRESE, AUTHOR, SPEAKER, TRAINER

Focus

When I talk to the team, I try to get them to focus on their sense of purpose, "Understand what you are trying to do. You are trying to graduate and trying to win." Period. Every decision has been based on that.

For people in business their decision has to be based on how can we satisfy the customer first, it's not how can we run the business.

That is why universities run into a problem because they don't understand why they have a university. We have a faculty for one reason, because we have students. We have coaches for one reason, because we have players. We don't have students because we have a faculty, let's understand why the faculty is here.
        —LOU HOLTZ

Ask, Ask, Ask!

When I heard Jack Canfield say to "ask, ask, ask." If you ask and are told no, things didn't get worse, nothing changed. You had nothing to lose. You didn't have it in the first place. But if you ask you might get a yes.

Immediately, I came home and tried it out with my administrator and got a big "Yes." Things in this case got much better. Now I ask with no hesitation.
        —JUDIE SINCLAIR, AUTHOR AND SPEAKER,
        PRESIDENT OF POSITIVE IMPACT

I purchased a set of Jack Canfield's audiotapes to listen to as I made my weekly eight-hour trek to Michigan State University to get my doctorate. I remember the experience so clearly. It was between 10 p.m. and midnight, when I had the highway virtually to myself as I drove home from class. I turned the tape off and thought for the balance of the two hours.

The statement was so simple . . . so basic, and it helped form the "me" that was evolving. He said, "If you want something . . . ask for it." I would typically get upset with my husband or my boss and preface the complaining statement with,

"Didn't you know _____." That blank could be filled in with many examples. For instance, "Didn't you know that I need to receive a remembrance on Valentine's Day? Didn't you know that I wanted to receive that job assignment?" The reality is that, no they didn't, because I never told them what was important to me or what I wanted from them.

I wrote that sentence on a piece of paper and taped it to the dashboard of my car. Slowly, I would gain the courage to ask for the things I wanted and, amazingly, I got most of what I asked for—promotions . . . remembrances that were meaningful . . . help with the housework.

Eventually, I became the educational leader of a school. The first day of the school year, I had cards printed and gave one to each of the staff persons with this printed on it:

"If you want something . . . ASK FOR IT!"

I told them the story of this quote and explained that over the years my skill in mind reading had not improved, so they would have to tell me what they needed from me for their personal and professional growth. I alerted them that they may not get everything they ask for, but they could guarantee they wouldn't get if they never let me know what it was. It was wonderful to see them come to my office holding their card as though it gave them permission to ask for things that would allow them to grow and become the professionals they wanted to be.

That one sentence has made such an impact on how I conduct my life. No longer do I have the self-defeating behavior of hurt feelings because someone didn't meet my needs. Now, if I want something, I have the courage to ask for it . . . I don't always get it, but at least it was considered.

        —DIANE HODGES, PH.D., AUTHOR AND SPEAKER,
        THRESHOLD GROUP

Smile to Get Through Anger

If I had my career to live over I would dream bigger and I would never lower my standards. I would be as demanding as I'd ever been, but I would do this: the madder I was, the more I would smile. The stronger my content of language, the more I would smile.

I used to be so intense. Everybody'd think I was mad, including my children. Now I would smile and say (with a gleeful tone), "If you do that one more time, I am going to grab you by the throat and I'm going to make you the most miserable guy you've ever been! You won't believe how miserable I am going to make you! Do you understand?"

And they'll walk away thinking, "Ah that coach, he is really a great guy!" And especially with my children the more intent I was about getting a message across, the more relaxed my facial expression would be.

    —Lou Holtz

Problems? No! Just Opportunities

When Christopher Reeve's body shut down and was forced to be still, his mind began compensating for the loss and getting stronger. Childhood memories have returned in sharp focus. He can now give 45-minute speeches without notes. He was able craft his autobiography, *Still Me* (Random House), which he dictated word by word.[1]

The Ancient Chinese Secret

In the Chinese language whole words are written with a symbol.
    Often two completely unlike symbols, when put together, have a meaning different than either of their two separate components.
An example is the symbol for "man" and that for "woman." These two symbols standing together, mean "good."
The two symbols for "trouble" and "gathering crisis," when brought together, mean "opportunity."

As the answers always lie in the questions, so the opportunities of life lie directly in our problems. Thomas Edison said, "There is much more opportunity than there are people who can see it."

[1]Quoted in Jeffrey Zaslow, "The Uncommon Strength of Christopher Reeve," *USA Weekend,* May 17, 1998, p. 4.

Great leaders emerge when a crisis occurs. In the life of people of achievement, we read repeatedly of terrible trouble which forced them to rise above the commonplace. In finding the answers, they discovered a tremendous power within themselves. Like a ground swell far out in the ocean, this force within explodes into a mighty wave when we overcome.

Then out steps the athlete, author, statesperson, scientist, the businessperson creating jobs for many people. David Sarnoff of RCA said, "There is plenty of security in the cemetery; I long only for opportunity."

People of achievement know this secret. The winds of adversity cannot shake them. Charles Lummis, first editor of the Los Angeles Times, *said, "I am bigger than anything that can happen to me. All these things, sorrow, misfortune, and suffering, are out-side my door. I am in the house and I have the key!"*

Hidden in trouble hides the shining key, our own magnificent opportunity.

*—*DOTTIE WALTERS

Don't feel that you have to be happy and cheerful all the time. Trying to "put on a smiling face," when you feel miserable, will only cause you more stress. Be yourself.

However, remember that everything happens for a reason, so every problem is, in fact, an opportunity in disguise. When you learn to recognize this, you will grow and move beyond those situations. If you don't allow yourself to learn and just see problems at the level of the problem, you will continue to be tormented by the same things over and over again until you do learn. Evolution requires patience, courage, and endurance. Stick with it.

*—*DR. DEEPAK CHOPRA

That Which You Resist, Persists

One of the things I heard Covey say was that we resist in others that which we are stuck on in ourselves. I may have heard that before, but the day I heard him, it must have really hit home because I can date my change in view of others to that talk.

I had a presentation myself that day, in a workshop, and I distinctly remember a woman who argued with my information, seeming to want to create a conflict in the session. I remember saying to myself, "Welcome her questions because resisting her will only keep you stuck."

I remember agreeing with her questions and inviting opinions from the other participants and in their responses, and the time to relax and let go, I found the ideas and the path for helping this woman begin to accept the suggestions I was sharing for dealing with volunteers.

I have continued to live by the concept. My colleagues can tell you that it has lessened the stress of staff meetings because I am less apt to argue right away.

Covey taught us that dilemmas are in our perceptions. I am now constantly clarifying my perceptions, especially when I feel some tension with another person. When I feel strong disagreement with another, I find myself wondering what it is about them or their content that is pushing my buttons. How is my perception of him or her related to an issue of my own?

Sometimes I don't even need an answer, because just being reminded about the concept is enough to clear my reactions so I can be more accepting. And sometimes I find the issue right away and can say, "Oh yes, there it is again," and naming it allows me to let go of it and my irritation for the moment. Then I can continue the interaction in a clearer mode.

—SARAH ELLISTON, CONSULTANT AND TRAINER
IN VOLUNTEER MANAGEMENT

God, Please Give Me Problems To Solve!

I heard Norman Vincent Peale at the Science of Mind Church in the sixties. I remember one thing he said—"If you do not have any problems, say 'God don't you trust me any more? Give me some problems to solve!' "

Many people get into the philosophy of positive thinking and believe that life from then on is smooth sailing, but it is not. You

*just look at it in a different way and know it is polishing your dia-
mond. You are not a victim but a volunteer and that you can handle it with grace and ease and with the help of angels or a higher
power of some kind.*

　　　　　—Dr. Tish Morgan, New Age minister
　　　　　　and author

A Place Where There Isn't any Trouble

*A client gave me a series of Norman Vincent Peale's tapes, and I
listened to them over and over again. One story that especially
inspired me was the one about the man who walked up to Dr.
Peale and said that the world is falling apart and he does not feel
that he can make it anymore.*

*"I have so many problems, and I do not want to deal with the
problems." Dr. Peale said to the man, "Please come with me, and I
will show you a place where people do not have to worry about
anything anymore." The man said "Really, where is that?"*

*They walked a few blocks to the cemetery. Where Dr. Peale points
out that people in the cemetery do not have any worries or problems.
Dr. Peale states, "If you are going to be on this Earth, problems will
be a part of life. Embrace them, and move forward. Don't make
problems your stumbling blocks, make them your stepping stone."*

*I have had many health and financial challenges and I reflect
on Dr. Peale's story. It gives me the strength to grow and move on,
without worry.*

　　　　　—L. Greg Voisen, president,
　　　　　　Sales Solutions Systems, Inc.

Learn the Lessons Failure Teaches

Failure is a detour, not a dead-end street.
　　　—Zig Ziglar

*I think everyone should experience defeat at least once during their
career. You learn a lot from it.*
　　　—Lou Holtz

Striving! It Is Better to Try and Fail

Groups clamored for my father to speak to them. I use parts of a longer quote from dad's speeches in my own talks.

What It Takes To Be Number One

Winning is not a sometime thing, it is an all the time thing. You don't win once in a while, you don't do things right once in a while, you do them right all the time. Winning is a habit, unfortunately so is losing. There is no room for second place. There is only one place in my game, and that's first place. I finished second twice in my time at Green Bay and I don't ever want to finish second again. There is a second-place ball game, but it's a game for losers played by losers.

It is, and always has been, an American zeal to be first in any-thing we do, to win, and to win, and to win. Every time a football player goes to ply his trade, he's got to play from the ground up: from the soles of his feet, right up to his head. Every inch of him has to play. Some guys play with their head, that's OK, you've got to be smart to be number one in any business. More importantly, you've got to play with your heart, with every fiber of your body. If you're lucky enough to find a guy with a lot of head, and a lot of heart, he's never going to come off the field second.

Running a football team is no different than running any other kind of organization, an army, a political party, or a business, the principles are the same. The object is to win, to beat the other guy. Maybe that sounds hard or cruel, I don't think so. It is a reality of life that men are competitive. The most competitive games draw the most competitive men, that's why they are there, to compete, to know the rules and objectives when they get in the game. The object is to win fairly, squarely, by the rules, but to win.

And in truth, I've never known a man worth his salt, who in the long run, deep down in his heart, didn't appreciate the grind and discipline. There is something in good men that really yearns for discipline and the harsh reality of head-to-head combat. I don't say these things because I believe in the brute nature of man, or that man must be brutalized to be combative. I believe in God and I believe in human decency. But I firmly believe that any man's finest hour, the greatest fulfillment of all that he holds dear, is that moment when he's worked hard on a good cause and lies exhausted on the field of battle—victorious.

That last phrase, "the greatest fulfillment of all that he holds dear, is that moment when he's worked hard on a good cause and lies exhausted on the field of battle—victorious," stands out as the message dad gave me that is emblazoned in my heart, and which I hope stays in the minds and souls of audiences after I leave.

—VINCE LOMBARDI, JR.

I remember Les Brown's story about the lazy dog. The canine sits uncomfortably over a nail, but it is too lazy to move. Instead it howls once in a while. This teaches us too often we vent about what life does to us without doing anything about it. Too often we prefer an uncomfortable inertia to an uncertain heaven of trying to achieve a goal.

I have used this anecdote in my life to say that instead of being passive, I should be reactive. Instead of letting somebody else or some event set my agenda, I can set it. What is the worse thing that can happen? I can fail. I may be no better off, but at least I tried to improve my life.

Because of Les Brown's words of inspiration, five years ago I changed careers. I became a tour guide instead of remaining a school teacher. While my former colleagues complain about teaching, I am now successfully earning an income from something that I truly enjoy doing.

—DR. PHILLIP SCHOENBERG, AUTHOR AND SPEAKER

Depend on God

I find myself faced with tasks demanding wisdom and courage beyond my own. And not just on the big decisions, I am constantly in need of God's grace to perform life's routine duties with the love for others, the peace, the joy, inherent in God's call.

I've had to learn that dependence is a good thing. That when I've used up my own resources, when I can't control things and

> *when I'm willing to trust God with the outcome, when I'm weak—*
> *then I am strong. Then I'm in the best position to be able to feel the*
> *power of Christ rest upon me, encourage me, replenish my energy,*
> *and deepen my faith. Power from God, not from me.*
> —ELIZABETH DOLE, SECRETARY OF
>   TRANSPORTATION, NATIONAL PRAYER BREAKFAST,
> WASHINGTON, D.C., FEB. 5, 1987

Common to the messages for these Superstars is that dreams are hard work, but absolutely worth it! Just go for it! Learn from these experts who all say to achieve, write down your goals, begin with the end in mind, then dream greater dreams! Attitude is a choice, until to reach your dream you can choose to fake it till you make it! You will become what you think about, think about achieving your dreams. For every action there is an opposite and equal reaction, so act! Visualize, focus, and ask, ask, ask for what you want. And to achieve what you want, give. What you give comes back, multiplied. Be with people—while you are with them. Smile to get through. You can do it—you have the power. Never give up. Problems in your path? Not so. They are just opportunities. Ask God or your Higher Power for some guidance to show you the difference.

PART II

Creating a Superstar Speech

A good, solid message, *without passion* from the heart, compassion, a well-defined purpose, for the right audience, will be a typical "academic" presentation. Academic presentations are notoriously dry with heavy—hardly remembered—content. So what makes the difference in messages that are remembered and those that have great content but are forgotten? Here in the second part of the book, we will show you!

Study the qualities of Superstar speakers that are remembered. By studying what has lasted in the hearts and minds of those who lives have been changed, you will have the basis of how to build your own talk!

Full Survey Results

Now, digging deeper into those very general categories from Figure 1, you have the following augmentation. There are so many qualities of great motivators mentioned that I have separated them into Figure 2 on issues of passion, purpose and

personality and Figure 3 on issues of skill and
character

NOTE: You'll think, "Wait a sec', many of these
overlap!" Yes, they seem to. Just take note of what
has remained in the minds of the listeners as the
reason the Superstar has lingered in the heart and
mind.

So? How Does the Survey Apply to Me?

In Part II of the book I will take each of the qualities
in Figures 2 and 3 and examine them in greater
detail.

As you work on your presentation, work on the
most important qualities first:

- "Motivate, or convince," them to _____
- Your message
- Becoming a real-life example

Then work your style, humor, heart stories, and
so on.

As you work on each of the qualities for your own
presentation, remember, the magic is in the mix. For
instance, Maya Angelou ranges from story to poem
to song and back again, using incredible presence
and long magical pauses to make her connection.

> *I once attended a presentation given by Maya Angelou at a mental
> health conference in Washington, D.C. Out strode Ms. Angelou
> full of life and brimming with confidence. She began by telling
> about her childhood in Arkansas.*
>
> *Words and emotions tumbled out in a gushing stream followed
> by deft reflection; verse recited from memory; a fragment from an
> old spiritual sung with strength and grace; then a humorous story
> about a childhood relative. I remember walking out of the church*

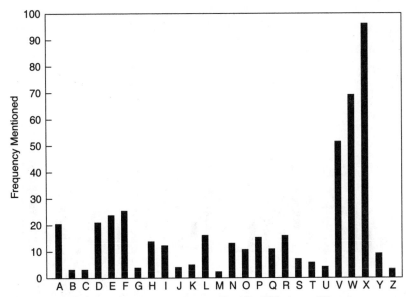

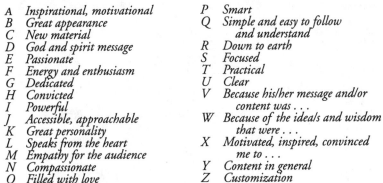

Figure 2. Qualities of Superstars Survey Result: All Issues of Passion, Purpose, and Personality

A   Inspirational, motivational
B   Great appearance
C   New material
D   God and spirit message
E   Passionate
F   Energy and enthusiasm
G   Dedicated
H   Convicted
I   Powerful
J   Accessible, approachable
K   Great personality
L   Speaks from the heart
M   Empathy for the audience
N   Compassionate
O   Filled with love

P   Smart
Q   Simple and easy to follow
       and understand
R   Down to earth
S   Focused
T   Practical
U   Clear
V   Because his/her message and/or
       content was . . .
W   Because of the ideals and wisdom
       that were . . .
X   Motivated, inspired, convinced
       me to . . .
Y   Content in general
Z   Customization

and feeling that I had just received a sermon on life and its excit-ing possibilities. It inspired me to think of new ways to record and synthesize the daily events of my life that would make them inspi-rational and worthy of future reflection. I was reminded of a quote by Aldous Huxley, "Experience is not what happens to a man; it is what a man does with what happens to him." My evening with Maya Angelou showed what one individual can

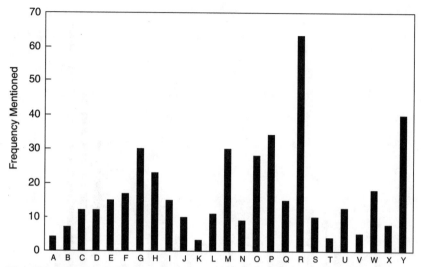

Figure 3. Qualities of Superstars Survey Results: All Issues of Skill and Character

A	Speaker thinks like me	M	Sincere
B	Speaker is like me	N	Genuine
C	Their example overcame adversity	O	Eloquent and uses words well
D	They were the first to . . .	P	Great story/ies
E	Character, integrity	Q	Voice
F	Just who he/she is	R	Style
G	Their life is an example	S	Presence
H	Walks the talk	T	Charisma
I	Uses true and personal stories	U	Talking just to me!
J	They are real life	V	Involves audience
K	Humble	W	Related, connected
L	Honest, believable	X	Creates tears and emotions
		Y	Uses humor, wit, entertaining

achieve when they focus their intellect and personal history through a lens of creativity and positive reflection.
    —DAVID RACHLIS, NATURALIST

You might not be the type of speaker to use the drama of Maya Angelou or Winston Churchill. Perhaps you are the type of "stand at the lectern and project magic" speaker that Dr. Peale was. There is no one right way. Note in these pages what they have done that is remembered to design what works for your own uniqueness, beliefs, and life experience.

5

Skills and Qualities of Superstar Speakers

In Chapter 5 we cover the attributes that are not directly connected solely with the message.

- Being a real-life example
- Style and eloquence
- Passion and purpose
- Involving the audience: humor, heart, and audience participation
- Compassion for the audience
- Connecting to the audience
- Stories and storytelling

The Power of Passion and Enthusiasm in Your Talks

> *I don't consider myself a great speaker, I consider I have a passion to share what I believe.*
> —Lou Holtz

Power, passion, conviction, dedication, and enthusiasm. Separate yet so closely related. For instance, a speaker who is propelled by the power and passion of his convictions, is always enthusiastic, filled with energy, and shows the dedication to his topic. That is motivational!

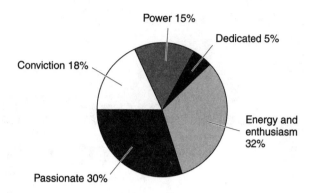

Figure 4. Qualities of Superstars Survey Results: Power, Passion, Conviction, Dedication, and Enthusiasm

What are you passionate about? What gets your soul soaring? Discovering what these things are in your life will be the first step towards becoming a Superstar speaker.

What! "I only need to speak at company meetings about paper clip usage! How can you be passionate about *that?!*"

OK, call it enthusiasm, call it power. But you can find "it" in almost *any* subject for which you spend time and soul studying.

> *Everything you do should have an emotional quotient. That is what helps you communicate with passion. Passion persuades, and it is a great incentive to action. I try to cultivate creativity most strongly through education. Franchisees and store managers participate in extensive training at corporate headquarters in England, while managers are taught in training sessions to unleash the passions of their staff.*
> —ANITA RODDICK

Passion Creates Experts

The world is willing to pay more respect to a brain surgeon than to a general practitioner. If you will only present on the subject once, bring in research of others to gain credibility. Create charts, graphs, and overheads of these findings.

As Mark Twain said, you've got to know 75 percent more about your subject than your audience.
   —**MARK VICTOR HANSEN**

[To learn about distributing the Suzuki four-wheel drive vehicles] I . . . thoroughly researched every detail of importation and distribution of Japanese vehicles. As in real estate development, I read every book, interviewed every specialist, studied every article, and "learned" from the experts.

At the end of the process, we had built what the Japanese had described as the fastest and most successful vehicle distributorship in their history.

This reaffirmed my favorite maxim, "You can learn anything you need to learn to achieve any goal you set for yourself. There are no limits except the limits you place on your own imagination."
   —**BRIAN TRACY**

Allow the Knowledge to Come to You

You already know the answer to what your passion is. The problem is you may have buried that knowledge long ago. Perhaps you thought that to follow your passion would be impractical or somehow unacceptable, when the only thing unacceptable is ignoring your innate desire.

Trying to discover your passion in a cognitive way is futile; it is like chasing a rainbow. Rather you should allow the knowledge to come to you. One way to become aware of your innermost desire is to open yourself to flashes of insight. This is not an active process. On the contrary, it is actually a process of inaction. Close your eyes and sit quietly. Don't try to figure anything out. Don't do anything. When a distracting thought enters your mind, let it pass. Be open to the images and signals your subconscious is sending you. After this mini-meditation, write down every thought that occurs to you. Then write down every desire you have, everything you want from life.

At this point you need to become clear about your dharma, or your purpose in life. We all have a reason for being here in the physical world, and that reason is made up of at least three objectives. The first is to discover our higher self. The second is to express our unique talents. The third component is that once you have ascertained your special talent, you need to use it in a way that benefits humanity.

One way to determine your special purpose is to ask yourself, "What would I do if I had all the money and all the time in the world?"

For example, suppose your answer is, "I want to travel all over the world and see different places." The law of dharma would then suggest that you literally fulfill that interest by first learning all about these places, traveling to those that you can, and then helping others to gain pleasure and knowledge from visiting these places. One possibility is to start a company that organizes traveling adventures.

I have found that when you are clear about your personal desire and how you can use your special talents to enrich someone else's life, every situation, circumstance, and person takes on a meaningful role in your life. And this starts to create "good luck." Good luck is nothing but an increasing frequency of synchronicities and coincidences that start to support your desire. It is opportunity meeting preparedness. The opportunity is in the situation, circumstance, and people that you meet; the preparedness is in the constant awareness of your desires and purpose in life. This, then, is the beginning of passion for life.

—Dr. Deepak Chopra

Passion Takes Practice

I am not a passionate speaker, at least not for many years in my career. I was told by expert coaches that my left brain had predominated over my right brain, the head was dominating the heart.

Albert Hubbard, in his book on great orators, wrote that you must hurl yourself into the message. Almost abandon yourself to the message, but with control. That is the key to great performances, control the passion.

> *It is a matter of practice. If you feel strongly about something,*
> *you make it clear you feel strongly. Don't be afraid to feel strongly*
> *and passionately about what you are saying.*
> *The question is, if you don't feel really strongly about it, why*
> *would you talk about it?*
> **—BRIAN TRACY**

You Can't Hire Other People to Do Your Push-Ups

Part of the fun of interviewing all the experts for my books, is that they don't all agree on "the" way to be great speakers. There are many roads to success! For instance, most are unbending in their beliefs about the need for extensive preparation and hard work, but not all agree.

> *I meditate, but beyond that do not use a script or prepare. I try to*
> *connect with the audience "live" and build on that positive energy.*
> **—DR. DEEPAK CHOPRA**

> *I took away from Jim Rohn[1] the importance of hard work. It's not*
> *just motivation, aspiration, information, affirmation. You've got to*
> *do your homework, do your doingness. I love his phrase that "you*
> *can't hire other people to do your push-ups for you."*
> *I also love what he said, "If you read a book a week, in 10 years*
> *you will be in the top 10 percent of your field." You will have read*
> *525 books. This affected me. I now read a book a week minimum.*
> **—JACK CANFIELD**

Winston Churchill used to say that there were only two things more difficult than making an after-dinner speech—one was climbing a wall which is leaning toward you, and the other was kissing a girl who is leaning away from you.

The reality is, creating great impromptu wit and brilliance takes hard, diligent, and smart work. Hard in that it takes effort that is new to you. Smart in that you need to find ways to study better, faster, and deeper

---

[1] A Superstar I will profile in a future volume.

than you, and others have before you. Diligent because you must carry on in what will prove to be a bigger task than you are anticipating.

Work Hard

Churchill estimated it took him six to eight hours to prepare a 45-minute speech. Many of my speakers, and I, say you can plan on 45 to 60 minutes of preparation time per one minute of speaking time.

> *The harder you work, the harder it is to surrender. . . . The difference between a successful person and others is not a lack of strength, not a lack of knowledge, but rather is a lack of will.*
> —VINCE LOMBARDI, SR.

> *Dad was an excellent speaker and in demand. He would talk about management issues, and conceptualize it around football. What really epitomized what he stood for was, "To accomplish anything worthwhile you must pay the price."*
> —VINCE LOMBARDI, JR.

> *Success is like anything worthwhile. It has a price. You have to pay the price to win and you have to pay the price to get to the point where success is possible. Most important, you must pay the price to stay there.*
> —VINCE LOMBARDI, SR.

Work Diligently

If you are coming from a place of passion in your heart, diligence won't be much of an issue for you. You'll stay up all night working on the words and be shocked at the sunrise.

> *You know we were just with Dave Barry, and Dave was saying, that, "It takes me one week to write a column." Most people think that because they are reading something in two minutes it only took two minutes to write. Lilly, you and Dottie write stories; we know that is not the case.*
> —MARK VICTOR HANSEN

Work Smart

Find ways to study better, faster, and deeper than you and others have before you. (See the discussion in Chapter 6 on becoming an expert.)

Og Mandino[1] was always carrying a pad with him. You'd be sitting in a board room together and he'd have two pads, one with the work of the meeting, the other with ideas he got that would be valuable for whatever book he was working on at the time. He was highly focused on his mission.

What impresses me most about Brian Tracy is his unquestionable determination to be focused. Brian gets more done in less time, and does it well, because of his ability to focus on the matter at hand. A perfect example of what one can do when one works smart, not just hard, and focuses their energies, like a laser.

    —NIDO QUBEIN, INTERNATIONAL BUSINESS CONSULTANT, SPEAKER, AUTHOR

How Do You Find "Passion"?

Anita Roddick said "Do business in an extraordinary way. Break the rules and go with your heart. Who needs cosmetics in fancy bottles? Give 'em urine sample bottles with a pretty label that can be refilled. Whatever you do, do it with style, boldly bend and break from tradition."

After ten years, I can still see her on stage . . . vibrant, passionately speaking from her guts, and spilling out her secrets. I couldn't take notes fast enough, her pace was exhilarating.

Anita inspired me to throw out my notes and my handouts, to design a brochure that reflected who I really was, and venture into the world of creativity, innovation and whole brain thinking. Anita started it all.

    —MAGGIE MILNE, KEYNOTE SPEAKER ON
      "OH!RIGINALITY" (TM)

---

[1]Another Superstar we will be profiling in a future volume!

"What are you passionate about?" Ninety percent of those who come to me for advice cannot answer that. So how do you find your passion? Here are ways some of our Superstars find passion.

Have a Burning Desire

People come to you because you have something to say and a burning desire to say it. You can't worry about grammar, or where your hands are, or what is acceptable. If you have a burning desire to tell somebody something, you will have an enthusiasm to do it, and you'll find the words to express yourself.
  —LOU HOLTZ

Use Your Heart Power

Unless a man believes in himself and makes a total commitment to his career and puts everything he has into it—his mind, his body and his heart—what is life worth to him? If I were a salesman, I would make this commitment to my company, to the product and most of all, to myself. . . . Once a man has made a commitment to a way of life, he puts the greatest strength in the world behind him. It's something we call heart power. Once a man has made this commitment, nothing will stop him short of success.
  —VINCE LOMBARDI, SR.

In What Do You Believe?

I've been speaking for about 20 years; the stories change but my philosophy really hasn't.

I hear what these great speakers and writers say. I don't hear their words and say, "Gee, that's my philosophy," I do say, "That will make my philosophy or belief stronger, I am going to incorporate that facet of it into what I believe and how I try to act and what I try to do." Hearing their words will help you discover what you believe in your hearts.
  —LOU HOLTZ

Develop Power Moves to Change Your "State"

I heard Tony Robbins say that one of the keys to success in anything is managing your emotions. He explained that a rapid technique for achieving this is to develop "power moves," i.e., the way you use your body. Essentially, you suddenly change the way you move, or the expressions you make, etc., and your state of mind changes immediately. I tried it and to my amazement, it worked instantaneously! It has become one of the single most effective tools I use to stay motivated and upbeat, even when the world seems to be crashing down around me.

I recently returned from vacation and was feeling quite overwhelmed by several personal and professional projects. My depression was so profound that it made me lethargic; I just couldn't seem to move forward. I employed Tony's technique and immediately became energized and focused; my thinking became crystal clear, and I was able to plot a course to successfully complete the projects.

—Maggie Munro, marketing events manager
at QAD, Inc.

Find Better Ways

Most creative people go through a period of desperate soul searching before they find their niche—the limitless world in which they can make the best use of what they have to offer, with no limit on ultimate growth. Being creative is nothing more than finding better ways of doing what you already do. The noncreative person is the person who just keeps doing his work the same way, without even thinking of better ways. . . . But the person who has found his dominant interest or his route to fulfillment, will never be boxed in for long. And he will find life interesting and rewarding.

—Earl Nightingale

Find Exciting Goals

So often I hear people say, "Tony, where do you get your energy? With all that intensity, no wonder you're so successful. I just don't have your drive; I guess I'm not motivated. I guess I'm lazy."

My usual response is, "You're not lazy! You just have impotent goals!"

Frequently, I get a confused look to this response, at which point I explain that my level of excitement and drive come from my goals. Every morning when I wake up, even if I feel physically exhausted from lack of sleep, I'll still find the drive I need because my goals are so exciting to me. They get me up early, keep me up late, and inspire me to marshal my resources and use everything I can possibly find within the sphere of my influence to bring them to fruition. The same energy and sense of mission is available to you now, but it will never be awakened by puny goals. The first step is to develop bigger, more inspiring, more challenging goals.

—Tony Robbins

Use Journaling and Hypnotherapy

In my book, Future Diary, *I have you ask yourself 128 questions to help you discover who you are. If you don't use my tool, use anything that is a "journal," and you just ask yourself, "What is my passion?" and you just start writing. It is almost automatic, your subconscious knows. Everyone of us is coded at birth with DNA and RNA, we are coded with what we are supposed to do.*

If journaling doesn't work to bring out those hidden passions, then have a hypnotherapist put you in a hypnotic state.

You need to ask yourself the small questions and the giant ones that are eternal: Who am I? What am I really dedicating my life's force energy to? When the game's over, what do I want written on my tombstone that says I made a difference and I was here? When the game's over, what will your obituary be? I have already written my obituary, 20 pages. Assuming I live the 127 years I plan on living, I plan on selling way over a billion books. Jack and I have 132 other books and three other series we want to write together! Lots of great stuff.

I'm in my passions of books, speaking, and entrepreneurship. Once you get into your passions, you will wish you were two or three people to do it all! You are so happy you can hardly stand it!

You wish you could clone yourself so you could pull off even more magic. It's because you know you are really helping people.
—MARK VICTOR HANSEN

Discover Whom You Envy

At my seminar I do a section on discovering your life's purpose. We start off by hitting it from the external, then we eventually approach it from the inside. We get them to answer questions like: "Who are you envious of?"

I was envious of Kenny Rogers, the singer. I had to ask myself, what is it I am envious of? He brings pro-athletes down to his ranch in Virginia. They divide up into teams and have a mini Olympics type event all week. They play all day, then at night they get massages and have gourmet meals. I realized it is that I love hanging out with people who are the best at what they do that made me envious. It helped me realize my passion is for information, for sharing, for generosity, for making a difference.

I start with the envy question, then I ask, "Think back in your life, when did you feel most alive? When did you feel most happy? When did you feel most loved? What was your greatest success? What was it about that success that made it a success?" As they answer these, people start to see some patterns.

Finally, we ask, "Whom do you admire most on the planet alive or dead? If you could be anyone on the planet, who would you be?" If someone says Tony Robbins, that is a real different statement than Mother Teresa. It helps define what they want to express.

With their eyes closed I have them imagine they are climbing a mountain, they go into a temple, and this wise person comes and brings them a gift. As they open the gift, it will symbolically represent their life's purpose. People open it and get things like a children's book, this because they are supposed to write a children's book. Some get little poor kids looking up a them with hope, this because they are supposed to go empower those kids. People get in touch with their passion and their purpose.
—JACK CANFIELD

Power, passion, conviction, dedication and enthusiasm. Separate yet so closely related.

Remember, passion creates experts. Experts are what audiences want to hear. Passion takes practice and you can't hire other people to do your push-ups. Work hard, work diligently, work smart.

Find your passion and share it with others.

They Are Sincere and Motivate by Example

As you see, being "a living example" is of enormous importance! People gave so many reasons for and examples of this category that I have an entire subsection devoted to this subject.

Achieving Sincerity, Honesty, Character, and Humility

You will often hear critics of presenters say, "They were not sincere." A valid point, but a lack of sincerity is usually a symptom of the true problem. They lacked sincerity because they were not speaking from their passion, from their heart. The audience must believe that you believe. They will believe you, *if you believe you.*

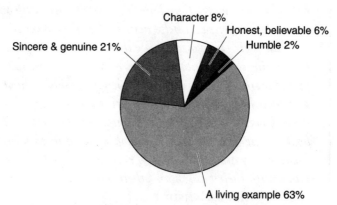

Figure 5. Qualities of Superstars Survey Results: Being Real and Sincere

"How do you *seem* sincere on the platform?" I am constantly asked. By being *sincere!*

> *We must ask ourselves if in pursuing life's options, we have left behind the fundamentals?*
> *This substitution of regulation for responsibility is a kind of Puritanism for people who no longer believe in character, who no longer believe in the wisdom and goodness of the people. But we will never write enough rules. Individual and national character is what we need.*
> —ELIZABETH DOLE

Talk Your Truth, Talk Your Belief

Even if the audience disagrees with your message, they will respect you if you speak what you believe in. Not everyone has a passion for Christianity, like Zig Ziglar does. But Zig was right at the top of my survey, as the best motivator of all time, because he speaks with sincerity—a symptom of his passion.

> *Even as Zig became so successful, so well known, he never compromised his beliefs. I know he always talks about God's presence in his life; he is unabashed about that, a wonderful frame of reference to say what you believe.*
> —NIDO QUBEIN, INTERNATIONAL BUSINESS CONSULTANT

> *Tell the truth and speak from your heart. If you do that, 85 percent of what you do will come naturally. Your body will move, you'll make eye contact, you'll penetrate the audience, you'll tell jokes if you're supposed to, you'll be vulnerable. People will connect with you because you are talking about your own life, your own heart, your own passion.*
> *People don't want to have someone stand up there and be a paragon of virtue, they don't think they can measure up. But if they can hear that in the midst of all of your success, you fell down, made mistakes, and right now you have problems too . . . they'll love you for it.*
> —JACK CANFIELD

What Is a Living Example?

Of course, the route to being honest and sincere is to talk honestly and sincerely about *who you are*. Then to become a "who you are" worth talking about, a living example of your message.

As you read audience comments on these "living example" related issues, you will see there is a huge overlap. Yet, they were mentioned individually. Looking at each will give you ideas on how you can become a living example, without being the first person on Mars, or the survivor of a horrific accident.

> *None of us can claim perfection and few can wear the mantle of hero or heroine, but each of us has the option of choosing a life of decency and self-discipline, self-reliance and diligence. From time to time, we all fail our own standards, but our standards will never fail us.*
> —ELIZABETH DOLE

Becoming a Living Example

> *The greatest compliment I have received after a speech was, "One speaker told us how great he was. Lou Holtz showed us why he was great." I'd never looked at it that way before.*
> —LOU HOLTZ

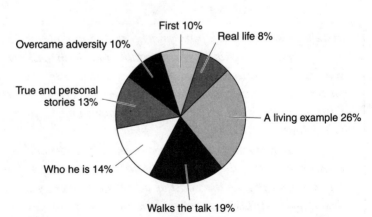

Figure 6. Qualities of Superstars Survey Results: Being a Living Example

In the prequel to this book, *Secrets of Successful Speakers,* I did not appreciate the overwhelming importance of presenters being a living example of what they preach. I didn't want to emphasize that too heavily because it is the most difficult thing to achieve! In doing a book on presentation skills, I want to give you simple ideas and skills you can easily learn. But this? This means you must work on *you* to create and discover greatness. That frustrates me as an author and consultant because "becoming" is so consuming. It terrifies me as a speaker because it means I must work on *me.* It means not just talking about it, but *being about it.* It means working on the core of who I am to prepare, earn, and increase my contribution as person to become a "sermon we see."

Sermons We See

I'd rather see a sermon than hear one any day;
I'd rather one should walk with me than merely tell the way.
The eye's a better pupil and more willing than the ear,
Fine counsel is confusing, but example's always clear;
And the best of all the preachers are the men who live their creeds,
For to see good put in action is what everybody needs.

I soon can learn to do it if you'll let me see it done;
I can watch your hands in action, but your tongue too fast may run.
And the lecture you deliver may be very wise and true,
But I'd rather get my lessons by observing what you do;
For I might misunderstand you and the high advice you give,
But there's no misunderstanding how you act and how you live.
—Edgar A. Guest (1881–1959)

The man who wants to earn a lot of money, but who has not prepared himself to do it, will not achieve it until he does. The parent who wants the love of his children, but who has not earned it, will never get it, and should not seek it. The man who wants higher wages and shorter hours without an increase in his contribution or service is only, over the long haul, kidding himself. He will end by paying the higher wages he seeks himself.
—Earl Nightingale

Be about It

> *One of the greatest moments in anybody's developing experience is when he no longer tries to hide from himself but determines to get acquainted with himself as he really is.*
> —NORMAN VINCENT PEALE

> *The speaker who never has done anything but sits in a "classroom of life," and says "I think this is the way a philosophy ought to work, this is what I think you ought to do," just isn't going to be trustworthy and believable to the audience. You have to have lived. You have to have believed it.*
> —LOU HOLTZ

> *Thousands of people want to be speakers, people come to me all the time and say, "I want to be a speaker." I give the same advice, first I ask, "Well, what have you succeeded in?" Which usually stops them cold.*
>
> *You cannot teach people something that you don't already know. You do not know how to succeed until you have succeeded. What you do is go out and succeed at something, then you can come back and say, "This is what I learned, this is how I applied it, these are the results I got." If you don't you will only be able to speak to young and immature audiences, and only once.*
> —BRIAN TRACY

> *I feel inspired. Inspired means to breathe in spirit. At some point I breathed in enough that I became inspirational rather than needing to be inspired by someone else.*
> —JACK CANFIELD

> *Five years ago, my company contracted Stephen Covey's organization to develop a one-week class for all of the employees in my division.*
>
> *This class caused me to really take a look at myself, my relationships with others, and my life in general. I came to realize that while I thought I was a "nice" person, there were some traits in my character that really needed "work." I also discovered that as I*

began to work on "me," my relationships with co-workers, my children and my husband began to flourish.
> —MICHELLE BENNING, LEARNING AND DEVELOPMENT MANAGER, XEROX CORPORATION, TEXAS

Who You Are Speaks Louder Than Words

Maya Angelou told us the story of a young mother who was illiterate, on her own, and facing a long hard road in life. She created her own business by selling hot meals to factory workers on opposite ends of a long road. Eventually, she created such business, that she was able to set up her own stand, then a store halfway between the two, and thrived there. No one would have believed in her, so she created a better life on her own, creatively. First going to her customers, using trial and error. Then letting them come to her and expanding her offerings.

Against all odds, today, I guide people in creating their dreams and I am writing songs and stories that speak to the frightened, injured parts of us and say, "You are not alone, you are precious just as you are."

Because, as Maya Angelou said, "We are women. We are amazing. And we make our own paths. If you don't like the path you are on, then step off. Create your own!"
> —ANNE E. TREMBLAY, WRITER, SINGER, LIFE-GUIDE

Champions of Hope

Speakers such as Christopher Reeve affect me not so much by their words, but by their example. Just by their willingness to step in front of an audience they say, "I am not going to give up . . . if I can do it, so can you." It gives new determination to millions of us who disable ourselves with self-limiting beliefs.

When I saw Christopher Reeve, he told the story of his recovery from his accident and that you should never for an instant be absorbed in self-pity. At that time I was an able-bodied person and connected with his message in a different way than I do today.

Today, I am paralyzed after being crushed by a falling tree. His words stayed with me. I kept them in my mind as I lay in my hospital bed grieving over my losses. Many times I did indulge in self-pity. I kept a picture of Christopher Reeve that was taken the day I heard him speak so I could see it from my hospital bed. Seeing his photo took me back to the day when he was speaking. Remembering his words helped me to pull out of pity and to focus on hope.

Today I am finding inner strength to view life with a fresh perspective. Now I am sharing my experiences with others as I speak and write about my firsthand experiences on how to deal with fear, disappointment, and changes in life.
—**ROSEMARIE ROSSETTI, PH.D.**

When I read an article on Christopher Reeve—knew at once I had discovered not only the best definition of "greatness," but was also inspired what to ask for in my daily prayer.

Reeve spoke of how he would respond to the question "What is a hero?" Earlier without hesitation, his answer would be, "a hero is someone who commits a courageous action without considering the consequences!"

He said, his definition now (after his horse-jumping accident which left him paralyzed from the shoulders down) was, "A hero is an ordinary individual who finds strength to persevere and endure in spite of overwhelming obstacles."

The new Christopher Reeve is now my new hero!
—**GERALD GREEN, AUTHOR OF** The Magic Of Public Speaking, **PENANG, MALAYSIA**

They Overcame!

Look seriously at what you have overcome. Your experience may not be as horrific as many of the Superstars, but your story may well give others the insight to say, "If she can do it, so can I!"

It's not whether you get knocked down, it's whether you get up.
—**VINCE LOMBARDI, SR.**

> *Show me anyone who is successful, and I'll show you someone who*
> *has overcome adversity.*
> —Lou Holtz

When we heard Dottie Walters speak at an NSA convention, she
told the story of persevering when things get tough. She quoted her
Scottish grandfather, "I lay me down and bleed a wee bit but I will
be up to fight again." Her story and quotation, as well as her per-
sonal example, have inspired me to hold steady to the course when
things get tough. I visualize that soda counter (which now has a
place of honor in her home) and am determined that I will also be
a survivor.

> —Sally Harrison, psychologist and widow of
> the late speaker extraordinaire Col. Gene
> Harrison

Tell Your Story, Personal Experience

Having said you must become a person of success *before* you talk about
being a person of success, don't discount your own successes. Each of
us has overcome, and accomplished. Tell your story and personal experience. Tell of your failures and triumphs. Tell of the lessons these
taught you. Then give your listeners strategies of how they can apply
these lessons to *their* lives.

One of the most perplexing aspects in working with speakers on
their presentations is they very often want to diminish their experiences in life that have brought them to where they are today. Why?
Why do we claim not to be experts at something for which we have
labored for years? I feel it is because we are too close to all the mistakes
and failures we know we make daily. Perhaps we feel like a failure for
wanting to leave that industry. Here is a secret of any Superstar speaker:
they make *more* mistakes and have more failures than the average person. Why? They do more than the average person. Babe Ruth had the
record for most hits, he also had it for the most misses!

Look at your life. What have you been doing for the past 20 years?
Chances are you have a great deal to bring to the platform, in addition
to the new expertise and knowledge you will acquire as you research
and develop.

I like to speak from memory and from my heart.

There are people who are fictitious about what they want to say. They've read this, or they've heard this at a speech, so they think "this" is what people want to hear. They don't have a passion and a deep down belief. When I talk about personal experiences, I can get excited about them because I've lived it, I've seen it.

If I find out that somebody needs me to get across a message in teamwork, it is foolhardy for me to stand up and talk to them about how they ought to have teamwork in their company and talk about their company. But I can stand up and talk about the importance of teamwork in the experiences I've had. Then they'll say, "You know, that's just like my situation. That applies to me."

—LOU HOLTZ

On Stage and Off

When you step on the speaking platform, you step into a fishbowl. You will be judged, not just as the person you show on stage and in print but, perhaps even more, on the person you are behind the scenes. Once you decide to take the platform, even for a small company speech, every move you make is talked about and scrutinized on stage and off.

I had the opportunity to have a private meeting with Christopher Reeve after he gave an incredibly inspiring talk at the Peter Lowe Success 97 Seminar in Indianapolis. What was so amazing to me was the concern I saw compassionately flash in his eyes when he discovered I was battling a rare form of cancer. He then proceeded to encourage and cajole me into never giving up no matter what the future was to bring me.

I was floored and my eyes teared. How could this man, a quadriplegic, still have the energy to feel so compassionately for others, for me, after what had happened to him?

Why didn't he bottle up every ounce of his personal energy to use solely for his own recovery?

It is the miracle of the human spirit personified in the heart and soul of Christopher Reeve.
    —BILL GOSS, SPEAKER/AUTHOR OF *THE LUCKIEST UNLUCKY MAN ALIVE*

The first time I got to "share the platform" with Zig Ziglar, he spoke first in the morning, and then finished up the daylong program as well. He closed out the day by giving his typical marvelous performance combining information, humor, and his signature storytelling.

After ending his program, many in the audience immediately rushed up to Zig for autographs, questions, and to compliment him on his fine talk, information, and share their own stories of how Zig's teachings have enhanced their own lives.

Zig patiently spoke with everyone, there were a lot of people. Finally, there was one person left, a thirty-something looking woman who looked as though she greatly needed advice.

Well, she really shared her story, telling Zig about her abusive upbringing, the anger she had toward her family, and her lack of confidence and self-esteem. Zig focused all of his attention on her, and I know he had to be tired and badly wanting to get off stage and rest, and allowed her to tell all.

I really admire Zig Ziglar and respect the fact that he has that priceless characteristic of "servant-leadership."
    —BOB BURG, SPEAKER AND AUTHOR,
    ENDLESS REFERRALS AND *WINNING WITHOUT INTIMIDATION*

Dr. Peale took my card and carefully put it in his pocket. I was so pleased that he kept it. Two days later, the mail came to my office bearing an envelope with Dr. Peale's name on the return address. I was so excited! Inside was a handwritten note. Dr. Peale said, "Dottie, I am proud of you and your business." I wept.

How many people gave Dr. Peale their business cards that day? How many hours did he spend writing to all of us? Dr. Peale walks the talk.
    —DOTTIE WALTERS

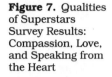

Figure 7. Qualities of Superstars Survey Results: Compassion, Love, and Speaking from the Heart

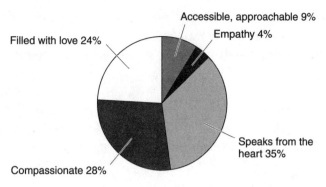

You are a living example of your message—a person who not only says, but shows us honesty, character, and sincerity. Your sincerity will shine through when you speak from your passion, from your heart. The audience must believe that you believe. They will believe you, if you believe you.

> One good man teaches many, men believe what they behold;
> One deed of kindness noticed is worth forty that are told.
> Who stands with men of honor learns to hold his honor dear,
> For right living speaks a language which to every one is clear.
> Though an able speaker charms me with his eloquence, I say,
> I'd rather see a sermon than to hear one, any day.
>   —Edgar Guest (1881–1959)

Becoming a Loving, Compassionate Speaker

Getting people to like you is merely the other side of liking them.
    —NORMAN VINCENT PEALE

The first time I shook hands with Mark Victor Hansen, and heard him face-to-face, only eight people showed up. I was there a half hour early to sit in the front row. I remember he treated the eight of us as if we were 800.
    —MIKE REDDING, AUTHOR AND SPEAKER

If you have a love for them, you will begin to speak from your heart. But the other side of compassion and speaking from the heart is listening to what your heart is calling you to do and say. Yes, we just circled back to those passion issues. They are closely related.

I heard Maya Angelou speak at Rutgers University in New Brunswick, New Jersey. After her talk, I waited in the receiving line to express my appreciation for her wonderful speech. Instead of just thanking me for my compliment to her, she said, "Thank you for being such a responsive listener. I really appreciate your being in the audience."

I have treasured her words to me over the years, and they have completely changed me as a speaker. I try to emulate Dr. Angelou's gracious humility by honoring my listeners in the same way that she honored me.

> —MARY SIGMANN, COACHING AND ORGANIZING
> SERVICES

Your mind won't really teach you anything but quieting your mind allows you to hear your heart and your heart is always ready to learn.

> —DR. DEEPAK CHOPRA

I had the incredible opportunity to participate in an intimate focus group organized by Newsday *Newspaper in New York. My husband, five other couples, Stephen Covey, and I met to discuss how we could incorporate the* Seven Habits of Highly Effective Families *in our marriage and family. My book was coming out and the pressure was affecting our family. When you start a new business you don't make money right away, and you work awfully hard to get what feels like nowhere fast.*

Stephen Covey listened to each of our stories. He wasn't just listening with kindness it was with an intensity and powerful active participation. Earlier, during the day before we met with him, we weren't feeling our "love." Mr. Covey offered his thoughts, much of which was in the book, but it was said with such caring and love. He made us see what we had and how we respected and applauded each other. That was two years ago. The impact has been evident in our relationship to each other. Stephen Covey loved us individu-

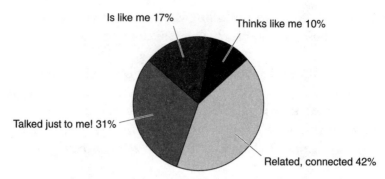

Figure 8. Qualities of Superstars Survey Results: Relating and Connecting

*ally and as a couple. He saw in us our depth and shared his views
with loving concern.*

> —PEGINE ECHEVARRIA, SPEAKER AND AUTHOR OF
> *For All Our Daughters: How Mentoring Helps
> Young Women and Girls Master the Art of
> Growing Up*

Cavett Robert,[2] founder and chairman emeritus of the National
Speakers Association, would always tell us, "They don't care how much
you know, 'til they know how much you care." If you have a love for
them, you will begin to speak from your heart. When you do, you
begin to relate and connect to your listeners.

> *Don't stand up there because you want to be the focus of that par-
> ticular meeting and that particular time, you stand up there
> because you genuinely have a concern for them. Your preparation
> shows you genuinely were committed to what you did.*
> —LOU HOLTZ

Becoming a Speaker Who Connects

> *There is a difference between impressing an audience, and connect-
> ing with an audience. But, once you have the connection, you can
> take them where you want to go.*
> —LES BROWN

[2]Cavett Robert is another fantastic speaker who I am profiling in a future volume of Superstars.

The number one reason speakers don't connect is they do not look right at the listener, one on one. Your eyes must penetrate the audience and never let go.

Practice delivering your talk with intense concentration on the message and audience. Don't play with your notes, or the microphone. Do stare right at someone, and *care* deeply that they understand the message. Now look right at someone else, grab them with your eyes, and say it again. You will catch the entire audience by catching them one at a time. My mother told me you look right into just one person, and wait for them to "lift." Your intense concentration on that one person makes you lose yourself. A bond occurs with the entire audience, even though you are with just the one.

Just to One Person

> *My job is to step into that room and capture every soul.*
> —Tony Robbins

The ultimate connection is when you make them feel you are speaking "just to them."

Rev. Bob Richards, one of our Olympic decathlon champions (the first guy on the Wheaties™ box!) tells of something that would happen to him over and over. After each of his wonderfully motivational talks—often to high school students—he would close with, "I know one of you will become our next Olympic champion. One of you will be willing to pay the price. You know who you are!" And he would leave the dais.

Invariably, some scrawny, least likely to succeed kid with horrible acne would come up to him afterwards and say quietly in the hallway, "Rev. Richards. Were you talking to me?"

He would smile. The child, encouraged, would then tell him, "Because *I am the one.*"

Rev. Richards told me, strangely enough he would hear from those kids years later. And they *were* the ones. They answered the call.

Go into a State of Communion

> *I plan my talks very tightly. But often, when I get into the talk, I hear this little voice in me that will say, "Tell them about your*

son . . . tell them about that time when you. . . ." People will come up afterwards and say, "I really needed to hear that one thing you said about. . . ."

I feel I go into a state of communion with my audience. They draw out of me that which they most need to hear. You've got a computer full of messages in your mind that you could take six hours to share when you only have an hour's talk. God knows why certain things bounce into your head to say when you weren't planning on saying them. But I think it is because the audience needs to hear them. I trust the process of my intuition.
    —JACK CANFIELD

There are times when they are sitting down, I'm standing up, and suddenly I feel as if I'm ten feet tall. I feel like I'm taking up the whole room. I feel like I could put my arms around all of them.
    —VINCE LOMBARDI, JR.

Too many speakers are worried about how they are coming across, they lose touch with their audience and the message they bring. If you stand up on the stage and your number one concern is the impact you are going to have, then you don't care if your tie is crooked or your shoes need polishing, or your belt's not lined up with your zipper, or your earrings aren't the right type, or you've got the right haircut, or colors on.
    —JACK CANFIELD

Focus

It may take you years before you find yourself creating those magic moments of connection with the audience. Not one speaker I asked was able to say how he or she creates the moments, nor when they are likely to happen. The common thread is that all of them work very hard on ways to enhance the lives of the listeners, with intense focus on the message.

Connection and Customization

To effectively communicate, we must realize that we are all different in the way we perceive the world and use this understanding as a guide to our communication with others.

Quality questions create a quality life. Successful people ask better questions, and as a result, they get better answers.
—TONY ROBBINS

During her years at Labor and the Red Cross, I saw time and again that no matter the size or prestige of the audience, Mrs. Dole felt that they deserved her best. Part of the speechwriting process in working with Mrs. Dole was providing her with information about the audience. Who were they? Were there any people she should recognize in her remarks? Was there any special inside humor or "local color" they would appreciate? By taking time to find out about her audience, Mrs. Dole was sending a signal that she cared about them. She was not simply standing behind a podium giving a speech she could give anywhere—she had taken the time to learn about them.

It was an easy step from wanting to be emotionally connected to the audience to wanting to be physically connected to them, as well. During the early stage of the 1996 campaign, Mrs. Dole began to experiment with wandering through the audience as she spoke. The feedback was great. And, when it came time for her convention speech, it was her idea to deliver it from the convention floor. Many advisers warned against it, saying that it was too risky, and that too many things could go wrong. She listened to their concerns, and made the decision to go full speed ahead.

When Mrs. Dole was Secretary of Labor, she was part of a delegation of Cabinet secretaries who traveled to Poland in the earliest days of democracy there. . . . Before leaving, she looked at the schedule and noticed that there were three or four official dinners. Anticipating that the Cabinet secretaries might be asked to give a toast at these dinners, we spent some time developing three or four toasts that wove together the histories and the people of America and Poland. Word eventually reached us during the trip that Mrs. Dole was the "toast of the town," because the Secretaries were called on to give toasts, and she was the only one who had taken the time to prepare anything.
—KERRY TYMCHUK, SPEECHWRITER FOR ELIZABETH DOLE, AND CO-AUTHOR OF *UNLIMITED PARTNERS*

Is Just Like Me

After I heard Elizabeth Dole talk about her childhood and education, something snapped. When I went home I said to myself: "Here's somebody with a similar background to mine, similar childhood and education, and her name's a household word. That means there isn't any reason why my name can't also be one. I'm going to get back into writing and get a national reputation." (This was when I was still practicing law in Memphis, Tennessee.)

So I started back that very day, with one small step. She helped me push myself into what I'd always really wanted: a freelance nonfiction writing career (88 published articles so far with more coming all the time) and a speaking/training career which followed from the writing.

—PRISCILLA RICHARDSON, PROFESSIONAL SPEAKER, TRAINER, AND WRITER

Of course, doing your homework before the event will help you find ways to be "just like them," and to be a speaker to meet the struggle of the times. You will catch the entire audience by catching them one at a time. Go into a state of communion, lose yourself in giving your message as it best fits their needs, wants, and hopes. Focus so hard on them that you get into that magic "zone." Look right into just one person, and wait for them "lift." Magic begins to happen.

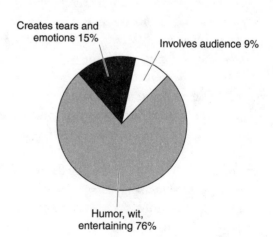

Figure 9. Qualities of Superstars Survey Results: Involvement

Creates tears and emotions 15%

Involves audience 9%

Humor, wit, entertaining 76%

How to Involve the Audience

Looking at Figure 9, you might think, "Yeah! Grab some jokes, and my talk will be a success!" But go back to Figure 1 and note that this takes up only 6 percent of important remembered qualities of Superstars. When people consult with me about their presentations, 99 percent of the time they want to work on how to be funnier up there. No, no, no! Business talks that are funny or heartfelt *without* a great content, "something they can use" message to build from, *are a disaster!*

Before you work on the humor, heart, and audience participation, work on your base, your message. Work on it some more. Then get fanatical about it for a few years. *Then* add some of the three best "involvement" strategies: humor, heart stories, and audience participation exercises.

I resolved that I would be the opposite of speakers that are only jokes, only humor, and only emotion. Insincere emotion, what I call gush, gush, puke, puke emotion, stories that will work the emotions of the crowd. But my weakness is that I don't give enough emotion and too much content.

Now I am working my way back to the center. I "romance the points" I want to make. I have developed what I call the windshield wiper method of speaking, it goes: left brain, right brain. Left brain, right brain. Left brain, right brain. Left brain, right brain. Fact, story/anecdote. Fact, story/anecdote. Fact, story/anecdote. Fact, story/anecdote. So it's practical, with the fact for the left brain, then the story or anecdote that illustrates it for the right brain. If you have too much content, it's like pouring water on the ground. It forms a pool. If you keep pouring water in the water, it doesn't get a chance to soak in. It just evaporates or spills over. If you pour content into the mind, and then you go to the right brain, it gives the material a chance to sink in.

The danger with stories is that they are so well received that they are like a narcotic. The audience laughs and smiles and "likes" the speaker. And all speakers want to be liked.
—BRIAN TRACY

Is Humor Important?

We are an entertainment culture, living in an entertainment age. Many educational enterprises fail to achieve the results they desire for lack of one simple idea: Most people would much rather be entertained than educated. The 21st century educator must be an extraordinary entertainer who educates people with the finest tools, and empowers them to act upon them. I call this philosophy, E3.
—TONY ROBBINS

Humor Is a Retention Tool

Everyone, in the average audience, has grown accustomed to communications of all kinds being more entertaining than was the norm even 30 years ago. All kinds of research has turned up benefits of humor in communication: retention of material, listener-presenter rapport, attentiveness and interest, motivation toward and satisfaction with learning, class discussion, creativity, idea generation, and creative thinking.

Behavior doesn't come from the head, but from the heart . . . as does laughter. Humor is wonderfully retained in the mind.

Research suggests that 85 percent of what we retain is visual. A good cartoon uses a visual image for retention. A good humorous story also creates a visual image in the listener's mind. Your listeners may laugh for only five seconds, but they'll think for five minutes on the meat of your message every time they remember it. As humorous speaker and researcher Joel Goodman, originator of "The Humor Project," puts it, "I can give 'AhHa's' through 'HaHa's.' "

Warning: Humor is a great tool for retention! Make sure the humor is deeply connected to your message. You don't want them to remember just the humor, you need them to remember the *point*.

For more on using humor in your presentations, read the prequel to this book, *Secrets of Successful Speakers* (Lilly Walters, McGraw Hill), and *What to Say When You're Dyin' on the Platform!* (Lilly Walters, McGraw Hill).

Humor Can Be Dangerous

As you saw from my survey (and is shown by other research), audience perceptions of the speaker, especially their expertise, are hardly affected by the use of humor. Work on your message for years before you worry about using humor; it has a great potential to backfire on you, when it is not interpreted as humor.

At one time The American Society of Training and Development created a code that states: "Presenters from any society podium must refrain from overt statements or pointed humor that disparages the rightful dignity and social equity of any individual or group." I applaud their valiant effort not to hurt, but humor is about pain. As Victor Borge says, ". . . humor is an insult itself . . . it's an insult to dignity—like the person slipping on a banana peel."

Sarcastic humor and ethnic jokes keep people apart, instead of bringing them together. Some people use sarcasm like a knife, inserting it quickly, turning it for effect, and then pulling it out before others have even realized that they've been stabbed.[3]

The trouble is, most people have no clue when, or why, people get hurt by their humor.

"I was just teasing you!"

"Hey, it was just a joke."

If you ever feel the need to say that sort of thing, you can bet the brunt of the joke was not the jokester.

I heard Maya Angelou speak five years ago. I was profoundly affected by the realization that the words we speak are powerful. I believe up until then I carelessly used my words in hateful ways against others. I stirred trouble among my family, co-workers and friends with just my words.

I looked at what was causing me to wreak so much havoc. When one part of your life is unhappy you act it out in other parts. Since words were powerful I decided to make my words positive and cheerful. It has enriched my life, and I see the positive effects on everyone around me. Since then I became a real estate agent. When I answer my phone I always have a "smile" on my face that translates over into my voice. I adapted her advice into my own life,

---

[3] *Sarcasm* is from the Greek *sarkazein*, to tear flesh (sarx); gnash teeth. It is a remark that leaves the object of the remark with a bit of self-esteem torn away.

and it has given me the reputation as one of the "nicest" Realtors in my town. People who haven't seen me in a while are always surprised at how "different" I have become.
        —DANA G. COLEMAN

What I remember most about Maya Angelou's speech is her talking about the power that words have on all of us.

There is no such thing as "Words can never hurt me." They can hurt, but better yet they can heal. She reinforced the lesson the Lord has been teaching me, Ephesians 4:29. That I must *use my words as instruments of healing. There is already enough hurt in the world.*
        —BRENDA GAYLE BRYANT, SMALL BUSINESS
         CONSULTANT

Audience Participation

Think of audience participation as anything other than your standing there talking, from the the subtle to extreme: reading, writing, sharing ideas, meditation, singing, snow boarding, walking on hot coals!

Tony Robbins is perhaps the master of extreme audience participation: the fire walk, exploding smoke machines, strobe lights, increasingly frenzied emotional exercises. In the first seconds Robbins often gets the audience out of their seats, then he pushes them higher. He starts comparatively small, telling the audience members to turn and greet their neighbor. He builds by having them give each other massages. Later he often orders the crowd to stand up *and maintain energy and focus!* Soon Robbins directs everyone in the crowd to greet their neighbor using emotions, ranging from loathing to fear, hopefulness, to adoration. He makes them do this three times, each time showing more energy and enthusiasm, so that the third time they're supposed to hug their neighbors as though they have just won the Super Bowl. He brings them higher by getting into what he calls a "peak state," wherein you have peak energy and peak joy and peak everything, and you become unstoppable. He explains the physiological process involved, and he helps them get there by jumping up and down and screaming. Tony gets the audience singing at the top of their lungs: "Born to Be Wild."

Silly? Well, it's very hard to argue with the amazing success of his presentations.

Another, and subtler, master of audience participation is Jack Canfield. He is gifted at the games that encourage the sharing of heartfelt emotions. Yet, he often has his group do an exercise where they run themselves, throat first, into an arrow and break it, rather than them!

> *I always have people at least talk to someone else in the room, stand up and do something, perhaps do a kinesiology or an experi- ence or shoulder massage, things that get them out of their chairs. In longer programs you can have them break into groups, talk about things, remember stuff from their childhood, set goals, share their dreams. I try to get people to "do" as much as possible.*
> **—JACK CANFIELD**

> *When I heard Stephen Covey speak he did an audience participa- tion activity. He asked everyone to stand, close their eyes, and using their right arm to point in the direction north. He then asked everyone to open their eyes and it was amusing to see that people had their arms pointing in every direction.*
>
> *Next, he asked only those who were absolutely certain which direction north actually was to stand, close their eyes and point north. To the audience's surprise, those standing for the second part had their arms pointing in many different directions! Dr. Covey took out a compass and pointed north, and said, "How many times have people said they absolutely know this is the right way to do it? How many times have we said this is absolutely the right way to do it? We say we are absolutely certain, but are we?"*
>
> *Dr. Covey's words motivated me to be 100% certain before I say, "I know this is right!" I now double-check all the facts before going on record to state them. I will only say, "I know what I'm doing"— when I really do know what I'm doing! Thank you, Dr. Covey!*
> **—EDWARD LEIGH, M.A., MOTIVATIONAL HUMORIST**

Heart Stories Touch Emotions

A story is also an audience participation device. (See more on story- telling in the next section.) Touch their hearts, their minds will follow. To touch their hearts, simply use what you have heard that touches your heart. We make decisions with our heads, we make commitments with our hearts.

> *Whenever we wanted to persuade our staff to support a particular project we always tried to break their hearts. At the next franchise holders' meeting we put on a real tear-jerking audio-visual presentation, with wonderful slides of the children against a background of Willie Nelson's version of "Bridge over Troubled Water." And to enable members of staff to experience what we had experienced, the next edition of "Talking Shop," the monthly video distributed throughout The Body Shop organization, was devoted to Boys' Town and what we could do there. The response was a joy. Everyone wanted to get involved in raising money and sponsoring boys, and from that moment onwards the International Boys' Town Trust more or less became an integral part of The Body Shop's extended family.*
>
> **—ANITA RODDICK**

Before you work on humor, heart, and audience participation, work on your base, your message. Get fanatical about it for a few years. *Then* add some of the three best "involvement" strategies: humor, heart stories, and audience participation exercises. These things are the gravy, not the potatoes.

All of these strategies go hand in hand with your development of the use of stories and storytelling.

Why Storytelling Is Important

Stories can be humorous, or heart stories, or just real-life examples.

Stories define nationalities and histories. Messages and morals are carried from generation to generation through stories: Robin Hood, the Wise Men following a star, Paul Revere and his heroic ride, a worldwide flood. They are the narrative lines we love; they trace our past to our present and point the way to our future.

Go back to Figure 1 and you will see that nothing is as important as the message. You will die a ghastly death up there if you have great stories, but have not first thought through your message and carefully defined exactly what you want the audience to remember.

If you have defined your message, then a humorous, or heart, story that happens to be a real-life example is a wonderful tool to sink that message into the hearts of the listener. Brilliant Superstars have taken years to first refine the message, *then* to use anecdotes that touch a deep, common chord. They play that chord through the delivery of the story.

> *One of the reasons* Chicken Soup . . . *is working is that the world is desperate for story. That is what the people in the speaking business do, they are in the business of storytelling. Masterful storytelling to help change lives from good to phenomenally good!*
> —MARK VICTOR HANSEN

How to Create Memorable Stories

To make your stories great, practice, keep the stories short and simple, and touch your own heart first and consider humor.

As you look at finding your stories, consider the criteria of the fore-master of the heart story, Norman Vincent Peale, for *Guideposts* magazine.

> *The main question we ask ourselves in selecting stories for* Guideposts *is: Is this story helpful? The experience related in the story or the wisdom gained by the storyteller must help the reader in some aspect of his or her life. Unless a story does that, it's not a* Guideposts *story.*
> —NORMAN VINCENT PEALE

Is Your Story Too Serious for Humor?

To make your story really memorable, add humor to it. Oh, your story is too serious? The best humor begins in the most horrific pain. Some of the funniest speakers I work with are POWs who have been tortured, rape victims, terrible accident survivors. Look for your humor in your pain.

Practice

The magical answer to a Superstar story is practice, practice, practice! Practice out loud, to real people. While practicing, make sure the story is more important than how good you look telling it. You want them to say, "What a great story, *it's* worth remembering!" not just "What a great storyteller *you are!*"

Stupendous Is Usually Short and Simple

> *Zig uses "down home" stories from his own Yazoo City, Mississippi, life. He says he speaks in a fast style of about 220 words a minute with "gusts of up to 550."*
> **—Dottie Walters**

In working with helping to select the *Chicken Soup for the Soul* stories on several projects, we have found the really fabulous stories are most often those that are very short. When you create a story, write the whole thing out. Go back and highlight what they must remember, those things that substantiate your message. Now cut the story in half! Leave those words that help make your point.

Touch Your Own Heart First

The most successful stories are the ones that make you, the teller, laugh or cry. If they touch you, they will touch the listener.

> *I have so many stories that move me out of 'Chicken Soup . . .'*
> *I can give you 10, but since I created it, I'd say Bobsy touches my heart the most . . .*

> **Bobsy**

> *The 26-year-old mother stared down at her son who was dying of terminal leukemia. Although her heart was filled with sadness, she also had a strong feeling of determination. Like any loving parent she wanted her son to grow up and fulfill all his dreams. Now that was no longer possible. The leukemia would see to that. But she still wanted her son's dreams to come true.*

She took her son's hand and asked, "Bopsy, did you ever think about what you wanted to be when you grew up? Did you ever dream and wish about what you would do with your life?"

"Mommy, I always wanted to be a fireman when I grew up."

Mom smiled back and said, "Let's see if we can make your wish come true." Later that day she went to her local fire department in Phoenix, Arizona, where she met Fireman Bob, who had a heart as big as Phoenix. She explained her son's final wish and asked if it might be possible to give her six-year-old son a ride around the block on a fire engine.

Fireman Bob said, "Look, we can do better than that. If you'll have your son ready at seven o'clock Wednesday morning, we'll make him an honorary fireman for the whole day. He can come down to the fire station, eat with us, go out on all the fire calls, the whole nine yards! And, if you'll give us his sizes, we'll get a real fire uniform made for him, with a real fire hat—not a toy one—with the emblem of the Phoenix Fire Department on it, a yellow slicker like we wear and rubber boots. They're all manufactured right here in Phoenix, so we can get them fast."

Three days later Fireman Bob picked up Bopsy, dressed him in his fire uniform and escorted him from his hospital bed to the waiting hook and ladder truck. Bopsy got to sit up on the back of the truck and help steer it back to the fire station. He was in heaven.

There were three fire calls in Phoenix that day and Bopsy got to go out on all three calls. He rode in the different fire engines, the paramedic's van and even the fire chief's car. He was also video-taped for the local news program.

Having his dream come true, with all the love and attention that was lavished upon him, so deeply touched Bopsy that he lived three months longer than any doctor thought possible.

One night all of his vital signs began to drop dramatically and the head nurse, who believed in the Hospice concept that no one should die alone, began to call the family members to the hospital. Then she remembered the day Bopsy had spent as a fireman, so she called the fire chief and asked if it would be possible to send a fireman in uniform to the hospital to be with Bopsy as he made his transition. The chief replied, "We can do better than that. We'll be there in five minutes. Will you please do me a favor? When you hear the sirens screaming and see the lights flashing, will you announce over the PA system that there is not a fire? It's just the fire department coming to see one of its finest members one more time. And will you open the window to his room? Thanks."

About five minutes later a hook and ladder truck arrived at the hospital, extended its ladder up to Bopsy's third floor open window and 14 firemen climbed up the ladder into Bopsy's room. With his mother's permission, they hugged him and held him and told him how much they loved him.

With his dying breath, Bopsy looked up at the fire chief and said, "Chief, am I really a fireman now?"

"Bopsy, you are," the chief said. With those words, Bopsy smiled and closed his eyes for the last time.

I go through the story, then I say, "What I think this teaches is that every one of us has a fireperson in him or her, and a person that has gone unfilled. You've got to figure out what that is, if you are young, old, black, white, male, female, you've got to go for it with gusto." This story carries me away. I have probably told that story a thousand times, and I cry every time. And when the story carries you away, it carries the audience.

—**MARK VICTOR HANSEN**

I've read perhaps 20,000 stories, putting 2000 of my favorites in about 20 books. So, if you read the Chicken Soup for the Soul *series, there are 2000 stories I love to tell. However, there are a few I tell more often than others.*

Like the Bobsy story of the little boy who had his dream come true and finish that story by saying, "Tonight you are going to be looking in the mirror and you will see two eyes looking back at you from the mirror. That is the Bobsy who lives in you. The little child whose dream hasn't come true yet. Just like they took care of Bobsy in Phoenix and made his dreams come true, you've got to take care of your dream. Nurture that child inside of you." The whole room gets goose bumps.

—**JACK CANFIELD**

"My Mama Used to Say . . ."

Lecturing at your audiences is often a bad way get the message home. But telling them how you learned a valuable lesson from some great person puts you in a much better position. This lets the listener know that you are humble and willing to learn from others, thus showing them an example they can following in listening to you. A masterful technique. Jim Rohn[4] uses Mr. Shoaf, Les Brown uses his Mamie Brown.

> *I listened to Jimmy [Jim Rohn] today. He is a master raconteur, and he does it so humbly that nobody catches the techniques he uses. I am told by those closest to Jim that although Mr. Shoaff did a good job in helping to get Jim on track, Jim actually uses Shoaff as the third-party endorsement. Jim uses Shoaff to teach everything. He is then able to talk to everyman.*
>
> *See, if I said, "Lilly tell me in last 5 years how many classes you've taken, show me how many books you've read, and let's go all the way back to when you were 18, so I can really beat up on you!"*
>
> *But Rohn tells the story of Shoaff talking to Rohn all those years ago, "Mr. Shoaff asked me, 'How much money have you saved in the last 5 years? Oh? Who sold you on that belief system? Whose philosophy were you following?'"*
>
> *The audiences gets it, yet they don't see how Jim is doing it. They don't see they have been touched by the master's hand. It is only now, this far along in my career, that I can appreciate the subtlety and brilliance of this masterful technique.*
>
> —MARK VICTOR HANSEN

They Have Style and Eloquence

Appearance is so often pushed as important, I found these results fascinating. Although appearance might easily fall under style, it was so

---

[4]Jim Rohn is a Superstar whom I will profile in future volumes.

rarely mentioned as a reason for audiences thinking a speaker was one of the greats, that I am not covering it in this book. Interesting to note that it was only mentioned with comments like, ". . . she was good looking *besides* . . ." or "a handsome man *that gave us.* . . ." For more on appearance, see the prequel to this book, *Secrets of Successful Speakers: How You Can Motivate, Captivate, and Persuade* (McGraw-Hill).

Becoming a Speaker of Style, Charisma, Eloquence

> *I learned how to tell a story better, I learned how to interject humor, I learned how to take a pause for timing, I learned how to modulate my voice, to use overheads, to tell a joke, use my body language, and to use neurolinguistic programming. All of that is great if I am doing it to help me reach my audience better. But if I am doing it because it is going to aggrandize Jack Canfield, then I think I have the focus on the wrong place.*
> —JACK CANFIELD

So, with the appropriate warning eloquently given by Jack, after you have worked for years on your "essence," and your "message," how can you work your style? Style, presence, charisma are all progeny of your passion, compassion, and purpose. They radiate confidence.

Having confidence and charisma just means you have done your homework, and done it again, and again! Then you just relax, love the

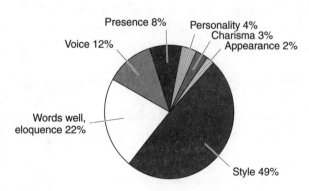

Figure 10. Qualities of Superstars Survey Results: Style, Charisma, Eloquence, and Voice

Presence 8%
Personality 4%
Charisma 3%
Appearance 2%
Voice 12%
Words well, eloquence 22%
Style 49%

audience, and work to help them. If you do, they just don't care if you make mistakes. In fact, they love you for them.

The father of the motivational movement, Dr. Peale, was still going strong in his 90s and beloved on the platform. Yet, in the middle of a story he would occasionally lose his place. But he was always able to make a joke about it, and everyone would have a hearty laugh, and he would continue on and be even more fascinating.

> *We are so afraid that people are going to judge us for being less than perfect. Everyone has had the experience of a speaker who goes off on a tangent and says, "Oh my God, where was I? What point was I making?" The audience starts to yell back, "You were talking about your wife . . . it was that vacation in Hawaii. . . ." "Oh, that's right. . . ." Everyone instantly bonds to you and loves you more because they know you're a human being.*
> —JACK CANFIELD

A Way with Words

Not all great speakers are gifted with words like Maya Angelou or Winston Churchill. If your message is passionately given from the heart, with compassion, with a well-defined purpose, and to the right audience, it will succeed, regardless of how well you craft your words.

However, we forgive many faults in those around us if they are humorous or eloquent.

If after you have done all the steps we have discussed, my, oh my, what magic you can create if you take the time to study the beauty of words. Study how they can combine them like poetry! How? Study poetry. Read the masters at crafting words: Shakespeare, Maya Angelou, Churchill, Confucius. As Earl Nightingale said, "You become what you think about." Read and rejoice in poetry, and you will begin to speak and create your own talks with eloquent words and brevity— the soul of wit.

> *When Maya Angelou finished speaking, we were all in love with her, each other and ourselves. I was aware that I had just seen words used in a way I never had before. Every line she uttered*

seemed like poetry, using only the essential words spoken in a dramatic and beautiful way, evoking deep empathic responses in all of us. I left the auditorium that night full of awe and wonder for the fullness and the mystery of life.

I went home and sat in front of my computer and wrote a what-seemed-to-me a very moving poem to the love of my life telling her what a phenomenal woman she was. You need to know that I do not usually write poetry, much less show it to anyone, but this phenomenal woman—Maya Angelou—had awakened a shameless poet inside of me, one that could now express love and appreciation more clearly on paper than ever before. To this day it stands out as one of those mountain top moments that reminded me once again how profoundly we can all impact each other with our messages as speakers—a message for which I will always be grateful.

A week later I also noticed that my speaking from the platform had become more impassioned. My heart and soul were even more present than before. It was as if I were imbuing each word that left my mouth with a vibration of love and joy and wonder. My audiences noticed it, too. I received a lot of feedback about how much more dynamic and passionate I had become. I only hope that I am now doing a little more for my audiences of what Maya Angelou did for me.

—JACK CANFIELD

Poetry allows people to find the humor in life, the beauty in sadness.

—MAYA ANGELOU

Several of the other speakers had us talking to the people next to us and performing various actions that I found a bit tedious and even embarrassing—as though it was vital to get us up and active and laughing. Not Deepak. He just started to talk, and what he had to say was so mesmerizing, so exciting, that you couldn't hear a sound other than his voice. The audience was perfectly quiet, and he finished after an hour to a storm of clapping. His message was mov-

ing and exciting, and his delivery was a real testament to the power of words and words alone—not razzmatazz, no gimmicks, no let's-meet-our-neighbor. Just words.
—MARG MCALISTER, SPEAKER AND AUTHOR

Winston Churchill's love of, and fascination with, the English language successfully carried him through his speeches and writings. His words carried conviction and were given with eloquence, lasting eloquence. Arguably, his speeches are quoted more often by speech coaches than any other orator.

Churchill himself was well aware of the importance of imagery, metaphor, pithiness, idiom, colloquialism, antithesis, and epigram in his speaking and writing.

Especially important are his observations that "all the speeches of great English rhetoricians—except when addressing highly cultured audiences—display a uniform preference for short, homely words of common usage" and "the influence exercised over the human mind by apt analogies is and has always been immense. Whether they translate an established truth into simple language or whether they adventurously aspire to reveal the unknown, they are among the most formidable weapons of the rhetorician."
—WOLFGANG MIEDER, PROFESSOR, UNIVERSITY
OF VERMONT, AUTHOR OF *OF POLITICS AND PROVERBS*

Voice

I went to hear Earl Nightingale speak in person as often as he appeared in Los Angeles. He stood quite still as he spoke, no matter how big the crowd. Then that magical deep voice lifted our minds up into the air as he told us stories and gave us hope and courage.
—DOTTIE WALTERS

Some speakers are gifted with masterful voices; be grateful if you are one of those. Yet many more have strained and difficult voices that also work magic. Helen Keller was extremely difficult to understand, but she was one of the most sought-after, highest-paid speakers of her day.

If your voice is not a strong point, see a vocal coach, it can be changed. If you tend to get a hoarse throat, you *must* see a vocal coach. You are not using your voice correctly. You should be able to speak for hours, without strain. See *Secrets of Successful Speakers: How You Can Motivate, Captivate, and Persuade* (McGraw-Hill).

Tips on Style and Eloquence

If you ask 20 great speakers for their advice on speaking, you will get thousands of great ideas . . . some conflicting! Here are a few on acquiring style and eloquence:

> *When someone asks me what they need to give a talk, I tell them to keep it funny, keep it short, keep it passionate, and root it in your own experiences. Do slides, don't do PowerPoint. Never send your slides in advance. Know your audience—its age, its interests, and expectations. And last and probably least—check out the auditorium first; make sure you can see over the lectern! [Anita is short.]*
> —ANITA RODDICK

Movements and Gestures

I have heard it repeated—repeatedly—that you *must* move and gesture naturally every so many seconds. Nonsense!! You must be natural, which means you must not even *think* it. If you think about being natural, you will be incredibly *unnatural!*

Yes you say, but the great orators, move, and gesture, and have great eye contact! That is what makes a great speaker.

Really? Great eye contact, like Helen Keller? A top professional speaker of her day? Great movement like Christopher Reeve, whose quiet, unmoving body is moving the spirits of millions?

Yes, many great Superstar speakers move back and forth around the stage with a studied abandon. Zig Ziglar has movement down to a science. He moves every so many seconds to keep the audience attention. He alternates positions, standing, squatting, leaning. Yet, Norman Vincent

Peale always stood in a stationary position beside the lectern and brought the highest of decorum to the presentation. He was a masterful storyteller whose strength was in the "word pictures" he drew in the mind's eye and in hand gestures. They gave energy and imagery to his stories.

Work on *your* "connection" to meet the need of your listener; your own *natural* gestures will follow.

To have style, charisma, and eloquence, first and foremost consider the message you hope will linger, last, and transform the listener. With that uppermost in your mind, you will be charismatic!

6

Qualities and Creation of Superstar Messages and Content

As should be very clear by now, the message should be your first concern, before humor, stories, style, and eloquence. This chapter discusses the many qualities of the Superstar messages and helps you create your own.

Inspiring, motivational speakers are remembered not *just* because they were funny or eloquent or had style, but primarily and principally because the *message* and ideas caused a change in their listeners' actions and attitudes.

Figure 11 shows which qualities of "message" are most important. Note the most important are those which relate what the audience members took away from the talk, what they were motivated to do, what change they made in their lives.

Understanding what is actually being retained will help you create a talk that will be remembered.

I heard Stephen Covey in San Diego and was totally impressed by his opening. He told the audience that he is a "content speaker," that he was not there to entertain us. I was there to learn, not be entertained, so his statement really got my attention. It made me realize what is

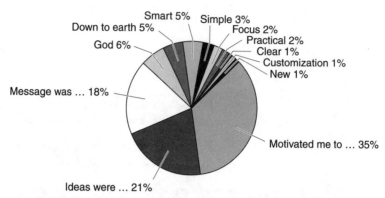

Figure 11. Qualities of Superstars Survey Results: Message and Content

> *really important—content!—and made me want to be more like*
> *him. And, as it turned out, he was pretty entertaining too!*
> —ROBERT MACPHEE, RELATIONSYSTEMS
>   CONSULTING

Creating Your Own Superstar Message!

Now we are ready to create the speech. As you have seen, we must create a message that will create change. Let's work on the steps, ideas, and questions to ask yourself that will help you decide what change you want to create.

Six Essentials Steps in Creating Your Speech

1. Decide what you are passionate about.
2. Become an expert in that subject.
3. Become a living example of the message.
4. Find those aspects of your audience about which you can feel driving compassion.
5. Decide what your presentation must accomplish.
6. Decide what three things your listeners must remember from your talk one year from now.

That's it. Those six steps. We have talked about the first four steps; now we'll talk about the last two.

What Must Your Presentation Accomplish? Change!

Some of us will do our jobs well and some will not, but we will be judged by only one thing—the result.
—VINCE LOMBARDI, SR.

Your talk must create a change in the listeners' actions or attitudes. Years later a Superstar talk is considered valuable:

- Because his/her message and/or content was . . .
- Because of the idea/s and wisdom, which was . . .
- Because I was motivated, inspired, convinced to . . .

The mark of a good speaker, a Superstar, is not how much the audience laughed, how much they listened, how much they learned . . . but how much they changed their thoughts and actions after hearing your presentation.

As you create your own message, start with the end in mind. What change do you want to create in your listeners?

When I heard Tony Robbins speak regarding his book Awaken The Giant Within, he emphasized "the new identity reference" principle. When you move to a new town, new job, or you are personally going through a "metamorphosis" that you can actually "re-invent yourself" . . . get a new "identity reference." Change your attitudes, behavior, appearance or name—become "new and improved."

At the time, I was going through some personal crisis, survived a business partner embezzling our business profits and was overweight. Tony Robbins was all I needed to hear that day! I reorganized my business plan, joined Toastmasters and then The National Speakers Association. With my first name "Joli" being French for "pretty," I changed my last name to "Andre," which is

French for Andrew meaning: "Strong." I began exercising and eating better, and lost 30 pounds. I cut my long frosted hair and colored it red. I feel fabulous,

> —JOLI ANDRE, SPEAKER AND AUTHOR, PRESIDENT OF
> POLISHED PROFESSIONALS

The first time I heard Anita Roddick speak, I was immediately moved to action. Ms. Roddick's company, which she founded, The Body Shop, is committed to making a difference on the planet. Her talks are not about her products; rather they are about the contributions that her company makes.

Anita inspired me to donate profits from my company, Golden Gate International Speakers Bureau, from day 1 and really drove home for me that, "anyone can give" even if it is "only time" and "there is no time to waste."

> —LAURA FENAMORE, PRESIDENT, GOLDEN GATE
> INTERNATIONAL SPEAKERS BUREAU

The most motivational speaker I ever heard was Dottie Walters. She was motivational in the truest sense of the word: her words made me actually do something. As a result of hearing her speak, and by using the clear-cut proven methods she outlined, I transformed my entertainment program into a presentation on creativity methods, assembled a demo video, and prepared my first back-of-room products. That's a lot of motivation!

> —TOM OGDEN, MAGICIAN, AUTHOR,
> AND CREATIVITY EXPERT

Define the Purpose,
Define the Change You Will Create

I must make each one see that in order to do something they have never done, you've got to be someone you have never been.

The audience will have a look on their face that asks, "What's in this for me? Why are you telling me this? What value does this have for me? How does/will this make a difference in my life personally? Professionally? Spiritually?"

> —LES BROWN

> *When I go in there, I just don't want to make them a better man-*
> *ager or better salesperson, I want to make them a better wife or*
> *husband, mother, father. I don't believe you can separate success*
> *professionally, spiritually, and socially. I think that all three of*
> *them have to enjoy success for you to really truly be a positive aspect*
> *for an audience.*
> —Lou Holtz

> *I began with a philosophy which was too many speakers are too*
> *shallow, they know very little, so they dress it up in stories. You may*
> *pass the entertainment test, but can you pass the note test? How*
> *many notes were taken at the end of the talk?*
> —Brian Tracy

First Create Your Mission Statement

So, your talk must create change. Define the purpose of that change in one clear concise sentence.

Wait, Lilly! You don't understand. I give just "informative" talks.

Rubbish. There is no such thing as "just an informative talk." After you give them the "information," then what? You must motivate them to do something with it!

Your purpose will be the seed from which the rest of your incredible talk will grow. If that sentence is weak, the whole talk will be weak. Creating a strong mission statement will go a long way to make your talk one of those that is timeless. It often takes many weeks to think through the purpose and mission and refine your defining! These questions will be a good place for you to start in creating that one clear sentence.

- After they hear my speech, what must they walk out and do differently?
- After they hear my speech, what must they walk out and feel differently?
- After they hear my speech, what must they walk out and know differently?
- How will the information you are giving them make a difference in their lives personally? Professionally? Spiritually?

What Must They Remember?

I would love to spend time with you, working on ways to make your presentation fantastic. But let me save you at least $1,000 in my consulting fees. Before you come to talk to me, first define your mission statement, then figure out what three things the audience must remember a year after they hear you.

"Wait! I have a ton of stuff they must remember!"

Too bad. They won't. On average they remember 10 percent from a talk. So, take control. What 10 percent must they remember about your talk? Think of three things. Once you work that out, the rest is easy!

> *Look at Les Brown, who I think is probably the best motivator in America. Les gets up there, and gives a historical talk, very emotional, very intense, giving powerful mental messages like: "It ain't over 'til I win! If you want to achieve something, you must become something more. If you want to earn more, learn more."*
>
> *These are things that we know, but the talk is built around critical success ideas that you write down and think about. Even though most of his talk is just pure emotion, it's built around key ideas.*
> —BRIAN TRACY

Use Words That They Will Remember for Years: Themes

Who said this . . .

We shall not flag or fail.
We shall go on to the end.
We shall fight in France.
We shall fight on the seas and oceans.
We shall fight with growing confidence and growing strength in the air.
We shall defend our island, whatever the cost may be.
We shall fight on the beaches.
We shall fight on the landing grounds.
We shall fight in the fields and in the streets.

We shall fight in the hills.
We shall never surrender!

Winston Churchill.[1] Were you even alive during World War II? Yet, there is very little chance that you have not heard reference to that speech. Why? Why that speech? He said tons of others we don't quote. It wasn't just the times; we have been through other horrible wars since. What great speech do you remember from the Vietnam War? The Persian Gulf War?

Right. Me neither!

Here is the big secret! That message has been remembered for the last 50 years, because . . . he made it so easy we *can* remember it! Things are remembered when they are easy to remember.

When Churchill found a theme that made impact, he used it over and over in many of his speeches. For instance, you might remember his saying, "This was their finest hour."[2] France had fallen. He needed the Britons to gird their loins, and the Commonwealth and the United States to be assured that Great Britain would not fall. The core and mission of the "we shall fight" and "finest hour" speeches are the same; he just uses new words to send the message into the soul.

> *Let us therefore brace ourselves to our duties, and so bear ourselves that, if the British Empire and Commonwealth last for a thousand years, men will still say, "This was their finest hour."*
> —SIR WINSTON CHURCHILL

Repeat What Must Be Remembered

Repetition insures that what must be remembered, will be remembered. It also creates a sense of poetry, which captures the attention of the heart and mind. Repeating a point six times or more increases the probability of its being remembered from 10 percent to 90 percent!

---

[1] Excerpt from speech given by Winston Churchill to the House of Commons on Dunkirk, "We Shall Fight on the Beaches," June 4, 1940.

[2] Excerpt from speech given by Winston Churchill to the House of Commons as the the Battle of Britain began, June 18, 1940.

Your audience is a group of minds. The mind is a brilliant computer, much grander, smarter, faster than anything man has yet created. Those brilliant minds will jump to where you point them for about a nanosecond. Then they are off on a thought of their own. As you attempt to capture their thoughts, think of herding cats. You must be clear and firm to get them all corralled. An often repeated theme is a great wrangler of minds!

Creating the Speech

Once you have the mission, and your three main points, you are almost done! That was the hard part. Just in case you whizzed through it, trust me, you'll come back to it soon if you want Superstar results.

But, assuming you did the hard part, just put it into this 25-second format.

Intro: Purpose, and three things they must remember to accomplish the purpose (about 5 seconds total).

Body: Thing 1 with a one-sentence explanation; thing 2 with a one-sentence explanation; thing 3 with a one-sentence explanation (about 15 seconds total).

Conclusion: Purpose and three things they must remember to accomplish the purpose, with a call to action (about 5 seconds total).

STOP! Don't skip the exercise above. Until you can create your talk in this 25-second format, *you are going to confuse and bore your audience.*

I know, I know. You want the drama, the tears, the laughter, the standing ovations, the great ad-libs, the terrific stories, like those Superstars! Those Superstars first baked the bread, then added the jam years later. Ever eat jam all by itself? OK in tiny doses, doesn't make much of a meal. Frankly, disgusting. The format above is how you will create a very tasty bread.

Once you are able to do it in the short version above, you can expand it like this:

Intro: Purpose and three things they must remember to accomplish the purpose (add as time permits: humor, quote, poem, story and/or visual that makes your point).

Body: Thing 1 with a one-sentence explanation.
- Three things about this they need to remember.
- Humor story that makes one of these points.
- Heart story that makes one of these points.
- Visual aid that makes one of these points.
- Audience participation exercise that makes one of these points.
- RECAP: Purpose, three things they must remember to accomplish the purpose.

Body: Thing 2 with a one-sentence explanation.
- Three things about this they need to remember.
- Humor story that makes one of these points.
- Heart story that makes one of these points.
- Visual aid that makes one of these points.
- Audience participation exercise that makes one of these points.
- RECAP: Purpose, three things they must remember to accomplish the purpose.

Body: Thing 3 with a one-sentence explanation
- Three things about this they need to remember.
- Humor story that makes one of these points.
- Heart story that makes one of these points.
- Visual aid that makes one of these points.
- Audience participation exercise that makes one of these points.
- RECAP: Purpose, three things they must remember to accomplish the purpose.

Conclusion: Purpose and three things they must remember to accomplish the purpose, with a call to action.

That format can take you through a full-day presentation. You just add more information to support the points they must remember. Or, add another story, or an audience participation exercise that helps them remember, understand, and apply the "things" you want them to remember.

Write It Out First

> *If I really want to know how I feel about a thing, I write about it.*[3]
> —MAYA ANGELOU

You must, must, must write out your talk. Preferably on a computer that has an "outlining" function. It will help you create and arrange with ease and creativity.

It takes time.

> *When I'm preparing a speech, I have a whole stack of paper, a pair of scissors, some glue. Also about 20 books I want to make reference to, the biggest dissenting thinkers, that sort of thing. Then I cut and paste. I work for hours on the opening and hours on the end. Then I put everything into slides.*
> —ANITA RODDICK

> *As a young writer, I've always tried to mimic the writing of someone I've admired in hopes to reach their level of excellence.*
>
> *Reading pieces from Dr. Maya Angelou has guided me to realize that it is not someone else's level of writing I must achieve, but my own. So now when I write, my poetry carries a more significant meaning, it's beyond words on paper, it's a smile, a breath of fresh air, joy, encouragement, tears, it's concurring fears, believing in your dreams.*
> —TANGELA WILLIAMS, SENIOR, SOCIOLOGY/POLITICAL SCIENCE, ILLINOIS STATE UNIVERSITY

Prepare Four Times the Material You Will Need

To be great up there you must be an expert. Prepare four times the amount of material and research you will need. Once you have done that research, you will be in the position to cut the material down to be short and simple. See more on becoming an expert later in this chapter.

---

[3]Quoted by Patti Thorn, in "Maya's Way: Maya Angelou's Zest for Life Continues to Fuel Her Creative Fire," *Denver Rocky Mountain News,* November 23, 1997, p. 1E.

Keep It Short

Norman Vincent Peale said to me, "I remember a young fellow who wanted me to advise him on how to be a good speaker! I told him, 'Be interesting, be enthusiastic . . . and don't talk too much!'" In other words, the less you say, the better chance they will have to remember it. Besides, they don't learn while you are talking, they learn while they are thinking. If you have been profound, they will begin to *think*. If you are still talking, they just ignore your new words. So, don't talk so much! It is very eloquent.

Keep It Simple to Make It Memorable

Mark Victor Hansen is a wonderful example of using "simple." He uses simple, easy words, in a happy unsophisticated manner. Much like Will Rogers with his simple countryfied words and thoughts, Mark seems very elementary. Then, just every so often these great presenters throw in concepts and verbiage that "punch" you. I would hear a word, and think, "Oh, come on, Mark! You made that up!" I would look it up in the dictionary, and son of a gun, it was right there!

That is the brilliance of "simple" speakers. They are brilliant enough to make it simple.

Lesson? Create speeches so simple that a bunch of it *can* be remembered; then they *will* be remembered.

> *There is no objection to anything being said in plain English, or even plainer, and the Government will do their utmost to conform to any standard which may be set in the course of the debate. But no one need be mealy-mouthed in debate, and no one should be chicken-hearted in voting.*
> —SIR WINSTON CHURCHILL, SPEECH TO THE
> HOUSE OF COMMONS, JANUARY 27, 1942

> *I was first inspired by the great Norman Vincent Peale, who became one of my close friends. Decades ago, following the death of my daughter, he urged me to devote my talents to speaking in the field of drug abuse prevention. The wonderful stories in his books and speeches have been an inspiration to me to make my serious points through illustrative anecdotes.*

Dr. Peale reminded me that the Bible's greatest sermons were parables, generally about everyday people whose lives were changed by faith. His words continue to inspire me with his warmth and understanding.

I will never forget the tremendous moment when he was called upon to speak at an imposing formal funeral that was presided over by high-ranking priests and archbishops from the Catholic church. The strict liturgy and reading of Latin words was dramatically altered by the simple, plain, heart-spoken words of Dr. Peale, who brought the high-sounding ceremony down to earth with his warmth and humanity.

—ART LINKLETTER, TV STAR, AUTHOR, AND LECTURER

First Make It Easy For You

I am always amazed that speakers want me to help them create a memorable talk, but they can't remember it themselves!

Just think of little ways to help you remember it—without notes—and you will be amazed at the neat little things you will come up with to help the audience remember.

One of my favorite and time-honored memory tools is the acrostic (for many others see *Secrets of Successful Speakers—How You Can Motivate, Captivate, and Persuade* (McGraw Hill). I love to help speakers come up with them.

For instance, I did one for Martha Campbell Pullen, international magazine publisher and national PBS television host, with whom I wrote, *You Can Make Money From Your Hobby: Building a Business Doing What You Love.* Martha is a Baptist, that is, with a really big *B.* After she answered my question, "In what do you base your business success?" I was able to create GRACE:

God. First in all things.

Resilience. Get up when you're down.

Action. It is not enough to dream, wake up and work at it!

Creativity. Allow the unusual to happen.

Enthusiasm. Allow the spirit of excitement to fill yourself and spread to your friends.

That is about 25 seconds of material. You now understand exactly what Martha is about, and what the talk will be about. After you have heard the message repeated six times: verbally, in an overhead, in a "fill-in-the-blank workbook," as a discussion with two other audience members, you would *really* remember it.

Superstars are brilliant enough to make their messages simple and short. Audience members don't learn while you are talking; they learn while they are thinking. They'll think better, and listen better, if you give them long, quiet pauses. Besides, the human mind doesn't remember much about speeches . . . except the easy, often-repeated stuff. So, make what you want your audience to remember easy, and repeat it often. Create speeches so simple that they *can* be remembered, then they *will* be remembered. Memorable talks are those that are easily remembered!

Finding Great Material and Becoming an Expert

As you work to become an expert, you will find great material and great new ideas! This section will help you find out where experts find knowledge, from on-line subscription-based database services, to "lifting" other people's material. (See *Speak and Grow Rich* by Dottie and Lilly Walters)

Getting New Great Ideas

I do a tremendous amount of reading, five or six books a week, in addition to the daily papers and magazines. I subscribe to some esoteric journals and newsletters. I never know where I am going to find an idea.
   —EARL NIGHTINGALE (*SUCCESS* MAGAZINE, JUNE 1983)

If you are to become a Superstar speaker, you will need to come up with great new ideas.

I asked Jack Canfield how they came up with one of the greatest ideas that has come into our industry, the title *Chicken Soup for the Soul.*

> *When the book was almost completed, we realized we did not have a title. Mark and I decided to use two different forms of receptive meditation to get the title. Mark would go to bed each night repeating the phrase "mega best-selling title" several hundred times. In the morning he would awaken with possible titles.*
>
> *I used a different method, I simply asked God to give us a title that would help us reach the greatest numbers of people. On the third day, the words chicken soup were written on a screen in my mind. As I contemplated its meaning, I remembered that my parents and grandparents always fed us chicken soup when we were sick. As I thought about it more, I realized it wasn't so much that our bodies were sick, but that our souls were sick. Within the hour the title wrote itself on that screen,* Chicken Soup for the Soul.
>
> —JACK CANFIELD

Nothing New on the Face of the Earth

Before you panic that you don't have hours and hours of brand-new, never-been-heard-by-anyone-before material, remember from my research results that new material really was not much of an issue.

Besides, even "new material" is usually old material delivered in a new light. Most of the wonderful new technologies we have are using the same old mathematics used by ancient genius, but with new application and understandings. That's what *you* bring to the platform: new enthusiasms, new applications, new insights, and motivation to actually apply the concepts in someone's life.

In the 1960s Earl Nightingale made famous, "You become what you think about." It was in his mega best-selling books, his records. Wow! What a great "new" idea. Yet I seem to remember the Bible telling us in Proverbs 23-7, "As a man thinks, so he shall become." But Earl brought such new excitement to this seasoned wisdom that he helped it become a catchphrase for this century. You can do as well with wisdoms that have impacted and changed your life.

True genius resides in the capacity for revaluation of uncertain, hazardous, and conflicting information.
—Sir Winston Churchill

In addition, many words of wisdom must be heard over and over before they finally "catch." Be confident that material, even though it is often-heard advice, can be profound. If it is usable to you, it will be to others.

Know the Audience and the Material

To be an expert, you need to explore your topic fully. You have also to explore the needs of the audience.

Ask those you are presenting for some in-depth questions. We send out a preprogram questionnaire. See a sample in *Secrets of Successful Speakers: How You Can Motivate, Captivate, and Persuade* (McGraw Hill).

Once you have done your research on the audience needs, you can look for the appropriate phrases, words, emphasis, and emotions, be it humor, laughter, tears. What story would be most appropriate to make a difference in their lives?

Understand as a communicator, what is the right speech, what is the right story, for this occasion that can drive the point home, that can help them to begin to see themselves in their circumstance differently.
—Les Brown

Become an Expert! Research!

The best way to find impactful, appropriate material is to become an expert! To become an expert, research! Research the audience, research their industry, research key players on their teams.

I read every book I can possibly get on success. I purchase 5 to 10 books each week and I subscribe to about 30 different magazines. I organize my time and my life so that I read and take notes about 3 hours per day, 7 days a week, 365 days a year. On some days, I get in 5, 6, and 7 hours of reading and note taking.

> *Today, as a result of more than 20 years of work, I have developed enough seminar materials so that I can speak for more than 20 days without repeating myself.*
>
> *In real estate the three secrets are location, location, and location; in speaking it is preparation, preparation, and preparation.*
>
> *In my opinion, a speaker needs to know 100 words for every word he or she uses in a talk. If the speaker has not done the many, many hours of research and study, the audience will know very quickly that the speaker is shallow and poorly informed.*
> **—BRIAN TRACY**

Be on the lookout for new material. Save material worth sharing and practice bringing the material to life with a hint of a gesture or a change in voice. A good experience is a treasure waiting to be discovered.

You must collect all material that strikes you as meaningful or humorous as it occurs. To keep it for use in your presentations, always carry a little notebook with you; the palest pencil notation is better than the best memory. As life goes on around you, look for the meanings and messages and the funny side. Keep asking yourself:

- What key learning point can I convey with this incident?
- Write down the message you imagine from the event before you capture the story! You can work backwards to re-create it later.
- Does the message warrant the time required to tell it?
- Will others be able to visualize the scene?
- Will they be able to relate to it?
- Develop transitions ("Recently, I had a chance to experience . . . ") and ways to set the scene ("It was.., and I was just . . . ").

Using Other People's Material

Using other people's material is done, and often. Using other people's tried-and-true material is the way every great speaker in history has grown. It is also the way millions of others have "died on the platform." If you use it, credit it, or be instantly *dis*credited.

You will find examples of great stories and anecdotes in books, such as the *Chicken Soup for the Soul* series, the *Complete Speakers and Toastmasters Library, Speakers Sourcebook* and *Speakers Sourcebook II,* and many others. This material is perfect for the novice business presenter or the presenter who must give a presentation only one time, then go back to their "real" job.

Credit the Source!

Using others' material in nonprofessional presentations is not a problem, as long as you *give credit.* If you are getting paid to give your presentations, credit the source and get the author's permission before you lift a story.

Either way, lifting without crediting is stealing.

If someone is sitting there who heard it before, and knows you are stealing the material, you lose all credibility. They won't hear another word you say.

Reading a wonderful story will often remind you of an actual experience you had that was similar, and you won't have to lift other's stories at all.

When You Don't Know the Source

As a credible expert, you need to know who said what. But sometimes the original source is lost in obscurity and you just can't figure out who it belongs to.

The Internet is making things ever worse. I get wonderful material sent to me daily, with no attribution to the source or the author. Very frustrating. Worse, when a speaker says something often, it gets repeated as "theirs." My mother often says, "Bill Marriott says 'Failure? I never encountered it. All I met were temporary setbacks.' " I have never heard her say that without crediting Bill. Yet I have often seen it attributed, much to her frustration, to Mom!

Do your best to credit the source, the real source. When you can't, acknowledge it with a line like, "As a wise person once said . . ." or "I wish I knew who it was that said . . ."

When People Lift Your Material: Scarcity Consciousness

If your material is good, people are going to repeat it. If you are lucky, they will credit you. Consider it a compliment and don't waste time complaining.

When I was gathering stories for this book, I had one speaker tell me, "I can't allow you to tell my story. Others will try to repeat it, not telling it as well as I do!" Interesting that of the top 50 Superstars whom I have profiled so far, none had this attitude. Besides, if that is the last story you ever have, you are in trouble anyway.

> *One of the big things in the National Speakers Association is to say, "I don't want to put my signature story in your book. When I go to tell it, people will have already heard it!"*
>
> *The reality is, people come up to me and say, "You're going to tell that Bobsy story, aren't you? . . . You're going to tell that Markita Andrews story, aren't you? . . . You're going to tell that puppy story aren't you?" They want to hear it again.*
>
> *Why do you go to a James Taylor concert? You've heard all of his songs on his records. You want to get close to the energy and feel the charisma of it.*
>
> *I think most people have a "scarcity consciousness," where they are afraid to let go of anything. They think it's the only great story they are ever going to have in their life. Ken Blanchard once said to me, "If people are afraid that someone is going steal their idea, that is a reflection of low self-esteem, because it implies they are only going to have one good idea in their life." The same is true with stories.*
>
> **—JACK CANFIELD**

> *Nature is lavish and abundant through these laws and that in fact if you truly tune into the spiritual laws that would be a solution for you to get out of poverty. Nature is truly abundant. Every seed is the promise of thousands of forests. If we follow how nature expresses herself, we would also be able to create an abundance in our personal lives that nature creates. Look at the magnificence, extravagance and lavishness of the Universal Mind as it imagines the cosmos into existence.*
>
> **—DR. DEEPAK CHOPRA**

> *People are always coming up to me and asking me if they can have permission to quote from my programs in their own work. I always tell them that anything that they hear from me can be considered*

"public domain." I give them my enthusiastic permission and encouragement to take any of my ideas or concepts and use them to help other people, with or without attribution.

Some people are very jealous of their material and insist that no one use their ideas without permission, if at all. I take exactly the opposite viewpoint. I base my life on a philosophy of abundance. I encourage everybody and anybody to take anything of mine that they can use and share it with anyone who it can help.

If our major purpose in life is to help other people to be happier and more successful as the result of our teaching, then I believe that we are duty bound to encourage everyone, everywhere, to take our ideas and spread them freely wherever they can do some good.

—BRIAN TRACY

As you work to become an expert, you will find great material and great new ideas! The best material comes when you also research the audience as well as the subject.

There is nothing new on the face of the earth. Be confident that material, even though it is often-heard advice, can be profound. If it is usable to you, it will be to others. It may be the gem that finally catches in someone's heart that helps turn that person's life into new and better directions.

Your fans can only hear your story so many times before they need new material. Don't worry. When you look for new material that makes you and others laugh, think or take action, you will find all you need to replace those that others lift. Besides, by the time it is being repeated that much, it is time for you to get new stuff. In case you ever want to tell my story, *please*, feel free. As P. T. Barnum said, "Just spell my name right!"

Messages That Return to the Spirit

Talking about God in your speeches has been taboo for the past 30 years. Today I see us circling back; it is a powerful trend of those at the top of the speaking industry. A majority are talking about "a Higher Power." Some, like Norman Vincent Peale, Mark Victor Hansen, and Jack Canfield, call it just that, "a Higher Power." Some, like Zig Ziglar and Elizabeth Dole, enjoin the Christian doctrine. But all point to the spirit and a Higher Power as the source of their success, and they suggest that their audiences do the same.

> *[I read] Norman Vincent Peale's* The Power Of Positive Thinking *cover to cover. I read the book two pages at a time so that I could absorb each vignette separately and benefit fully from each one. Even though Norman Vincent Peale always refers to Jesus Christ and even though I am Jewish, I substituted the words Jesus Christ in my mind with the word God. That made it work for me and showed me that his writings could be applicable to any religion.*
>
> *This concept of providing yourself with positive thoughts that can take the place of negative ones is powerful. In addition, this idea of living with faith, the belief in the good will of our Creator, has a power much stronger than any other good advice I have heard or read.*
>
> *When I read Norman Vincent Peale, he said that faith has the power to make great changes in people. After I started to put that idea into practice, I developed a strong relationship with God that continues to help me as I struggle through the problems of daily life. Because he once suggested to take God as a business partner, I decided to take Him as a life partner. It is amazing how helpful it is to have God to work with every day.*
>
> —DR. SALLY GOLDBERG, PROFESSOR OF EARLY
> CHILDHOOD EDUCATION, AUTHOR, SPEAKER

In creating your own Superstar message, remember, there is no such thing as just an informative talk. If you want to "inform," then define the purpose of the change your information will create. The worth of a speaker must be measured years after the speech, by the change the words created in the actions and attitudes of the those whose lives they have touched. The human mind just doesn't remember much about speeches except the easy, often-repeated stuff. Take control, decide what three things your audience must remember a year after they hear your talk.

Be an expert on your subject. The search for expertise goes on every moment of your life.

7

Putting It on the Platform!

Now you are ready to take these Superstars qualities and put them on the platform! How do you appear natural and unrehearsed? How do you overcome stage fright? This chapter shows you.

Appearing Unrehearsed

How? By an incredible amount of practice and rehearsal. Rehearse, out loud, until your talk is second nature. Literally.

In the first week that good comedians work on a new piece, they will often tell it 70 times to anyone who will listen. During this process they shorten and sharpen. That witty ad-lib you hear great entertainers throw out is often the same one they have used for decades. Being natural takes a great deal of unnatural practicing, preparation, and practice.

> *After hearing Elizabeth Dole speaking at the Republican National Convention, I was humbled. I had heard that she was a perfectionist in her presentations—practicing over and over, polishing and perfecting. But the way she did her "Dole Stroll" made me committed to more perfection in my own presentations. My family and friends say I should "lighten up" and relax more before a program. Instead, I now realize that my obsessing, practicing, and perfecting of my craft is a good thing. Obsessive preparation enables me to be so "ready" that I can mingle and work with the audience in a relaxed manner.*

Yes, Mrs. Dole is my hero in the performance category—for the way she's feminine, strong, personable, and perfectionist.
   —CONNIE MERRITT, SPEAKER, AUTHOR, FORMER
   NURSE

They pay a speaker 10, 20, 50 times what they pay a teacher. There is an enormous difference between carrying a tune when you run the lawn mover and Pavarotti. The difference is immense in terms of preparation and practice.

Most people seem to think I just decided to make a talk last week, and here I am. I tell everyone that asks me about getting into this business, to "read Speak and Grow Rich[1] *and* Secrets of Successful Speakers.[2] *I have read them from cover to cover and I recommend to run, don't walk for those two books. If you need more advice after you read those two books, call me." It takes almost as much time to become a brain surgeon as it does to become a successful professional speaker. Once they discover that from your book, I never hear from most of them again!*
   —BRIAN TRACY

Practice Time

Plan on one hour for every minute of a new talk. After that, I personally need two hours for each hour of a talk I have not given recently, in perhaps the past three months.

It takes a thousand hours in front of critical public audience to find out if you can be a paid professional speaker. It takes a second thousand hours to find out if you are any good at it. It takes a third thousand hours to develop your skill to the point you can make a living at it. It takes a fourth thousand hours, assuming you made it through the first three thousand, to make it into a career. All of the great speakers I know are in their fourth or fifth thousandth hours.

To put together a new one-day seminar on selling or management, I invest fully 300 hours of research in the best books, articles

---

[1]By Dottie and Lilly Walters, Simon & Schuster, 1998.
[2]By Lilly Walters, McGraw-Hill, 1993.

Before acknowledging the crowd, Maya Angelou strides to center stage and moves the audience with a compelling poem sung in various languages. She flows from Spanish to Hebrew to French, and finally into English, in the form of a slow spiritual. Then she bridges the opening song to her audiences and message by saying that someday she will grow to be a composer. Maya also explains in her opening that each of us, whether we admit it or not, has the talent to be a composer of the music of our world and of other worlds. Her opening therefore motivates, it is unusual, and it shows off her amazing versatility, without direct bragging.

Connect to the Audience

Bridge yourself to them. Maya's opening is also a brilliant way to connect right into the heart of the listeners because it is easily adaptable to specific groups. For instance, when she was addressing a Wisconsin state teachers convention in 1998, she told the teachers they were composers, too—of their students' lives. "You want to compose a good world. . . . People's entire lives are in your hands. Somebody's going to help rid ourselves of the plague of AIDS and cancer . . . of this blight of racism and sexism. She's in school somewhere. He's in school somewhere. And you might be his teacher."

> *There you are a complete stranger to them, they have never seen you before, you have never seen them. You have a few seconds to make this connection and to create the level of credibility and acceptance so that they can embrace these words that you are going to give, which will move them to another place. It is the moment of truth.*
>
> *To get into their minds, research them thoroughly! Then you can create that opening to move them to another level. Key phrases or statements might be very good, but they might not be the "right" phrase for that particular audience or person. You need to understand the difference in the expectation of those who invite you to speak and those who are being spoken to. Then you craft the message to meet the needs of both.*
> —LES BROWN

*and tape programs ever produced. It is quite common for me to
read an entire business book, investing 10 or 12 hours, to find
5 minutes of inspiration I can add to my own ideas.*
—BRIAN TRACY

Rehearse for Real Audiences

Better than just giving your speech out loud, do it for other re
ple. Consider giving parts of it to your friends, clubs, or associat
which you belong. Nothing is better practice than giving it live
people. Get out, and get among 'em!

*Lay it out on paper to see how it looks,
Give parts of it at dinner tables and with friends. See how it
will be received.
Lincoln's Gettysburg Address was given several times in several
different ways at small groups and social gatherings. He just pulle
together the pieces that had really worked.*
—BRIAN TRACY

Openings—Making the Connection

The opening of your talk is when you will make your second connec
The first came when they walked in and observed you talking to the s
But your opening will set the mood for the talk. The best reten
is in the first and last 30 seconds. Make sure those main points are
there, as well as in the body of the speech.

Find ways to make your opening connect with them, to mak
unique, and to show off your skills (See much more on openings
*Secrets of Successful Speakers: How You Can Motivate, Captivate,
Persuade* by Lilly Walters, McGraw-Hill.)

Be Unique and Show Off Your Skills

For instance, sometimes Zig Ziglar starts his talk when he's not on t
stage. The audience hears his voice, but doesn't see him; they all sta
looking for him. It grabs their attention, adds a bit of interest, ar
helps to create the mood of, "This will be something different."

You get them to like you by showing them that it is an honor to be with them. I say, "You are here because you are the top people in this company. What an honor to share a couple of ideas with you." Or you could say, "I have spoken to many, many groups, but you are one of the most important of all, because you are some of the most important people in this business." Or, "I have been looking forward to coming here for a long time. I have spent hours thinking of ways to make this time more valuable. I promise you we are going to share some great ideas." Anything that tells them that you care, that you've spent the time, that you value them. Sometimes I'll open with, "Thank you for coming. I know how busy you are, I know how many other things you could be doing right now. So I promise you that I will make the next 3 1/2 hours some of the most enjoyable and helpful of your life. I will give you ideas you can use to dramatically improve your life."

The bridge is next. The bridge is one of the most important things speakers miss. The bridge of commonality. You must cross the bridge to their side of things. The way you do it is to draw a parallel between yourself and them. I did a talk for the top sales people from BMW recently. I began the talk by saying, "I'm happy to be with you. You represent the finest automobile in the world, the ultimate driving experience (which is their advertising line), I've been driving German cars for 25 years. I also imported $25 million worth of foreign vehicles and set up 65 dealerships. I've attended every tradeshow in the country, and I've spoken to thousands of car purchasers." From then on they knew I was not an outside speaker with a "canned" message.

—BRIAN TRACY

Your opening connects you to them. It takes intense focus.

To appear natural and unrehearsed, do an incredible amount of rehearsal. Rehearse out loud, until your talk is literally second nature.

The best retention is in the first and last 30 seconds. Make sure your main points are told there!

Find an Inspiring Teacher

I still get coaching as a speaker, and it hurts! But it is the only way I can grow in my craft. I am still not the speaker that I am going to be.
                    —LES BROWN

1. *Listen to whomever you perceive as a great speaker. If you can't listen to them live get their tapes.*

2. *Find a great mentor among greats.*

3. *If you get any chance at all, write them a letter and say, "Look, when you fly into town, it would be my great honor to pick you up." Get as close to him or her as you can. Apprentice to him or her. Carry his suitcase. Do the drudge work: sell their products at the back table, meet all her friends, meet the friends of their friends. Learn what they are doing to market themselves.*

4. *Make sure it is in tune with who you are and how you are going to out-picture your success at your highest and best picture of yourself . . .*

5. *and for humanity.*

That is what I used to do for Cavett Robert.[3] I would pick him up in New York back when I was bankrupt and upside down in a beat-up, old Volkswagen. He never got uptight, even though his foot was going through the hole in the floorboard. I was totally embarrassed, but he never humbled me. He was so good at exalting people. He would tell me, "You've got it, boy!" And he'd write me little letters. He took me on as an honorary son. He was superbly helpful.

If you have a great inspiring teacher, the student becomes great in that subject. I didn't do well in high school in geometry. Then I got with Bucky. Bucky finished Albert Einstein's unified field theory because he created a change in math based on triangles rather than squares, called synergetics, and I got it! I got it because Bucky

---

[3]Cavett Robert is a Superstar star I am profiling in a future volume of Superstars.

*was so great. I could give you a 12-hour class in synergetic geome-
try, and you'd love it because you'd experience it, because Bucky
was totally experiential and inspired me.*
　　　　　—MARK VICTOR HANSEN

Stage Fright!

*To be a good speaker you have to speak a heck of a lot. I have done
5,000 talks in 38 different countries to 2 million people, and I still
get scared. The fear of every speaker is "I'm not going to be good
enough." I've done 5,000 speeches; I've had it at least 4,000 times.
Cavett [Cavett Robert, founder of the National Speakers
Association] called it, "the tortures of the damned."*

　　*In Taiwan, three hundred people were waiting to greet me at the
airport at 12:10 a.m.! The next day they take me into this IMAX-
like theater. The top persons in the audience seem to ascend up to
the heavens! I'm thinking, give eye contact to everybody? How? The
people in my audience paid $500 each in American currency, that's
a lot in Taiwan. I was sweating cold and I've been doing this for
25 years. I was terrified I won't be able to deliver. You might say,
"You shouldn't be sweating." I say yeah, I've got the best interpreter,
she works for the prime minister, we spent three hours together
going over my style and language and ways and get in synch. But it
all doesn't matter, if you care about the audience, you are going to
have stage fright.*
　　　　　—MARK VICTOR HANSEN

Mark was a smashing success in Taiwan, because he has the answer to
fear on the platform: fill your mind with caring for them. The caring
causes the fear, it also causes its cure.

*When you become detached mentally from yourself and concen-
trate on helping other people with their difficulties, you will be
able to cope with your own more effectively. Somehow, the act of
self-giving is a personal power-releasing factor.*
　　　　　—NORMAN VINCENT PEALE

Use things you love in your talks. For Angelou, it's poetry. From the platform she uses those poems and poems set to music that make her feel fabulous, she might recite and sing 10 or more about the topic of the day: feeling sexy, proud, positive, and powerful. Linking to something she loves so deeply, lets her pour her love back into the audience.

Most speakers develop their own courage-strengthening technique to use just before they go on. Some do deep breathing. Others do exercises to escape the demon of fear.

As I wait off stage with my mental motor roaring, straining against the minutes before I can let my energy flow, I do mental visualization.

First I ask my Heavenly Father for help, using the words of Saint Francis of Assisi: 'Lord, let me be a channel of Your love.'

I visualize the people sitting in my audience. I see them coming from a long distance. They are hungry, tired, discouraged. My modules of material are platters of delicious, steaming, nourishing food. With all my heart I want to give these people this good food they are hungry for.

When I hear my introduction, I mentally "jump up in my mind" as I walk on stage. Instead of fear, I become full of anticipation, excitement, happiness. I leave all those "self" thoughts in the wings.

    —DOTTIE WALTERS

You will experience stage fright. Just fill your mind with caring for the audience. The caring causes the fear, it also causes its cure.

Tough Crowds

Everybody gets to experience tough groups occasionally. You get to go home, and you cry, and think I should never speak again. Everybody is going to get melted down. You know you are in trou-

ble when, as Bill Gove says, "They are the type of crowd that will eat their young!"

If I could give anything to any speaker, it would be that you are going to go through a bunch of "dustors" before you hit the oil. In the oil business a dustor is an empty well. In speaking it's an audience that doesn't care if you're there, i.e., an empty well. It's not that in a dustor presentation the audience is bad; it is that you and the audience don't synchronize. My advice is to go to the most user-friendly audience to get your confidence back.

I got to speak to 8,000 school principals and superintendents here at Anaheim Convention Center. One of them comes up to me afterwards and says, "You're so good. I gotta' school where nobody goes to college. Would you come out and talk to our high school, just our 1,700 seniors?" Well, I get out there and I'm dressed in what I thought were cool clothes. Right before I go on, the principal tells me, "You're all alone. I've pulled out all the teachers, it's just going to be you and them. I know you'll get 'em'!" I did the whole talk, incorporating everything I knew that would inspire these kids! "There are 37,000 occupations, you have more opportunity than ever! You live in America, the land of opportunity . . ." all this cool stuff. I didn't get them, they got me! Well, they melted me down. They came up to me afterwards and gloated over the fact that they had gone out of their way to get me. It wrecked me for at least three days.

Thank God I had other talks to do. Everyone is going to hit a place where you strike out. It's not just Babe Ruth who had more strikeouts than he had hits.

We know when we are melted down. The danger to us is that we don't know what we really accomplished, and it just kills us. But I happened to meet a kid in an airport that told me he was in a talk where I got melted! I was embarrassed, "Oh my God, that was the worst talk I ever did." He said, "You may not know it, you may not have helped those other kids that day, but I intended to kill myself that night. Your talk pulled me through. It helped me figure out who I was."

—Mark Victor Hansen

Before You Step Out on the Platform

Very few Superstars just walk out in front of the crowd. They have ways they "psyche-up" to a state of readiness. From doing a preshow workout, to prayer, to taking time to prepare themselves.

Preshow Workout

To fire up Tony Robbins' blood, and bring himself into a peak state for his audience he does a preshow workout, with isometric squats, jumps on a portable trampoline, and even lying on an electric massage table. On-stage and off you will see him pound his chest, exhaling through his nose deeply. His thrusts his arm into the air and yells, "Yes!" Offstage and in private he uses this to create power and enthusiasm. On stage he repeats the move which helps him re-create the emotional intensity for which he is famous.

He has been known to stay up in this state by spinning up on his toes, beating his fists on a wall and shouting. He repeats an affirmation over and over, "I now command my subconscious mind to direct me in helping as many people as possible today by giving me the strength, the emotion, the persuasion, the humor, the brevity—whatever it takes!—to show these people and get these people to better their lives *now!*"

I prepare by going out with a very clear idea of what I want to do. I work hard, gathering as much information as possible. I create an outline in my mind. However, rarely does it end up exactly that way. I get up before the crowd and I absolutely trust in my Creator and my unconscious mind. I am totally and completely focused on delivering to my audience what they really need at that moment.

That's why my speech changes sometimes. I am out there on stage looking at how people respond. I watch my audience very closely. I have so much passion that it just flows. Unlimited examples of stories flow through me at any moment.
—TONY ROBBINS

Call on a Higher Power

*Before I speak I do an invocation. I call on God. I say,
"Father . . . Mother God, I ask you to be here with me now, surround me, and fill me, protect me with the Christed white light of
the Holy Spirit, and lead me and guide me to say only that which
is for the highest good and for the greatest enlightenment of the
people that I am now going to be addressing. Make sure I get my
ego out of the way and that I am willing to be vulnerable and tell
the truth, and let my heart and my vulnerability show. Let me
uplift these people so they can leave and live more fulfilling lives.
Thank you, Lord, for this opportunity to be of service." When I do
that I feel I am being used for a higher purpose and I trust, I trust
that I will say the right thing.*

—JACK CANFIELD

*In sports we call it being in that "zone." It's where you can really
"have" somebody, then take them to the next level. Every speaker
can create magic moments, if in their heart of hearts they are
speaking on their passion. If they are passionately and on purpose
doing their livelihood. I am doing what I have spent my whole life
sculpting. My mind spends my whole time saying, "What can I cut
in? What can I cut out of the talk so I can get the wind beneath
their mental and spiritual wings?*

*The spiritual body moves the mental which moves the physical.
If I can do my magic, I get out of the three dimensions of height,
breadth, and width, and into a spiritual space, which controls all
the rest. And that is where miracles happen. I try to live in the
spiritual space first.*

*I would never, ever, go into a talk without praying
first . . . invoking the Lord's Prayer, invoking white light. Making
sure I light all the candles inside. If their metaphorical candle has
been blown out, I use prayer to ready myself to light it. I'm not
there to light mine.*

*I assume I am prayed up, aware, my candle lit, ready to light
theirs if they give me permission.*

—MARK VICTOR HANSEN

The satisfaction that I get now is to help people to set some goals, and to raise their standards and maybe to make them more proficient in their everyday lives. I say a prayer before each speech, and hope to God that I can say something that is going to influence people.
　　　　—Lou Holtz

Want *memorable* results? Go back in the last half of the book and study the qualities being *remembered.*

As you put all of these skills on the platform, remembering to appear natural and unrehearsed, takes a great deal of preparation and practice. Practice all your talks out loud, especially your openings and closing to better make the connection.

Find an inspiring teacher to help you achieve your speaking goals. Model others, but be yourself and be unique.

Fill your mind with caring for the audience. The caring causes the fear, it also causes its cure. Everyone is going to hit a place where you strike out with tough crowds. It's not just Babe Ruth who had more strikeouts than he had hits. Preparation, practice, and prayer, before you step out on the platform will increase the times that you hit home with your audiences.

Curtain Call

Are you ready? Will your message be remembered? Can you be a merchant of hope? Are you ready? I think so, just do it. You have hoped you could be a wonderful speaker. After hope, comes work.

Are you ready to succeed in doing what is necessary? Do you have the courage to do it? Do you have the power?

> *When Maya Angelou spoke, she said that "courage is the greatest of all gifts. . . . for without it, nothing else is possible." At those times in my life when I've felt at my lowest and have lost sight of my true purpose, her words have resonated within my soul reminding me why it was important to "keep on trucking."*
> —FRANCINE WARD, J.D., SPEAKER/CONSULTANT

> *You are now at a crossroads. This is your opportunity to make the most important decision you will ever make. Forget your past. Who are you now? Who have you decided you really are now? Don't think about who you have been. Who are you now? Who have you decided to become? Make this decision consciously. Make it carefully. Make it powerfully. Commit to CANI—Constant And Never-ending Improvement!*
> —TONY ROBBINS

Just Do It!

> *Set it as a goal for yourself. Set a deadline, make a plan, take action on your plan and persist by holding your own feet to the fire. The average person will be astonished at how much they will accomplish if they begin to act in an above-average way.*

Mark Victor Hansen gave me a good piece of advice back in 1984. He said, "Get it 80% right and then go with it. You can improve it and upgrade it later, if you like, but the most important thing initially is to get it done!"

Los Angeles, especially Hollywood, is crawling with would-be script writers. The editor of the Los Angeles Times *sent a reporter out onto the sidewalk in front of the building on Wilshire Boulevard to stop people and ask the following question, "How is your script going?" Three out of five passers-by responded with "Almost done!"*

Just do it!
        —BRIAN TRACY

After Hope Comes Work

What change has occurred in your life as the result of hearing the words of a great speaker? I kept in my heart that no matter how dark the day, there is always hope. But after hope, comes work.

When we do the best that we can, we never know what miracle is wrought in our life, or in the life of another.
        —HELEN KELLER (1880–1968), BLIND AND DEAF AUTHOR AND LECTURER WHO TYPED HER OWN MANUSCRIPTS AND SPEECHES

Since my story came out in *A Second Helping of Chicken Soup for the Soul,* I cry a great deal.

"... I just read your story in *Chicken Soup* . . . I didn't know there was hope . . ."

"... my child lost the use of his arm, we didn't think he would ever be able to use a computer until . . ."

"... our Doctor told us Mary would just need to learn to hunt and peck on the keyboard. That typing manual you talked about in *Chicken Soup.* . . ."

". . . The therapist said there were other things Johnny could do besides typing . . ."

Other things besides typing? In today's cyber-gotta-use-a-keyboard-world? What was happening to these handicapped children? Children are being taught in kindergarten to use a computer! "Oh, except you. You, the wired kid with the funny hand, you just 'hunt and peck.' " Hunt and peck? I cry when they tell me.

I type over 50 words per minutes because I was taught a real typing method.

It's not just "typing," in my family, it's art! It is the beginning of great speeches. It's stories, laughter, tears. It's taking the letters of a keyboard and making pictures in that note to Auntie Ruth.

Mom taught me the love of life, as painted by words. I would snuggle up to dad, while mom read fairy stories. She made them magic. For her, everything revolved around those typed words.

Then, when I was 11, laying in that hospital for two months, she asked, "Will she be able to type?" They told her, "Don't worry, she can do other things."

"Other things?" All the best things she was able to give in her life were created with those magic keys. Keys I would never be able to use. Her heartache was all-consuming. It caused her to come down with horrible pneumonia. I remember she and daddy came to see me every day in the hospital. Dad, as always, was the rock we could all lean on. But mom, my Mother the Warrior, was ill of heart and body. I was so worried about her. I kept trying to reassure her, "Mom, it's OK. It's only one finger." She would cry and leave the room. I thought she was being pretty silly about it all. I didn't realize she and dad hadn't gotten up the nerve yet to tell me how bad it really was how much of my hand was lost from the accident.

Hope is a good place to start. But you need to *start*. When yet another counselor told her I would not be able type, mom got going again.

She called up the biggest name in typewriters at the time, IBM. They put her call through to the manager. She told him my story and asked if he knew of a one-hand typing manual. He happened to have one on his desk! Just one, he wasn't really sure why it was on his desk or what he was supposed to do with it. But mom was. This kind manager even sent out a rebuilt electric typewriter for me too.

My hand was bandaged inside a huge cast, I hadn't seen it myself yet. Mom was so excited, she came running down the hall in the hospital to where I was sitting in a wheelchair to tell me what she had found. I was confused, "Why will I need a one-hand typing manual?" She had forgotten she hadn't told me yet. She started to cry again, and with a very broken voice told me it wasn't just my pinkie, "In the last operation, they had to amputate your ring finger and most of your palm."

I got teary too. Then all those messages of hope I had been hearing all my life from people like mom, Norman Vincent Peale, Earl Nightingale, just kicked in. "Mom, it's OK, I don't want to get married anyway." She started sobbing and left the hospital. (I must admit, I changed my mind on that getting married thing by the time I hit about 18!)

Hope is a good place to start. Now that I knew the truth, it was time to get started. I learned to paint pictures with those magic keys. She pulled me through with her love of the words. Look in a bookstore. Those books bearing my name, were typed with my one hand.

Then *Chicken Soup* told my story to the world.

> I read your story in *Chicken Soup*, . . . I didn't know there was hope . . . please help me find that manual.

All these years I had just assumed that everyone would be using the new, updated, really terrific version of that old one-handed touch-typing system I had learned with. I told the first two callers, "Just call the local rehab department at the hospital in your area, they know!"

They called; then called me back, no luck, no manuals, no hope. More called, asking for help.

> Mary is so shy since the accident, she would love to learn to type so she can play with the other kids. They told her there is a special keyboard we could buy for her. But I was hoping she could learn to use a standard keyboard, like the other kids use.

I cried.

Over the next five days I called over 50 rehabilitation experts, occupational therapists, hand surgeons, hospitals, associations, and typing teachers. Only two people were even aware that a one-handed person might *want* to type. These two had never ever persued it for their patients. I asked—over and over again—"What do you tell kids with the use of only one hand about learning to type?" They had no answer.

Hope is a good place to start, but then you must get to work. I started to work. I found that typing manual, the only one in print, the same one I had used 30 years before! The copies were gathering dust in a warehouse. Until I finish my own manual, which I will create for these kids, we sell that easy, simple little manual and what a return we get! Not in our accounting department; we barely break even. But now when these parents call we can open the door to so much more than hope.

I am very grateful for a life experience with Superstars speakers around the world. They have taught me the value of these messages that begin with hope and succeed with work.

Speakers call and ask if I think they are ready to be a Superstar speaker. I ask, "What is the message your audience must remember? Can you be a merchant of hope?"

They say, "I hope so."

Before I go back to finish *typing* the last page of book eight, *Secrets of Superstar Speakers,* I tell them, "After hope, comes work."

For more about Lilly Walters' other books, albums, seminars, and private consultations:

Phone 626-335-8069, Fax 626-335-6127,
E-mail Lilly@Walters-Intl.com
http://www.walters-intl.com

Index